KNOWING AND HELPING YOUTH

CONTRIBUTORS

Dan Boling
Golden Gate Baptist Theological Seminary
Mill Valley, California

William R. Cromer, Jr.
Southern Baptist Theological Seminary
Louisville, Kentucky

Gloria Durka
Boston College
Chestnut Hill, Massachusetts

John H. Peatling
Union College Character Research Project
Schenectady, New York

Robert E. Poerschke
Southeastern Baptist Theological Seminary
Wake Forest, North Carolina

G. Temp Sparkman
Midwestern Baptist Theological Seminary
Kansas City, Missouri

Stanley J. Watson
New Orleans Baptist Theological Seminary
New Orleans, Louisiana

Margaret Webster
Ewart College
Toronto, Ontario, Canada

G. TEMP SPARKMAN, editor

knowing and helping youth

BROADMAN PRESS

Nashville, Tennessee

4232-19

ISBN: 0-8054-3219-1

Dewey Decimal Classification: 259

Subject Heading: CHURCH WORK WITH YOUTH

Library of Congress Catalog Card Number: 77-075621

Printed in the United States of America

INTERNATIONAL CHRISTIAN GRADUATE UNIVERSITY

CONTENTS

BV
4531.2
K67
1977

All Scripture quotations marked KJV are taken from the King James Version of the Bible.

All Scripture quotations marked RSV are taken from the Revised Standard Version of the Bible.

Introduction
G. Temp Sparkman

A book is its own best advertisement. However, its distinctive features are not always evident. Therefore, it is appropriate to point out that this work goes beyond the many excellent books on youth development already on the market. The first of these features is the unusual amount of space and religious application given to the theories of Erik Erikson, Jean Piaget, and Lawrence Kohlberg. In addition, an entire chapter is devoted to the developments in religious thinking among adolescents, reporting especially on the seminal research of Ronald Goldman and John H. Peatling.

Add to these assets the discussions of the church youth as a member of family and youth culture, the suggestions on how to be a sympathetic counselor to youth, the description of the elements of a personal affirmation of faith, and the suggestions of meaningful ways youth may be involved in education, worship, mission, and witness—and you have a very helpful book.

When this book was first proposed, the table of contents was much larger than the one you find in this final version. Problems too complicated to deal with here made it necessary to trim the contents. In the process we simply had to omit some important material and to combine other material that rightly deserved treatment in separate chapters. Here are some of those omissions.

The Meaning of Adolescence

What is the phenomenon of adolescence? What are the major theories of adolescence?

Adolescence is the time of life between the end of childhood and the beginning of adulthood. However, its very "in-betweenness" means that persons in the adolescent years exemplify behaviors and reveal characteristics that are both holdovers from childhood and anticipations of adulthood. The word itself comes from a Latin word, *adolescere*, which means to grow up. The boundaries of the period are marked by a physiological development—puberty—to the full assumption of adult roles. While the notion that it is of necessity a time of turmoil and rebellion is not universally held, there is no doubt that it is a time of facing and, we hope, resolving some new conflicts not known in childhood.

Rolf E. Muuss writes in *Theories of Adolescence* (Random House, 1966) that adolescence is "sociologically, . . . the transition period from dependent childhood to self-sufficient adulthood; psychologically, . . . a marginal situation in which new adjustments have to be made, namely those that distinguish child behavior from adult behavior in a given society."

A new use of the term *youth* has appeared in recent years to denote the period after adolescence, or what some will label young adulthood. In such a case youth means those persons who, because of a continued pursuit of education or adoption of an alternative life-style, have not yet entered completely the world of the adult.

In the present book we are using the terms *adolescents* and *youth* interchangeably. In the chapters on theory and development the reader will note that the descriptions of the years of adolescence or youth differ with the various theories. But while the psychological boundaries vary, functionally we are dealing with the school student in grades seven through twelve.

Perhaps the confusion in terms is but an indication of our confusion over the meaning of the period in our culture and our uncertainty about how to aid our children's movement from childhood to adulthood.

The confusion and uncertainty notwithstanding, there are some things that we know and some strategies that we feel confident with. This book is about some of the theories and approaches that can be recommended. There are, of course, many other important theories, such as the psychoanalytic theories of Sigmund Freud and his daughter Anna; Kurt Lewin's field theory; Robert Havighurst's developmental tasks; and other applicable theories. For discussions of these see the books *Theories of Adolescence* by Rolf E. Muuss and *Understanding Adolescence*, edited by James F. Adams (Allyn and

Bacon). Also see *Youth*, the seventy-fifth yearbook of the National Society for the Study of Education.

The Physiology of Adolescence

Many will wonder how we could hope to produce a book on understanding adolescents without a chapter on physical development. Such an inclusion lost out in the end because there are a number of excellent chapters in other books dealing comprehensively with such development. The reader is referred to updated editions of youth psychology works such as *Adolescence and Youth* by John Janeway Conger (Harper and Row) and *Understanding Adolescence*, edited by James F. Adams (Allyn and Bacon).

Of special interest to all of us should be the psychological effects of physiological development, as for example in the case of the youth who is late in maturing physically.

Gloria Durka in chapter 1 of the present book refers to some aspects of physical growth, and the importance of neurological development is critical in Jean Piaget's cognitive theory, chapter 3.

Research

While relevant research is included in the book, there was not room for an entire chapter. The reader is referred to psychological and educational abstracts and to centers that focus on religious research, such as the Character Research Project, Schenectady, New York or the Youth Research Center, Minneapolis, Minnesota. There is some relevant research in *Research on Religious Development*, edited by Merton P. Strommen.

Stanley Watson's chapter 6 has some suggestions about counseling with youth and can be complemented by a clear picture of the dynamics involved in the problems of belief and doubt, prayer, and so on. Such is, of course, also an interest of professionals in the psychology of religion, and the reader can turn to their bibliographies for help.

Learning Theory

Currently, learning theory is being discussed under several rubrics, among which are behavioral theory, psychoanalytic theory, humanistic theory, and cognitive theory. See chapter 3 on Piaget for a cognitive bibliography and *Toward a Theory of Instruction* (Harvard University Press) by Jerome S. Bruner; *The Conditions of Learning* (Holt, Rinehart, and Winston) by Robert M. Gagne and *Principles of Instructional Design* (Holt, Rinehart, and Winston) by Gagne and Leslie J. Briggs (behavioral); *Psychology of Learning* (Markham) by William S. Sahakian and *Freud and Education* (C. C. Thomas) by Seymour Fox (psychoanalytic); *Freedom to Learn* (Merrill) by Carl Rogers (humanistic). For a treatment of several teaching strategies deriving from various theories see *Theories for Teaching* (Dodd, Mead and Company) by L. J. Stiles and *Models of Teaching* (Prentice-Hall) by B. Joyce and M. Weil.

Programs in the Church

Most readers will wish that the Cromer and Boling chapters had been longer, for their subjects deserve separate treatment. For further help with these areas see the resource lists at the end of the chapters. More than likely the various denominational headquarters will have materials on worship, education, mission, and witnessing among youth.

The exciting and effective ministries being done through church recreation and music in some denominations are another means of involving and helping youth. Recreation settings provide opportunities for utilizing the concepts and strategies of education, mission, and witness presented in this book. Youth involvement in music also has a significant educational dimension, contributes to the worship of the church, and can be utilized in mission and witness settings. The editor is most familiar with the good work being done in recreation and music in his denomination through the Baptist Sunday School Board, Nashville, Tennessee.

A chapter might have been given to the planning and implementation of the youth ministry. Again, each denomination has its own approach to church's comprehensive program involving youth. Stanley Watson has a helpful book on the subject *Youth Work in the Church* (Broadman).

Social Problems

Beyond the discussion by Robert E. Poerschke in chapter 2, there is a pervasive field of social problems. The following quote from Charles S. Ireland in *Reader's Digest*, June 1976, and referred to by newspaper columnist Carl T. Rowan, points up the problem and at the same time exposes our book for its middle-classness. "If an inner-city youngster survives and makes it to adulthood, he or she is likely to be angry, embittered, enraged. The repeated failures in school, the discriminations, the constant roadblocks, the menial jobs available—all take a terrible mental toll. The youngsters grow up feeling self-hating, worthless . . . . Their lives are so barren of hope that they have no fear of a jail sentence, a prison term, or even death." Besides the great social pathos in these words, there also is a challenge for doing more effectively what Boling is discussing in the chapter on witness and mission.

The Book's Unity

A critical test of a multi-authored work is whether it achieves any semblance of unity or is merely a series of disconnected essays. As you read this book from chapter to chapter, you will find two expressions of a genuine unity. One, the logical progression and relation of each subject was planned and to a degree attained. But the more important element of unity was uncontrived. It simply shows through in the concern of the writers that what we are to be about in youth ministry is helping the youth toward a meaningful Christian experience that shows in some integration of personality and in being involved in God's work.

G. TEMP SPARKMAN

Kansas City, Missouri

1

Identity—the Major Task of Adolescence
Gloria Durka

Identity and Human Development

The crisis of adolescence is the crisis of identity. During this period, for the first time adolescents seek to clarify their understanding of who they are and what their role in society is to be. They hope to chart for themselves a perspective and direction. They hope to achieve an effective integration out of the remnants of childhood and the hopes and dreams of their anticipated adulthood. Failure to resolve this crisis results in a generalized sense of role diffusion. In extreme cases, failure can result in neurosis, psychosis, or delinquent behavior.

But the problem of identity is not merely a problem of adolescence. In our culture it is a problem that spans adolescence and is usually not resolved until adulthood, if ever. In this regard, we can distinguish between the identity crisis and identity formation. Identity formation is a lifelong process. It involves a process of simultaneous reflection and observation as well as a process of increasing differentiation. For this reason identity should never be viewed as a static established achievement but as a dynamic achievement. We should remember that the identity crisis does, however, typically occur at the end of adolescence.

During any or all of the adolescent years, the young person is fluctuating—in and out of middle childhood—in and out of maturity—in and out of adolescence. That adolescence is a confused period of human development should come as a surprise to no one, especially those who work with persons who are at this stage. Consensus on the factors that contribute to the problem appears hopeless. In the meantime, certain facts are clear:

—By middle adolescence physical growth is almost complete, sexual maturation is established, and mental development—in the sense of ability to do logical reasoning and to understand historical perspective—is adultlike.

—Age thirteen (approximately) begins a new stage of learning and growth. Childhood is over. This new phase of growth has its own special characteristics and distinctiveness from either childhood or adulthood—youth's capacity for religious questions, abstract thinking, and so forth.

—American youth are reaching the stage of religious doubt earlier than ever before, many by the age of fifteen and some as early as thirteen.

—American society recognizes a self-conscious youth culture as a distinctive feature of the twentieth century. This phenomenon is apparently here to stay for the foreseeable future.

—Large numbers of Christian youth are not currently enrolled in any type of religious instruction program. Research indicates that current participation in religious instruction is a major factor in ability to predict devotion to religion.

—Generations of baptized Christians may be lost to the church unless a massive and more effective ministry to youth is begun soon.

—Top priority must be given to youth ministry. This means primarily the training and development of persons who specialize in ministering to youth.

—There has been a decline in traditional orthodoxy among youth. Youth today do not pray; nor do they attend weekly worship services as often as they formerly did. Christian youth are active in some church youth activities, but drop out earlier than youth in other generations.

—There is a breakaway from moral standards previously and more generally accepted. This is especially true in the areas of premarital sex; theft and shoplifting; the use of drugs and alcohol; and the taking of one's life.

—Surveys show an increased number of runaways from home, a greater degree of conflict with parents being resolved by escape means.

But in the realm of self-understanding an adolescent is uncertain and insecure. This condition is brought on by several factors: rising prosperity, the further prolongation of education, the enormously high educational demands of a postindustrial society. For example, since 1900 the average amount of education received by children has increased by more than six years. In 1900, only 6.4 percent of young Americans completed high school, while today almost 80 percent do; and more than half of them begin college. In 1900 there were only 238,000 college students; in 1970 there were more than 7,000,000 with 10,000,000 projected for 1980.[1]

And behind these measurable changes lie other trends, less quantitative but even more important: a rate of social change so rapid that it threatens to make obsolete all institutions, values, methodologies, and technologies within the lifetime of each generation; a technology that has created not only prosperity and longevity but also power to destroy the planet, whether through warfare or violation of nature's balance; a world of extraordinarily complex social organization, instantaneous communication, and constant revolution. The generation that came of age in the 1962-1972 era both reflects and reacts against these trends.[2] Few would dispute the claim that these individuals have been deeply affected by the civil rights movement, the successful revolt against the war in Vietnam, and the first overthrow of an American president.

The passage from childhood to adulthood begins with puberty—the beginnings of sexual maturity. At the beginning of puberty a person has a well-established personality structure, including a rhythm to life, attitudes toward work and other people, self-image, and scholastic record. Then comes the experience of sexual maturation. The outward signs of sexual maturation are obvious enough. The first menstrual period for girls occurs at about the age of thirteen, although it can vary from ten to sixteen and a half. A boy, however, grows more slowly into adulthood. Sperm production and initial ejaculation come closer to the fifteenth year. The young glands are secreting a new mixture of chemicals into the bloodstream, which causes rapid and uneven growth. This upsets the emotional balance of older children. Countless psychological problems as well as numerous social difficulties may arise simply because of these physical differences.

In educational settings, groups may form within larger groups. Or the total group may take on a personality that does not fit a small minority. These minority persons in turn can feel left out—and can drop out. It is the physical change that causes so many of the characteristics that are assigned to adolescents. They are bored with themselves—tired of being children but scared about becoming adults; they are anxious to be independent but too listless to assume responsibility. They are preoccupied with sex but are afraid to talk to adults.

Not only is this experience so powerful that it changes a person's body in size and function; but it is also so thoroughgoing that it forces teenagers to look ahead to their roles in adult life. Thus, these young persons are required to rework their lives in the light of their new situations. The major part of their lives that has to be reconsidered is their experience in the family. These family influences are very strong, as almost every study has pointed out. Yet, the teenagers are in struggle with the beliefs, patterns of conduct, and attitudes they experienced as children.

This means that the profound adjustment that individuals must make when their bodies begin to become sexually mature will be made when they as persons are less experienced and less capable of self-direction. Since the awakening of sexual impulses is also social, an excess of feelings, relationships, and fantasies are directed toward others. The process of self-understanding is rushed. The values and customs that have been inherited from childhood are put to the test prematurely. Because sexual maturation is also the experience that causes persons to move away from the influence of parents to that of their peers, individuals are exposed to general cultural conditioning at a younger age.

For American youth late adolescence begins a protracted psychosocial moratorium—a phenomenon which is found in other cultures, but which in the United States has become a way of life. It is a period when society allows, even encourages, young people to explore possibilities without committing themselves to any one of them. They are, for example, to have many friends of the opposite sex; yet they are discouraged from an exclusive pairing off until they are more ready to assume the responsibilities that such a relationship entails. They are counseled to investigate different colleges or different fields of employment before they invest themselves too deeply in any one.

In the past, when societies were more homogeneous as a whole or in their different ethnic and religious groups, this invitation to choice did not extend to religious belief. It was assumed that adolescents would continue in the religious tradition of their families. Today, in our pluralistic, heterogeneous society, the psychosocial moratorium extends to religion as well as to choice of a marriage partner, a field of employment, a life-style, and so forth. No one has planned it this way; yet it has become a fact of life for a vast number of American adolescents. During this period youngsters can be compared to trapeze artists who, having let go of one trapeze, have not yet grabbed on to the other. They are between trapezes.

Another source of tension comes from what has been described as cultural discontinuities. The anthropologist Ruth Benedict has suggested that such discontinuities can provide a possible explanation of the origin of some of the conflicts of the adolescent period.[3] The theory emphasizes the sharp discontinuity American culture establishes in the development process from childhood to adulthood. For example, our society demands that children be taught certain patterns of behavior which must be discarded later if they are to be successful adults. To mention one, children are expected to be irresponsible. They make no labor contribution to the industrial society. Yet as adults they are expected to assume the responsibility of earning a living and keeping a home. In other societies this kind of discrepancy does not exist. There is a more continuous training for a responsible role because at an early age children participate with adults in performing tasks essential to the community.

Another discrepancy centers around behavior. Children are expected to obey adults until the time when they as adults are required to assume the role of dominance. This is in contrast to societies in which it is expected that a child who is docile or dominant will be accordingly a docile or dominant adult.

Sexual roles illustrate yet another discontinuity. In American society children are really expected to be sexless until they are physically mature. Adults must accept their sexual role to function as integral persons. But there is a strong resistance to the notion of childhood sexuality in our culture.

Such discontinuities may severely affect the developmental process by resulting in regression and lasting emotional distortions. Childish tendencies can tend to reappear in adulthood, and the person can remain emotionally immature.

Erikson and the Identity Crisis

Erik Erikson, a prominent contemporary psychologist, identified the crisis of youth as one of establishing identity and the task of youth as growth into responsible freedom. By crisis Erikson means a crucial time or turning point of increased vulnerability and heightened potential, which becomes either a source of generational strength or maladjustment. If a person does not sufficiently develop an identity, then identity confusion results. In identity confusion the person experiences a lack of direction in life and a sense of uprootedness that leads to various forms of human apprehension. Essentially the person becomes a stranger to self and to others, as well as to the larger historical processes.[4]

Erikson's research seems to indicate that in some young people, in some classes, at certain periods of history, the identity crisis is minimal. In other people, classes, and periods, this crisis is clearly marked off as a critical period. There is a great deal of evidence to suggest that in contemporary American culture, the identity crisis is of maximal importance. American youth feel a desperate urgency, often concealed under the camouflage of social conventions, to resolve the problem of what they are to believe in and who they are to become. But since a number of forces working in combinations have extended the period of adolescence, individuals may not experience the crisis until their twenty-fifth or even their thirtieth year.

Situating Erikson's Research

There have been different emphases in psychological theory throughout its brief history. Sigmund Freud, for example, introduced the will to pleasure through the study of sexuality. Alfred Adler has made contributions with the will to power as a main factor in the formation of neurosis. In the present, it seems as though the will to meaning is more dominant. Literature, drama, and art are replete with the theme of personal identity. In his earliest volume, *Childhood and Society,* Erikson builds upon the Freudian foundations, elaborating the psychological dimensions of physiological relations with important objects of affection.[5] But he went much further than Freud.

Erikson shows through clinical observations, anthropological studies, and experimental play situations that human interactions are culture bound even as they yield to a presumably cross-culturally valid psychodynamic interpretation. So even though Erikson begins with the biological and psychological data furnished by Freud, he gives this data his own interpretation. Thus the *oral* stage (in which the sucking and eating instincts are developed) becomes the time in which the person faces the conflict between trust and mistrust. During the *anal* stage (in which control of the excretory functions is developed), the growing child is confronted with a challenge to balance autonomy and control with a sense of doubt and shame. The *genital* stage (in which children must learn to identify with parents of their own sex) becomes a conflict between initiative and guilt. The *latency* stage (which is not marked by the development of any particular biological function) is reinterpreted as a crisis in which the person must face the challenge of industry and overcome any feeling of inferiority or inadequacy.

In reinterpreting or extending the basic four stages developed by Freud, Erikson moves from the biological development of the person to the psychological development of the individual ego. His ego psychology focuses on the development of the individual's personal identity. For Erikson, the pattern of development through the life span is called *epigenesis*. This notion has its basis in the step-by-step physiological development of fetal organs. Each organ has its appointed time for emergence. If it does not arise at that time, it will never be able to express itself fully because the appointed time for some other part will have arrived; and this will tend to dominate the less active organ. Moreover, failure of one organ to fully develop tends to impair the whole developmental schedule and the hierarchy of organs. By analogy and extension of this physiological model Erikson has proposed that lifetime ego development follows an epigenetic schedule through eight major stages. Each phase is characterized by a critical opposition in the sense of self and, as the phase passes, resolves the opposition with a dominance of one side over the other.

Each crisis is a step taken in the direction of the next and is a link in the chain of development. The solution of any one crisis is prepared for in previous phases and worked out to its completion only in subsequent ones. Erikson has described these phases in terms of their extremes of successful and unsuccessful solution:

(1) basic trust versus mistrust (birth to 1+)
(2) autonomy versus shame and doubt (2 to 3 years)
(3) initiative versus guilt (4 to 6 years)
(4) industry versus inferiority (school age)
(5) identity versus identity diffusion (adolescence)
(6) intimacy versus isolation (young adulthood)
(7) generativity versus stagnation (middle adulthood)
(8) integrity versus despair (older adulthood)

In his book *Identity and the Life Cycle* Erikson delineates these phases and suggests how their resolution contributes to healthy personality.[6] Each crisis in the developmental sequence involves a change in perspective. There must be a radical adjustment. For example, children fear separation from their mother in one phase of their development. At another stage of development this fear has vanished, and the children's greatest desire is to be independent. This is to say that they have faced the critical alternative between being a dependent creature and an autonomous one and have resolved it in favor of autonomy. Each crisis ideally is resolved in such a new adjustment. At each stage of its development, the ego comes up with a new sense of itself—that is, the individual senses the patterns of ego formation and tests these out in the social and cultural context of the environment. Each ego state has a kind of multidimensional equilibrium, which for all of its interrelatedness to physical, psychic, social, and cultural factors has a relatively stable autonomy of its own. Development in Erikson's scheme follows a conflict-resolution process throughout life. Unlike Freud, he stresses the identity crisis and generativity as much as or more than the early years of development

The Process of Identity Formation

According to Erikson, the fundamental problem of the youth stage is how one forms a wider, more all-embracing and inclusive identity. Self-esteem gradually grows into a conviction that the ego is capable of taking effective steps toward a tangible, collective future and that it is developing into a well-organized ego within a social reality. In a later work entitled *Identity, Youth, and Crisis,* Erikson calls this sense *ego identity.*[7] While he maintains that the identity crisis is the particular problem of young adults, its roots lie deeper—in a lifelong development that he calls the process of *identity formation.* These roots extend to the first instance of self-recognition that adolescents experienced as infants and develop throughout their childhood. However, the sense of ego identity is seriously threatened during adolescence.

Erikson claims that young people must become whole people in their own right, and the wholeness to be achieved at this stage he called a sense of inner identity. Young people, in order to experience wholeness, must feel a progressive continuity between what they have come to be during the long years of childhood and what they promise to become in the anticipated future—between what they conceive themselves to be and what they perceive others to see in them and to expect of them. Individually speaking, identity includes, but is more than, the sum of all the successive identifications of those earlier years when the children wanted to be, and often were forced to become, like the people they depended on.[8]

To put it another way, the integration now taking place in the form of ego identity is more than the sum of childhood identifications. It is the accrued experience of the ego's ability to integrate all identifications that are both positive and negative. Positive elements reflect those things that a person wants to become. On the other hand, negative elements mirror potential futures that are to be avoided. On a deeper level, they reflect a past that is to be lived down, a past that may mirror failures in competency and goodness which a person may have been made to feel guilty about, been shamed for, or been punished for.

So it can be said that, in a sense, adolescence is part of childhood and part of adulthood. Children identify with those particular aspects by which they are most immediately affected—the significant adults who touch their lives. By the end of adolescence these identifications merge and become subordinated to a single identity which includes all significant past identifications, but which also alters them to make a unique and coherent whole. Adolescent identity in its final development lacks the playfulness of infancy and the zest of childhood. There is a seriousness, an adult sense of purpose and direction.

In America cultural forces act to bring the adolescents to choose once and for all what their identity is to be. Such a task imposed by society is formidable, and in our culture it necessitates a long intermediate period of preparation. Erikson referred to such a period as a psychosocial moratorium during which individuals go to school to learn the technical and social requirements necessary for the professional situations to which they eventually will be committed.[9] Usually adolescents experiment during this time with various professional roles, looking for the ones they feel suited for. If it is found, they gain a sense of inner identity and continuity because the role allows them to bridge what they were as children and what they are about to become. It also allows them to reconcile their conception of themselves with that of society.

In general it is the inability to settle on an occupational identity which most disturbs young people. To keep themselves together, they temporarily overidentify with the heroes of cliques and crowds to the point of an apparently complete loss of individuality. Yet their search for something and somebody to be true to can be seen in a variety of pursuits more or less sanctioned by society. It is often hidden in a bewildering combination of shifting devotion and sudden perversity, as Erikson puts it, sometimes more devotedly perverse, sometimes more perversely devoted.[10] Yet in all youth's seeming shiftiness, a seeking after some durability in change can be detected.

Erikson gives several other characteristics of identity formation that should be mentioned here. For example, at this stage, not even "falling in love" is entirely or even primarily a sexual matter. To a considerable extent, adolescent love is an attempt to arrive at a definition of one's identity by projecting one's diffused self-image on another and by seeing it thus reflected and gradually clarified. This is why so much of young love is conversation.[11]

Another frequent characteristic of this period is prejudice. Young people can become remarkably clannish, intolerant, and cruel in their exclusion of others who are different in skin color or cultural background, and often in entirely petty aspects of dress and gesture arbitrarily selected as the signs of insiders or outsiders. They persistently endeavor to define, overdefine, and redefine themselves and each other, in often ruthless comparison. The restless testing of the newest in possibilities and the oldest in values are also indicators of their search for reliable alignments.[12]

Erikson sees rebellion as another typical characteristic of adolescence. He suggests that it is the logical outcome of young people's attempt to resolve discontinuities and to find a personally authentic philosophy of life. This rebellious attitude is frequently accompanied by a period of idealism that causes them to reject the existing values of family, school, church, and society. Frequently they seek oversimplified and unrealistic solutions and/or ideals that are impractical and rarely held for any duration of time.[13]

Erikson maintains that when self-definition, for personal or for collective reasons, becomes too difficult, a sense of role confusion results. Young people counterpoint rather than synthesize their sexual, ethnic, occupational, and typological alternatives and are often driven to decide definitely and totally for one side or the other. On the other hand, when young people successfully define themselves, they experience an optimal sense of identity—that is, a sense of psychosocial well-being. This sense of identity is characterized by a feeling of being at home in one's body, of knowing where one is going, and an inner assuredness of anticipated recognition from those who count. It connotes the resiliency of maintaining essential patterns in the processes of change. Thus, strange as it may seem, it takes a well-established identity to tolerate radical change. The adolescent crisis of identity is resolved not by the child who was but by the adult who is to be.

When identity formation is relatively successful in youth, psychosocial development leads through the fulfillment of adult phases to a final integrity, the possession of a few principles which, though gleaned from changing experience, yet prove unchangeable in essence. Erikson suggests that without old people in possession of such integrity, young people in need of an identity can neither rebel nor obey. He concludes that beyond childhood, which provides the moral basis of identity, and beyond the ideology of youth, only an adult ethic can guarantee to the next generation an equal chance to experience the full cycle of humanness. And this alone permits the individual to transcend personal identity—to become as truly individual as he ever will be, and as truly beyond all individuality.[14]

Other Contributions

Since Erikson cited the crisis of adolescence as the attempt to achieve identity, there have been numerous others who have joined in the discussion. Lyman Coleman has developed strategies that are aimed at helping young people grow in their own sense of self-worth as well as in esteem for others.[15] Coleman maintains that through experiences in groups, individuals can discover new information about themselves and others—that is, their strengths and weaknesses. According to him, the air of honest, helping relationships in a group reflects God's own inner life and can become a supportive, healing, Spirit-filled communion. For Coleman, identity is as much determined by the community as by the individuals. Personal identity and self-understanding are relational and are built in the context of a person's association with a group or community.

Lawrence Kohlberg, whose main concern is moral development, has contributed much by way of his explanations of moral dilemmas. By a process similar to the one Erikson described, Kohlberg suggests that one phase of moral equilibrium breaks down when the complexity of moral crises becomes too great to manage with the present level of organization. Thus Kohlberg further rounds out Erikson's theory because he describes an integral task of identity formation—that of mature moral reasoning.[16]

John R. McCall has directly applied Erikson's schema to religious and value education. In his works, especially *Growing Up*, McCall describes the identity crisis in terms of everyday experiences that are directly related to religion and values.[17]

The implications of Erikson's work in identity for religious development have also been explored by Barry McLaughlin.[18] He shows how Erikson in his treatment of Luther's life, *Young Man Luther,* proposes that all data—events, processes, actions, and personal relations—may have either or both a religious or a secular significance.[19] McLaughlin claims that though many may prefer to avoid assigning any particular religious dimension to these crises, Erikson points out that for a religious person like Luther, these events must have a deeply religious significance. He sees Erikson presenting Luther as achieving inner unity and integrity (identity) through his religious development. McLaughlin himself then proceeds to explicate these ideas even further, drawing out specific ramifications for religious life.

Although still in an embryonic stage, the work of James Fowler in faith development must also be mentioned here. A structural developmental theorist himself, Fowler's research centers around the inner structure of personal faith. He has identified six stages of faith-knowing that roughly correspond to Erikson's stages of psychosocial development. His third and fourth stages help clarify an important aspect of identity formation—that of the crisis of faith. By naming the specific tasks adolescents have to face with regard to faith-knowing, Fowler helps to focus on an area of development that is crucial to helping persons arrive at ego integrity.[20]

These are just a few theorists whose works have extended Erikson's interpretation of the identity crisis. Given the current scene, concern with the problems of youth will continue to increase; and with it there will surely be further attempts to elaborate Erikson's ideas.

Implications for Working with Youth

Teachers, counselors, and ministers who deal with youth come to be significant representatives of that strategic act of recognition, the act through which society identifies and confirms its young members and thus contributes to their developing identity. As has been pointed out earlier, basic to the adolescent's struggle for identity is the need for a coherent philosophy of life. They are not old enough or experienced enough to formulate such a philosophy, but they feel compelled to make a beginning to do so. This need becomes more intense under the conditions of a rapidly changing society in which many parents and teachers find it difficult to resolve conflicting values.

Adults working with children in church settings claim they want to teach the faith in such a way that children will appreciate it because they see its value in their lives. The hope is that in adolescence they will be able to discover it afresh for themselves, and it will become a central element in their lives. Negatively, these adults do not want to transmit the tradition to children in formal, dogmatic terms because they fear that in adolescence they may absorb it uncritically or have to go through a torturous process of rejection and realignment.

The church with its wisdom would like to be a significant factor in this crucial stage. But it finds itself with a new version of the problem. Adolescents have full mental capacity, so cognitive capacity is no longer the problem. Yet they have to deal with the depths of self-development and a range of social relationships at a time in life when they simply do not have the experience to make judgments that are needed. There is a social or experiential deficiency in dealing with the problems that are thrust upon them, and churches can help alleviate this deficiency.

Groups and Community

Erikson's work clearly shows that one does not establish his identity in a vacuum, but in relationship with others—that is to say, within some form of community. For the adolescent, the group (that is, community with others) is a most apt vehicle for self-discovery and self-extension. Group is defined here as a gathering of more than one person united in spirit and acting for a common goal. Such a definition includes the notions of community and service. Although the members are united, it is not a static unity—they are all moving toward some common end.

In a group, even adolescent rebelliousness can be used to advantage. The questioning of values, customs, and conventions can allow adolescents to gain insight through instruction, information, and guidance into the reasonableness of their values. Values can then become personally meaningful because they will be fundamentally rational. The idealism of this stage can aid this process because it can allow young people to accept challenges, and the supportive environment that the group provides allows them to be more secure in their quest.

It is helpful to note here that Jesus preached the good news first to his band of apostles. He worked within a small group; and once they had become a community, they were then sent by the Holy Spirit to serve all of humankind. What the apostles experienced then and what the church has experienced throughout all of its history must be experienced by its individual members.

If Jesus first worked with a small group and created a community before sending them out on their mission, youth workers cannot go wrong in imitating his example. The local church is the normal place where community can be created in full.

Because the creation of community teaches young people a new basis for identity—namely, the family of God—the church should use educational processes that are group-centered. Education is, of course, person-centered. But in American society it is generally used as a way for individuals to better themselves, and the motivation for learning and the reward system (grading) are individualistic. Perhaps little change can be made in the social system and in secular schools, but education under the control of the church could develop more processes that would help young people learn how to cooperate for group goals. Caring for each other should be a goal of church-related educational experiences.

Some Concluding Remarks

There is much to be gleaned from Erikson's theory for work with youth in church settings. This fact is evident from the very nature of youth ministry as it is currently evolving. Youth ministry is concerned with the total person, and those working in it help young people face and cope with the mystery of themselves and others. Therefore, youth ministry is rooted in relationships—relationships to self, others, and God. This makes it a call to community. Youth ministers call young people to community by helping them reflect on, evaluate, and understand their relationship to their various communities. The youth worker is also a force for healing and reconciliation within community experience. Youth ministry proceeds as an affirmation of gifts. The youth minister is sensitive to talents and personal gifts and tries to affirm them and nurture their development. Lastly, true ministry duplicates itself. Youth ministers encourage young people to minister to others by living out the church's mission to share the good news and by serving others in love and in justice.

All of the above characteristics are grounded in Erikson's principle of *epigenesis*. His exposition of the adolescent identity crisis can help focus the specific mission of church youth workers. Thus youth ministers would do well to undergird their goals with the insights of Erikson, who more than anyone has studied, defined, and explicated the identity crisis of youth and its ramifications for the broader community. These are especially important for the church, which by its nature ought to be an example of community.

Notes

1. Kenneth Keniston, "Youth: a 'New' Stage of Life," *American Scholar* (Fall 1970), p. 332.

2. Ibid., pp. 332-333.

3. Ruth Benedict, "Continuities and Discontinuities in Cultural Conditioning," *Psychiatry* 1 (1938): 161-167.

4. Erik H. Erikson, "Youth: Fidelity and Diversity," *The Challenge of Youth*, ed. Erik Erikson (New York: Anchor Books, 1965), p. 23.

5. Erik H. Erikson, *Childhood and Society* (New York: W. W. Norton Co., 1964).

6. Erik H. Erikson, *Identity and the Life Cycle* (New York: International University Press, 1959).

7. Erik H. Erikson, *Identity, Youth, and Crisis* (New York: W. W. Norton Co., 1968), p. 49.

8. Ibid., p. 87.

9. Erikson, *Identity and the Life Cycle,* p. 111.

10. Erikson, *Identity, Youth, and Crisis,* pp. 235-236.

11. Erikson, *Childhood and Society,* p. 262.

12. Erikson, *Identity, Youth, and Crisis,* p. 87.

13. Ibid.

14. Ibid., p. 42.

15. For an example of Coleman's work, see his *Program for the National Serendipity Workshops* (Scottsdale, Pa.: Serendipity House, 1971).

16. For an introduction to Kohlberg's work, see his "Stage and Sequence: The Cognitive-Developmental Approach to Socialization," *Handbook of Socialization Theory and Research*, ed. David A. Goslin (Chicago: Rand McNally, 1969), pp. 347-480.

17. John R. McCall, *Growing Up* (New York: Paulist Press, 1972).

18. Barry McLaughlin, *Nature, Grace, and Religious Development* (New York: Paulist Press, 1964).

19. Erik H. Erikson, *Young Man Luther* (New York: W. W. Norton Co., 1958).

20. For a succinct presentation of Fowler's research, see his "Faith Development Theory and the Aims of Religious Socialization," *Emerging Issues in Religious Education*, ed. Gloria Durka and Joanmarie Smith (New York: Paulist Press, 1976), pp. 187-211.

Bibliography

Benedict, Ruth. "Continuities and Discontinuities in Cultural Conditioning." *Psychiatry* 1 (1938): 161-167.

Coleman, Lyman. *Program for the National Serendipity Workshops*. Scottsdale, Pa.: Serendipity House, 1971.

Elias, John. *Psychology and Religious Education*. Bethlehem, Pa.: Catechetical Communications, 1975.

Ellkind, David. *Children and Adolescents, Interpretive Essays on Jean Piaget*. New York: Oxford University Press, 1970.

Erikson, Erik H. *Childhood and Society*. New York: W. W. Norton Co., 1964.

_____. *Identity and the Life Cycle*. New York: International Universities Press, Inc., 1959.

_____. *Identity, Youth, and Crisis*. New York: W. W. Norton, 1968.

_____. *Insight and Responsibility*. New York: W. W. Norton, 1964.

_____. "Life Cycle." *International Encyclopedia of the Social Sciences* 9.

_____. *Young Man Luther*. New York: W. W. Norton Co., 1958.

_____. "Youth: Fidelity and Diversity." *The Challenge of Youth*. Edited by E. Erikson. New York: Anchor Books, 1965.

Fowler, James W. "Toward a Developmental Perspective on Faith." *Religious Education* 69, no. 2, pp. 207-219.

_____. "Faith Development Theory and the Aims of Religious Socialization." *Emerging Issues in Religious Education*. Edited by Gloria Durka and Joanmarie Smith. New York: Paulist Press, 1976, pp. 187-211.

Keniston, Kenneth. "Youth: a 'New' Stage of Life." *American Scholar*, Fall 1970, pp. 631-648.

Kohlberg, Lawrence. "Stage and Sequence: the Cognitive-Developmental Approach to Socialization." *Handbook of Socialization Theory and Research*. Edited by David A. Goslin. Chicago: Rand McNally, 1969.

McCall, John R. *Growing Up*. New York: Paulist Press, 1972.

McLaughlin, Barry. *Nature, Grace, and Religious Development*. New York: Paulist Press, 1964.

Strommen, Merton P. *Bridging the Gap*. Minneapolis: Augsburg Publishing House, 1973.

_____. *Five Cries of Youth*. New York: Harper and Row, 1976.

2

Adolescents in the Family and Subculture
Robert E. Poerschke

What's with Church Youth in the Family and in the Subculture?

If, as it is often described, the period of youth is the transition [1] between childhood and adulthood, then the passageway must be described as having at least two playing fields marked off on it. Often at least two games are going on in its boundaries. Imagine the Astrodome playing surface marked off with a football field and a baseball diamond and covered with at least twenty-two football players, eighteen baseball players, six umpires, and five referees! Youth feel compelled to be out there. They're not sure if it is baseball or football they want or ought to be playing, or if they might better try the role of the official. After such decisions are made, they still have to deal with the question of position.

As youth discover the wide variety of identity roles that they would like to claim and that are imposed upon them by others, their search for identity often becomes exceedingly frustrating. The frustration is probably most evident in adolescents' two most intimate areas of relationship—the family unit and the subculture. Here the youth are working their hardest to achieve identity, to accomplish self-determination, to become somebody. And precisely in these two areas parents, church leaders, ministers to youth, ministers of music, and pastors have the greatest opportunity to understand, provide support, keep resources and viable alternatives readily available, and encourage youth to work through their problems for themselves.

Father and Susan were in the kitchen talking about her allowance and other privileges. Mother, washing dishes, and younger sister, Doris, doing homework, were partly involved. Father tried to wrap up the conversation by saying, "So, Susan, if you want more privilege and freedom you have to earn it—you have to 'shape up'!

You have to 'be somebody'!" "Right!" said Mother. Susan's instant retort was, "But Daddy, I *am* somebody!" And Doris chimed in with, "Yeah!"

It is very important to study these "somebodies." Who is the somebody Father wants Susan to be? Is Mother thinking of the same somebody? Does Susan know either of these somebodies? If she does, would she care to be such a person? Who is the somebody Susan feels she *is*? What somebody does Doris see and affirm? Susan's friends, at school and church, would have their own comments to make about each of these somebodies, and especially about the somebody Susan insists she is.

Being or becoming somebody in their own eyes, in the eyes of parents and family, and especially in the eyes of friends, is the major developmental task of adolescents. Achieving emotional, psychological, and social maturity is "where it's at" for youth. Physical, mental, moral, and religious maturations are also taking place, but these areas are the subjects of other parts of this book. In this chapter we will be considering the personality growth part of becoming somebody as it is affected by and takes place in the family and the subculture (particularly the peer group).

The family was, in childhood, and may continue to be the more dominant factor of the two. The subculture is increasingly important and influential in the life of the youth. The family tends to reflect and emphasize the importance of the roles and relationships of childhood and continues to be supportive and affirming in matters of developing trust, autonomy, initiative, and industry.[2] The peer group, the subculture, the community, and the world are fields to explore and conquer. They provide challenge as well as opportunity for developmental growth in identity, intimacy, generativity, and integrity. The tasks of developing identity and intimacy are especially important to achieve during youth years.[3]

On the one hand, youth are determined to have all the security, support, and material advantage that they can claim from the family. These are routinely available to them in the home. On the other hand, youth show equal determination to have all the freedom for intimacy, exploration, productivity, and independence that they can claim from the peer group and subculture. These parallel demands of youth bring to surface a tension of trust, acceptance, and communication that is deserving of serious attention at the least and capable of being destructively separating at worst. The family and the subculture are two major playing fields, superimposed upon each other, upon which youth develop themselves. The skills they will cultivate during their adult life are also formed on the larger playing fields of total culture.

If these arenas are important to youth, those who are seriously interested in ministering to youth will do well to understand and perceive in detail what goes on here. Such understanding will make it more possible to provide encouragement and support as well as resources to facilitate what is happening. It is important for leaders to stay out of the way and to allow youth the chance to try, to bomb out, and most of all to put it all together their own way.

Then What Goes On in the Home of the Church Youth?

Parents in the homes of church youth have a variety of behavior patterns. Three sets of variables are frequently used to identify parental behavior: Rejectant-Acceptant; Autocratic-Democratic; and Indulgent.[4] The spectrum of these variables in parental behavior has been described as follows:

Actively rejectant
   Nonchalant-rejectant
      Casually autocratic
         Casually indulgent
            Acceptant-indulgent
               Acceptant-casually indulgent
                  Acceptant-indulgent-democratic
                    Acceptant-democratic.[5]

Yet another set of variables deserving attention is the relative dominance of the father and mother in the home. The absence and/or presence of the two parents because of work, travel, or other reasons enters into this factor, along with the personality strength and inclination of each parent to want to control. Range of control, from Mother dominant to balanced control to Father dominant, coupled with quality of relationship (autocratic, laissez-faire, indulgent, democratic), suggests still another range of authority patterns in the home:

Mother-controlled—autocratic pattern of authority
  Mother-led—democratic pattern of authority
    Balanced control:
        Equalitarian—democratic pattern of authority
        Equalitarian—indulgent pattern of authority
        Equalitarian—laissez-faire pattern of authority
        Equalitarian—conflicting pattern of authority
    Father-controlled—autocratic pattern of authority
  Father-controlled—pseudo-autocratic pattern of authority
Father-led—democratic pattern of authority.[6]

The socioeconomic level of the home of the church youth is also of consequence. There is evidence to suggest that more often than not the home of the church youth will fall in the lower-middle-class to middle-class range. Upper-lower-class homes and upper-middle-class homes will also be represented frequently. Lower-class, lower-upper-class and upper-class homes will be least evident among church youth.

The youth in these homes must also be seen in variable groupings. At the obvious level they will be either female or male; and chronologically they will be in early, middle, or late adolescence. Many of the developmental characteristics of youth should be viewed in even greater detail and definition, for this is a time of many changes in a multitude of combinations. Orientation of developmental characteristics will be either toward childishness or toward adultness. The eternal tension between achieving personal freedom and privilege while at the same time avoiding, so far as possible, the concommitant duty and responsibility, is the essence of the struggle in which the adolescent is involved. Change in the characteristics of youth may take place in any of the following areas: from dependent to independent; from acceptant to assertive; from lethargic to energetic; from passive to active; from irresponsible to responsible; from family oriented to extra-family oriented. Usually such changes begin in and, to a large degree, take place in the family; but they may also happen outside and beyond the family.

Much has been written about the individual problems youth deal with. The early adolescents are becoming grown-up persons physically. Height, weight, complexion, sexual development, strength, and agility are some of the individual problems with which early youth struggle. The middle adolescents are focused upon areas of psychological growth, such as personality, sexuality, and relationships. In older youth the problems are more nearly in the range of doing something with this grown-up body and this developing personality. Experimentation and coping with other persons (particularly the peer group, but progressively more and more with adults), new ideas, and exciting adventures and experiences claim the attention of youth in this period.

In all three periods of youth the underlying and basic struggle is with putting it all together, with making sense out of life. Youth are not always aware of what they are about. Church youth are rarely able or willing to name themselves philosophers or theologians. They are, however, involved in a desire to hook on to something solid. Self-determination includes the struggle to establish a capacity for devotion and loyalty to something bigger than themselves and even bigger than the family in which they have been formed. It is an effort to stop or at least slow down that part of the formative process that is from without and to emphasize that part that is from within. The family is still important in some degree; but now self, others, work, play, and some unifying force—a ground of being, a God— must have first attention. The youth seem to want to believe in something that will make it possible for them to believe in themselves!

This feeling of self-determination is enhanced or impaired by youth's sense of control or authority. One facet is control over physical and material environment (as opposed to being controlled by the environment). A second facet is control over other people (as opposed to being in the control of other people). Another facet is control over the time factor. The question of the future and its influence (positive or negative) upon the present also has bearing.

The nature of youth's struggles, the intensity of the struggles, and indeed whether or not the youth are even involved in specific struggles are highly dependent upon the family in which the youth live. Far too few youth have available to them the best of family support, resources, and challenges. Homes in which parents are unable to resolve differences, in which parents act immaturely or are negligent or absent for whatever reason, and in which there is separation or divorce are quite obviously deterrents to youth's ability to put it all together. There is evidence that problems and struggles (especially as they involve relationship to other members of the family) are least frequent and severe in democratic homes; and they are progressively more frequent and severe in intermediate and authoritarian homes. There is some evidence to suggest that this progression is more evident among girls than boys.[7]

Generalizations are precarious. There can be no substitute for knowing the family background of each youth as a basis for understanding that youth. However, in situations where such individualized understanding is not possible, an overview and general understanding may have some value. Professional and managerial-class parents seem to provide greater opportunity for youth to achieve independence. Youth of such parents tend to discover, even as children, that they are of worth and have skills and abilities that will make it possible for them to control their environment. It is possible for them to feel that they need not necessarily feel inferior or subordinate to other people. For these youth the future holds promise; and preparation during youth for a job or career in the future is an acceptable and even desirable idea.[8]

Working-class parents tend to be more autocratic and rejectant. They are less likely to provide opportunity for their children to participate in the formation of their own lives and future. Physical punishment is evident in these families more frequently and at older age levels. Independent action and thinking is discouraged, and obedience and conformity are more often expected. Being or becoming somebody and putting it all together for youth in these families is in many instances more of a struggle and may even take on the form of a rebellion. The process of growth, then, is more likely to take place outside the home than within it.[9]

Neighborhoods, clusters of families, constitute a pattern of living, a general life-style, a subculture that has significant influence on the individual families and, through them, on the youth who are members of these families. There is, however, another pattern of stratification that has even more influence on youth. It is the youth subculture, which develops as youth move out of family– and other adult-dominated places and gather in "youth places," such as public schools, youth centers, recreational establishments, and churches. Here in the youth subculture, individual youth are usually most comfortable and secure in working at being or becoming a somebody they can affirm.

And What Goes On in the Youth's Subculture?

Interestingly, in the youth subculture, organization is again by family, though here they are described as gangs, cliques, groups, and crowds. In early adolescence the cliques are generally family sized and unisexual in nature. They tend to be neighborhood oriented, and conformity to the clique's standards and expectations is the primary prerequisite for membership. Leadership is casually selected by wide varieties of criteria (athletic skill, possession of money or a place to meet, assertiveness, and so forth). Still in early adolescence, these cliques begin to cluster. The larger family units, the crowds, that result are at first still unisexual in structure and are still from a relatively small neighborhood. However, interaction between crowds, and to some degree even between cliques, of opposite sexes begins.

In middle adolescence advanced individuals in these interacting crowds, as they become attracted to one another heterosexually, begin organizing overlapping and closely related heterosexual cliques. Soon, still in middle adolescence, these cliques enlarge to become heterosexual crowds. In such crowds, during late adolescence, as maturity in personhood and relationship is achieved, the security and support of the group become less important. Couple relationship becomes progressively more prevalent.

Though this description of group development during youth is brief and rather superficial, this period must, nevertheless, be viewed as one of major significance to youth. Youth who do not feel that they have a group of their own are generally very miserable people. Family does not adequately provide this sort of opportunity to get freed up, to get away from adult (and especially parental) judgments and directives, and to feel genuinely wanted and accepted. Youth must have the chance to develop conversational techniques, to practice getting along with people, to improve social skills, and to try out relationships with the opposite sex without too much apparent danger of serious consequences. Gaining such opportunities without peer support and help seems to youth an impossibility. The peer group in the youth subculture may well seem to youth to be more important than family or church or school.

Parents and youth leaders who view the peer group objectively also see its values and importance. There is no better place than the youth group for the youth to learn the skills of interpersonal relationships between equals. Social adjustments are more frequently made in social situations than in classroom or academic learning experiences. Learning to relate by relating in an accepting surrounding is the better way. A basic part of this learning is the "untying of apron strings"—the moving from a parent-centered world to an other-centered way of life.

Especially important in this learning of relationships is the sexual and heterosexual aspect. The need to be aware of maleness and femaleness and then to practice being male or female with someone of the opposite sex is highly important. In our larger culture, where the family and the school often are overbalanced with female leadership, influence, and model, it is particularly helpful for boys to live in a group and culture in which there is challenge to be an adult male.

The peer group and the youth subculture also present problems to youth in their struggle to become somebody. While on the one hand it seems that they find freedom from the imposition of family and parents in their peer group, youth often also discover that they must now conform to the expectations of their group instead. The individualism and personhood they are seeking may be denied even more by their peers than it is by their parents.

The fact that peer groups are usually exclusive poses another set of problems. True, when a youth is accepted by a group, the acceptance and the status of being in are affirming and supportive. But there are always those who are not accepted. The frustration of having rejectant parents or of needing peer affirmation must then be directed toward another group or another process for resolution. Even to the accepted youth, the exclusiveness of the peer group may be a handicap. If loyalty must be only to one group (as is often expected), and if relationships with other persons and groups are inhibited, youth's becoming process is forced to be narrow and restricted.

Status in groups and the membership of groups are rarely defined with clarity. The socioeconomic level of the family and neighborhood is often the primary criterion for membership. Upward mobility from these levels and membership in higher status groups are not frequent occurrences. Role concepts, interests, backgrounds, and activities seem more often to be the organizing forces than any choice or preference on the part of youth individually. Ethnic and racial features are strong forces in determining groups, so broadening and new experiences and relationships are apt to be beyond the grasp of individual youth. It is interesting to note, however, that athletic skill and maturity are often the exceptions that may allow a person to cross bridges and break through barriers in gaining admission to and leadership in peer groups.

Behavioral Problems in the Church Youth's Subculture

Serious behavioral problems (especially in the use of automobiles, alchohol, drugs, and involvement in theft, violence, illegal sexual activities, and so forth) in youth's subculture are not formally identifiable until adolescents having them are actually caught in the act. Much evidence exists to suggest that only a very small percentage of youth (5 to 10 percent) having various problems are actually apprehended and convicted. Of even greater significance is the evidence that suggests that behavioral problems of youth are quite regularly a reflection of the behavioral problems of the youth culture and the larger culture in which their peer group and family are located.[10]

Statistics that compare only those who have been caught with those who have not been caught (but who may actually have been equally involved in the same behavioral problem) cannot provide an adequate base from which to deal with either those caught or not caught. Only when we see the very close parallel in behavioral characteristics between youth and their peer groups with the behavioral characteristics of parents, the larger subculture, and the youth subculture of these same youth will we find ways to deal effectively with behavioral problems in church youth's subculture.

Then What Can Christian Parents and Church Leaders Do for Church Youth?

Psychologically, the answer is to provide for youth the possibility of becoming somebody. The answer is not to provide for youth the chance to become the somebody we want them to be. We may, however, claim the right and must assume the responsibility of telling them about and modeling that somebody. Better still, the answer is that we must provide for youth the chance to become somebodies:

—who can accept themselves as they are.

—who are aware of their aptitudes and are willing to develop them to the highest possible level of skill.

—who are unafraid of work and able to enjoy to the fullest all wholesome play.

—who are aware of others and sensitive to the needs of others to become and be somebodies, too.

—who will claim for themselves and be committed to the task of providing for all other selves the chance to try, to fail, and to put it all together for themselves.

Theologically, Christian parents and church leaders can provide for youth the chance to become new persons in Christ—the somebodies God intends they become. *Note:* we can't make them be such persons. We can't push the idea in their ears or cram it down their throats. We only can give them the room, the freedom, the resources, and the chance to gain for themselves the knowledge, the understanding, and the commitment to be such persons as they discover God intends them to become!

And How Can Christian Parents and Church Leaders Pull This Off?

This is the hard part! It is not as hard to know what to do as it is to be able to do it. Sociologically, the answer is simply to provide model communities (general subcultures, families, and the resultant youth subcultures and peer groups) in which youth can experience becoming somebody in an encouraging, challenging, and affirming atmosphere. Subcultures, families, and churches must be available to youth in which parents and adults are authentic model somebodies with whom youth can work.

Theologically, the answer to pulling this off is in the often used and only faintly understood word *koinonia*. *Koinonia* is a relationship:

—that includes God himself, as counselor and guide though the direction of the Holy Spirit.

—in which all members are consciously seeking to know and to model after Jesus Christ, who is "the way, and the truth and the life."

—that is committed to joining with God in revealing his searching, forgiving, affirming, blessing, reconciling love.

—and that warmly and genuinely welcomes and accepts every person.

Parents and church leaders must see to it that youth have available to them family *koinonia*, youth *koinonia*, congregational *koinonia*, and world *koinonia*. In such environments youth may experience becoming and being real, ultimate and eternally living as somebodies—"new persons in Christ." [11]

Notes

1. James S. Coleman, chairman, *Youth: Transition to Adulthood; Report of the Panel on Youth of the President's Science Advisory Committee* (Chicago: The University of Chicago Press, 1974).

2. Terms describing developmental characteristics taken from Erik H. Erikson, *Identity, Youth, and Crisis* (New York: W. W. Norton Co., 1968).

3. Ibid.

4. Karl C. Garrison, *Psychology of Adolescence* (Englewood Cliffs, N. J.: Prentice-Hall, Inc., 1965), p. 270.

5. Ibid.

6. Ibid., p. 273.

7. Ibid., p. 275.

8. Arlyne Lazerson, ed., *Developmental Psychology Today* (Del Mar, Calif.: CRM Books, 1971), p. 385.

9. Ibid., p. 387.

10. Ibid., pp. 391-396.

11. Sara Little, *Youth, World, and Church* (Richmond, Virginia: John Knox Press, 1968).

Bibliography

Cole, Luella, and Hall, Irma Nelson, eds. *Psychology of Adolescence.* New York: Holt, Rinehart and Winston, Inc., 1971.

Coleman, James S., chairman. *Youth: Transition to Adulthood; Report of the Panel on Youth of the President's Science Advisory Committee.* Chicago: The University of Chicago Press, 1974.

Erikson, Erik H. *Identity, Youth, and Crisis.* New York: W. W. Norton Co., 1968.

Garrison, Karl C. *Psychology of Adolescence.* Englewood Cliffs, N. J.: Prentice-Hall, Inc., 1965.

Gordon, Thomas. *Parent Effectiveness Training.* New York: Peter H. Wyden, Inc., 1970.

Gleason, John J., Jr. *Growing Up to God—Eight Steps in Religious Development.* Nashville: Abingdon Press, 1975.

Hansel, Robert R. *Like Father, Like Son—Like Hell!* New York: The Seabury Press, 1969.

Havighurst, Robert J., and Dreyer, Philip H., eds. *Youth.* Chicago: The University of Chicago Press, 1975.

Jersild, Arthur T. *The Psychology of Adolescence.* New York: The Macmillan Company, 1963.

Lazerson, Arlyne, ed. *Developmental Psychology Today.* Del Mar, Calif.: CRM Books, 1971.

Lidz, Theodore. *The Person—His and Her Development Throughout the Life Cycle.* New York: Basic Books, Inc., 1976.

Little, Sara. *Youth, World, and Church.* Richmond, Virginia: John Knox Press, 1968.

Miller, Derek. *Adolescence: Psychology, Psychopathology, and Psychotherapy.* New York: Jason Aronson, 1974.

Murphree, T. Garvice, and Murphree, Dorothy. *Understanding Youth.* Nashville, Tennessee: Convention Press, 1969.

Richards, Lawrence O. *Youth Ministry: Its Renewal in the Local Church.* Grand Rapids, Michigan: Zondervan Press, 1972.

Strommen, Merton P. *Bridging the Gap.* Minneapolis, Minnesota: Augsburg Publishing House, 1973.

_____. *Five Cries of Youth.* New York: Harper and Row, 1974.

3

Cognitive Processes in Adolescence
G. Temp Sparkman

It is generally recognized that the adolescent is doing a higher kind of reasoning than the child. An old problem for the child—how a person can be in Atlanta and Georgia at the same time—is no longer one for the adolescent. Excitement in childhood about the adventure in the parable of the good Samaritan changes in adolescence to an interest in the meaning of the parable. When the syllogism "All boys are sissies; Jim is a boy; therefore, Jim is a sissy" is shown to a child he will respond to the primary premise by contending that not all boys are sissies. But the adolescent, even though believing the premise to be untrue, will be able to accept it in order to follow the logical operation involved in the syllogism.

The conversations, the books being read, the subjects being studied in school—all show a thinker advanced past childhood. The most influential theory back of this phenomenon is that of Jean Piaget. Piaget, born in 1896 in Neuchatel, Switzerland, is most generally called a psychologist, but genetic epistemology (or the development of knowledge) is his enduring interest. He is equally known as biologist, philosopher, and logician.

Although Harvard recognized him in 1936 with an honorary degree, Piaget's influence in America has come late. English translations of some of his works came in the 1940s, and in 1958 a significant one on adolescent thinking appeared. The major American interpretation came in 1963. Piaget's influence is now very much with us; and his work deserves serious attention.

The most complete work on Piaget's cognitive psychology is *The Developmental Psychology of Jean Piaget* by John H. Flavell (1963). This work is in three parts: "The Theory," "The Experiments," and "Critique." The Foreword is by Piaget himself. Piaget writes that Flavell has successfully described and integrated his work. On the other hand, Piaget says of the Critique section, "It is difficult for me to find them all convincing." [1]

Another important book is *The Origins of Intellect: Piaget's Theory* by John L. Phillips, Jr. (1975). This work outlines the periods of development put forth by Piaget and has a section on the educational implications of the theory. There is a helpful section on terminology and concepts utilized by Piaget.

One of the best brief treatments of Piaget's theory, and the one to read first, is *Piaget's Theory of Cognitive Development* by Barry Wadsworth (1971).

There are, of course, other books by interpreters of Piaget besides Piaget's own works. Flavell and Phillips give complete bibliographies of Piaget's writings and of the translations and interpretations. The most significant English rendition of Piaget's own writings on adolescent development is found in *The Growth of Logical Thinking from Childhood to Adolescence* by Piaget and Barbel Inhelder, a longtime colleague of Piaget.

Overview of Periods of Cognitive Development

The primary concern of Piaget's research is with how a person thinks. Thus it is thinking, not how much a person knows, that Piaget is studying and theorizing about. The research has revealed that thinking is related to age, hardly a surprising finding. But the significant aspect of the finding is its insight into the kinds of thinking being done at various stages of development. This means that in addition to knowing that a child does not reason as an adolescent, we now also have some reliable information about the ways in which that reasoning is different.

Four periods of cognitive development have been suggested from the research findings: Sensorimotor Period—Birth to Two Years; Preoperational Period—Two to Seven Years; Concrete Operations Period—Seven to Eleven Years; Formal Operations Period—Eleven to Fifteen Years. For this chapter on cognitive processes in adolescence, the period of most importance is that of formal operations. However, it will be helpful to summarize the other periods.

The sensorimotor period, birth to two years, is one of significant development—mental as well as physical. The physical growth can be seen; the cognitive is more subtle. Piaget has found in these two brief years several stages of development. The best discussions of these findings are in Flavell and Phillips. During this period the child moves from reflex actions to deliberate actions. Instead of merely responding to the environment, he begins to take the initiative in experimenting with the environment. The child learns that objects are permanent and distinct from the self, that these objects exist even when unseen.

The preoperational period, two to seven years, does not leave motor development behind; rather, it builds upon it. The child moves from self-centered activity to genuine social activity. This is reflected, toward the end of the period, in the ability to play with and not just alongside others and in the child's language, which is now more dialogical and meaningful. However, thinking during this period is very limited. The child has difficulty taking the viewpoint of others, making real conversation difficult. He is erratic in behavior because of an inability to balance between current behavior and external interests. He has distorted perceptions because of being distracted by a single detail of an event.

The concrete operations period, seven to eleven years, is one of marked growth. The child can easily take the viewpoint of others and is thus a more social, cooperative person. A new kind of logical ability is perceived now that the child can reverse thought, as seen in the mathematic problem $7 + 3 = 10$, $10 - \underline{\quad} = 7$. This development also makes it possible for the child to perceive that water, when poured from one container to another of different size or shape, retains its original quantity—an insight that the preoperational child does not exhibit. The child in this period is still very much tied to operations in the concrete and is not yet capable of abstract reasoning, though he is grasping for such abstract ability; but the observer will note that this reasoning is still closely wed to the actual and begins there rather than in the potential.

Further elaborations and examples of thinking in these first three periods will be a part of the discussion of the final period, formal operations, for it is not possible to talk of the advanced nature of cognitive development in adolescence without talking of the kind of thinking over which adolescent thinking is advanced.

Adolescent Reasoning: Formal Operations

To operate on something is to apply tools and techniques to that something. We know from medical surgery what it means to operate on someone. Operations in thought, then, are the cognitive tools and techniques we use in thinking. The reason these operations are called formal is that they assume a form that goes beyond the thought of the child, which is concrete bound and without deliberate form. It is similar to the difference in *education* and *formal education*.

"The adolescent," by Flavell's interpretation, "performs these first-order operations, too, but he does something else besides, a necessary something which is precisely what renders his thought formal rather than concrete. He takes the results of these concrete operations, casts them in the form of propositions, and then proceeds to operate further upon them, i.e., make various kinds of logical connections between them. Formal operations, then, are really operations performed upon the results of prior (concrete) operations." [2]

The first characteristic of formal thought, then, is that it is propositional. Children, although they often wonder about possibilities and the unknown, deal primarily with what is. And while they apply a certain logic to matters, they do not exhibit a formal approach. The formal thinker, according to Sund, "may express a series of hypotheses in propositional form and reason as follows: "It is this or that./It is this and that./It is this but not that./It is neither this nor that." [3] You can see immediately that the ability to deal with possibilities by the making of propositions greatly expands one's world. It is necessary for systematic and scientific thinking.

One of several experiments illustrates this kind of thinking. There is a billiard table with targets placed in various positions. Instead of one's using a stick that can be carried and moved, the table has a screwed-down tubular plunger with a spring in it. The plunger can be turned to get different angles from the shots of the ball. The participant is asked to try to hit the various targets by angling the shots off one wall of the table. As the activity proceeds, the experimenter asks questions about why one target was hit and another target missed. Or the experimenter asks where the plunger would need to be aimed to hit another target.

> KAR (Age 9 years, 6 months) "The more I move the plunger this
> way (to the left), the more the ball will go like that (extremely
> acute angle), and the more I put it like this (inclined to the right),
> the more the ball will go like that" (increasingly obtuse angle).
> KAR reaches the point of discovering that the ball returns to the
> starting point when the plunger is "straight," i.e., perpendicular
> to the rebound wall.[4]

> LAM (Age 15 years, 2 months) "The rebound depends on the
> inclination (of the plunger), . . . Yes, it depends on the angle. I
> trace an imaginary line perpendicular (to the buffer): the angle
> formed by the target and the angle formed by the plunger with the
> imaginary line will be the same." [5]

The two responses above are not all that different on the surface.
Other, more divergent examples could have been chosen, but the
similarity of these illustrates the point of formal thinking. KAR
discovered the same things as LAM, but LAM was able to submit
the experiment to analysis and form hypotheses about it.

An important point made here is that the formal thinker performs
these systematic operations mentally, whereas the child's operations
are concrete bound. This is why logic-syllogisms are difficult for the
child. Particulars of the real situation prevent the child from accepting the assumption in the first premise. Adolescent reasoning, on
the other hand, can accept assumptions in order to pursue an
argument. This ability is a cornerstone of mature reasoning.

Also involved here is the ability of system or theory-building.
Inhelder elaborates: "The child does not build systems. His spontaneous thinking may be more or less systematic (at first only to a
small degree, later, much more so); but it is the observer who sees
the system from the outside, while the child is not aware of it since
he never thinks about his own thought . . . . In other words, the
child has no power of reflection, i.e., no second-order thoughts
which deal critically with his own thinking. No theory can be built
without such reflection." [6]

Scientific studies and humanities subjects are examples of
second-order thinking in that adolescents can imagine scientific
systems and evaluate them and can assume positions on matters of
concern to humanity, such as the problems of evil, suffering, and so

forth, and reflect on those thoughts. The scientist, philosopher, theologian, and intellectual social reformer, exemplify this ability in a highly advanced state.

This new reasoning ability leads to a recurrence of a limitation on thinking that showed up in the preoperational period. This limitation is labeled *egocentricism* and refers to the inability of the child to take another's viewpoint. It is a hindrance to socialization during the preschool years. And now in adolescence it retards the full development of reasoning power.

In its new form, however, it is cognitive or idealistic egocentricism. It comes out of an overconfidence in the systems or theories that the adolescent has devised, a belief that because something is possible it is real. You have seen young people who have become engaged by a religion or movement of some kind and who believe that new thing to be beyond error. There is a kind of blind loyalty to the ideology or the ritual. This makes it difficult to entertain competing ideologies or movements. One of the causes of this new egocentricism is at the same time one of the positive factors in the development of adolescent reasoning, according to Inhelder and Piaget. They believe that in the anticipation of adult roles, "the adolescent's egocentricism comes out in a sort of Messianic form such that the theories used to represent the world center on the role of the reformer that the adolescent feels himself called upon to play in the future." [7] This is not believed to be a deliberate egotism, but a genuine part of cognitive development—a part responsive to the new situation in which the adolescent is found.

In normal development, cognitive egocentricism eventually breaks down, just as did its counterpart in early childhood. The more the adolescent converses with others, the sooner this egocentricism begins to dissipate. Ideas, as they are tested in dialogue with peers, parents, and others, undergo some scrutiny and a certain amount of alteration.

Inhelder and Piaget say that while these social relations help in overcoming cognitive egocentricism, the final blow comes when adolescents enter the real world of work. At that time what seems possible is tested against what actually is, and adaptations are made. This is not to suggest that the adolescent does all of the giving in, for

that would not be true or desirable. It is just such clashes between
the ideal and the actual that militate against the status quo and lead
to progress.

Thus egocentricism is not to be viewed as a negative force or
equated with egotism. It is a necessary step in full, reasoning
maturity. It does have an early crippling effect on thinking; but it is
soon overcome, and its residue can be very positive.

This ability of second-order reasoning enables the adolescent to
store thoughts and then to retrieve them for the solution of a
problem. Sund refers to this ability as reflexive thinking and
suggests that it is done by scientists and writers who think back over
their work as they are completing it. One of the best illustrations of
reflexive thinking is in the solution of the problem "Bob is fairer
than John; John is darker than Bruce; who is the darkest of the
three?"

Second-order thinking also changes a person's historical perspective. The past is now longer, and persons and events in history are
put into better order. The formal thinker—with experience, of
course—begins to differentiate between what happened in Old and
New Testament times and to see that because of certain events
Abraham is before David, David before Jesus, and so on. The formal
thinker also begins to take note of historical parallels, such as that
Martin Luther nailed his theses to the Wittenburg Cathedral door
before there was a United States. The fact of infinity, backward and
forward, while never understood, is at least a major part of the
consciousness of the formal thinker.

Implied throughout this discussion is that the adolescent is no
longer bound by the *content* of a problem but can now deal with its
form. This was seen in the mastery of the syllogism in logic. It also
can be seen in a new ability to understand allegory or parable. A
child allows the details of a parable to obscure getting at the meaning behind the details, whereas the formal operational thinker, free
of the content, can perceive the meaning.

To the concrete thinker the Exodus in De Mille's *The Ten Commandments* is a high adventure in which the good guys got away,
albeit with some unusual assistance. The formal thinker sees beyond
the adventure to the meaning of the deliverance and even integrates

this into a larger picture or system of belief as to how God deals with his creation. The details do not become insignificant; rather, they are dealt with as parts of a whole, but are not allowed to replace the emphasis that the whole has inherent within it.

The Origin of Formal Structure

Now that we have seen what characterizes adolescent thought, we can deal briefly with what must be a question all of us have asked after reading such descriptions. The question is that of origin: Where do these structures come from?

Inhelder and Piaget present the best discussion of this question, and the inquirer is referred to their book for a more detailed examination. They admit that formal thinking waits upon puberty, but then quickly discount it as an explanation for the new advance in thinking. Rather, they contend, formal operational thought depends upon two developments: the anticipation of adult roles and the maturation of the nervous system. The exact linkage with the nervous system, which includes cerebral development, cannot be specified. But it is certain that this maturation within the individual, plus the influence of the social dimension through the anticipation of taking up adult roles, are the chief ingredients in the origin of formal structures.

Inhelder and Piaget ascribe three elements to the key concept of the *adult role*. One, the adolescent, although still very much attached to childhood, assumes an equal status with adults. Parents of teenagers have seen their children suddenly become their judges, often to an irritating degree. Two, a *life program* becomes important to the adolescent; the future and the adolescent's place in it becomes a concern. Three, the adolescent entertains and may develop plans for changing the society, either a small segment of it or the whole of it.[8]

Cerebral development sets the limits of formal thought. That is to say, until this development occurs, the person cannot perform formal operations. However, this potential for formal operational thinking is not realized apart from environmental factors. The adult role anticipation is the primal factor involved. Thus, while this advanced kind of reasoning is possible in adolescence, it is not realized automatically. Perhaps this answers another question that many have about Piaget's theory: "If Piaget is right, why do so many adults still reason at lower levels, especially where religion is concerned?"

The following observation sums up this interplay between individual givens and social influences: "Formal structures are neither innate *a priori* forms of intelligence which are inscribed in advance in the nervous system, nor are they collective representations which exist ready-made outside and above the individual. Instead, they are forms of equilibrium which gradually settle on the system of exchanges between individuals and the physical milieu and on the system of exchange between individuals themselves." [9]

The word *equilibrium* denotes a state of cognitive balance and has behind it the key concepts in Piaget's theory. To complete our understanding of the origin of formal structures, we will now examine these concepts: *function:* adaptation, assimilation, accommodation, and equilibrium; *structure:* schema.

Function refers to what is happening when we are thinking. Piaget suggests that as we confront a new experience, we go through a process of adaptation and organization.

First, let us look at adaptation. Adaptation involves changing the way we behaved before. It also involves an alteration in the experience itself. Thus both our behavior and the experience are changed in some way and in differing degrees.

When, in the face of new experience, behavior, or thought we work the new into existing behavior, we are assimilating, according to Piaget. We are, in such cases, adapting the environment to our own way of doing things. An example of this concept is children at play. While the children are doing a certain amount of imitating of adults or an adult environment, they are actually recreating the situation to fit their own abilities. Watch young children playing school, and you will see assimilation working. The children are taking what they perceive from the actual school situation (the teacher's demeanor, assignments, chalkboard activity, and books) and dealing with these perceptions within their own capacities.

When, in the face of a new experience, behavior, or thought we do most of the changing, we are accommodating, Piaget says. Accommodation refers to bringing into our way of behaving whatever new thing is presented to us. When we imitate others, we are accommodating to their way of acting or thinking, with only slight changes. An actor, though possessing a unique style, accommodates to the role that the script calls for. When young children show a marked, seemingly new behavior, they have accommodated to the extent that former ways of doing are no longer adequate.

While assimilation and accommodation can be separated for purposes of discussion, in actuality they cannot be so neatly distinguished. Together they form a complex of give and take, of reception and integration, which adds up to an adaptation of behavior. As this interplay takes place, we develop new behaviors, concepts, values, and attitudes.

We attain the equilibrium mentioned earlier by Inhelder and Piaget. This equilibrium is essentially a state of cognitive balance, when the conflicts of change required by the environment and by the strength of the individual are resolved. Phillips writes that this is a dynamic rather than a static balance. "It is a system of compensating actions that maintain a steady state . . . a condition of the system in which the internal actions of the organism completely compensate for intrusions from without." [10] Wadsworth defines equilibrium as "a balance between assimilation and accommodation. Disequilibrium is an imbalance between assimilation and accommodation." [11]

This interplay between assimilation and accommodation brings us to the second aspect of the function of development, *organization*. Thus we have adaptation and organization as the descriptions of the developmental function. That is to say, it is through adaptation (assimilation and accommodation) and organization that we develop cognitive structures.

The introduction of the concept of organization is simply to note that as we adapt to our environment, we do so from some kind of position or condition. The adaptation cannot take place in a vacuum. That aspect of adaptation called assimilation assumes that there is already something within us to which something else is being assimilated. Like the process of adaptation, organization is inevitable.

From biology, an analogy of organization is the digestive system. Although the state of that system will vary from time to time as we grow, it remains relatively unchanged as a system. Analogies from the cognitive area are not found so easily. However, the matter is somewhat clarified by Flavell: "All intellectual organizations can be conceived of as totalities, systems of relationships among elements . . . . An act of intelligence, be it crude motor movement in infancy or a complex and abstract judgment in adulthood, is always related to a system or totality of such acts of which it is a part." [12]

We have been discussing adaptation and organization. These are what are known as nonvarying developmental functions. While these do not vary with age, there is an important part of Piaget's theory that does provide a changing dimension with increasing age. It is called structure.

Structure represents levels of cognitive ability or levels of thinking. Structure is not content. It is not specifically what we think or do. Rather, it is how we think or behave. In the beginning of this chapter we referred to the fact that adolescents no longer have difficulty with the fact that Atlanta is in Georgia and that a person can be in both at the same time, whereas children cannot quite understand that. The reason for the gap in understanding is one of cognitive structure.

Probably the key element of cognitive structure is Piaget's notion of the *schema*. Flavell writes of the difficulty of defining a schema, a situation due partly to the fact that Piaget himself nowhere makes a definitive statement about it. Flavell, however, attempts a definition: "A schema is a cognitive structure which has reference to a class of similar action sequences, these sequences of necessity being strong, bounded totalities in which the constituent behavioral elements are tightly interrelated." [13] And in another place: "A schema is a kind of concept, category, or underlying strategy which subsumes a whole collection of distinct but similar action sequences." [14]

The student who is interested in more precision on the meaning of schema and the distinction between schema and organization is referred to the books mentioned at the beginning of the chapter.

Further readings in these books will give more detailed information.

Credibility of Piaget's Theory

Some persons have approached Piaget's theory with a kind of cognitive egocentricism, having become infatuated with the theory on first reading but not bothering to ask critical questions or to read criticisms of the theory. Of course, the theory ought to be read first without undue critical thought, with the attempt being to understand what Piaget and his interpreters are saying. Then should come the reading of Piaget's critics.

Piaget has been evaluated at several points: the experimental sampling, the experimental techniques, the reporting of the findings, and the postulating from the data. Flavell devotes considerable space to a critique of Piaget, much of which is technical and beyond the interest of most of us, who can utilize Piaget without getting into such high-level questions.

Sund and others, adding to Flavell's body of evaluation, report on research that both corroborates and challenges Piaget. Sund, for example, reports on a David Elkind study which found among 469 junior and senior high school students many who were unable to do formal operational thinking in reference to quantity and volume. Sund also reports a John W. Renner study of 588 junior and senior high students' ability to deal with conversion of a solid, weight, volume and some other tasks. Renner suggested that there is a kind of transitional stage, what he labeled "Post-Concrete-Operational," ranging from twelve to thirteen years, with formal thinking coming in the fourteen- to seventeen-year range.[15]

Of special interest to religious educators are the experiments and studies of Ronald Goldman, John Peatling, and others, discussed in the chapter on religious thinking (chapter 4).

Implications for Youth Education

Piaget did not concern himself with a theory of education. However, his theory of cognitive development has several implications for education. As far as religious education is concerned, Piaget's work has application to curriculum materials and to teaching approaches. Curriculum materials for youth can take advantage of the developing ability of youth to do formal thinking. In fact, some youth are already applying new intellectual tools to religious doctrine and are raising challenging questions.

Then there is the matter of teaching technique. Piaget's findings affirm the wisdom of educators who have called for dialogue in teaching rather than teacher-dominated instruction. As we discover how as well as what a student is thinking, we can be of greater help to the youth.

If Inhelder and Piaget are right about the influence of the anticipation of adult roles, does this not mean that mature adults will need to be placed with our youth? And does not this also mean that adequate vocational guidance is critical? In addition, this influence of mature adults calls for youth to be involved with the whole church community in worship and other activities rather than being isolated in their own interests and activities.

Chapter 4 of this book is really an extension of this chapter on Piaget, for it deals with the thinking of youth when religious materials are being utilized. It represents the most direct application of Piaget to religious education. Chapter 7 applies the theory to the affirmation of faith. The theory is related to Kohlberg's work as reported in chapter 5.

Notes

1. John H. Flavell, *The Developmental Psychology of Jean Piaget* (New York: D. Van Nostrand Co., 1963), p. 4iii.

2. Ibid., p. 205.

3. Robert B. Sund, *Piaget for Educators* (Columbus, Ohio: Charles E. Merrill Co., 1976), p. 50.

4. Jean Piaget and Barbel Inhelder, *The Growth of Logical Thinking from Childhood to Adolescence*, trans. by Anne Parsons and Stanley Milgram (New York: Basic Books, 1958), p. 8.

5. Ibid., p. 12.   6. Ibid., pp. 339-340.   7. Ibid., p. 343.

8. Ibid., p. 339.   9. Ibid., p. 338.

10. John L. Phillips, Jr., *The Origins of Intellect: Piaget's Theory* (San Francisco: W. H. Freeman and Co., 1975), pp. 14-15.

11. Barry J. Wadsworth, *Piaget's Theory of Cognitive Development* (New York: David McKay Co., 1971), p. 18.

12. Flavell, p. 47.   13. Ibid., p. 53.
14. Ibid., p. 54.   15. Sund, p. 75 ff.

Bibliography

Bower, T. G. R. *Development in Infancy*. San Francisco: W. H. Freeman and Co.,
   1974.
*Flavell, John H. *The Developmental Psychology of Jean Piaget*. New York: D. Van
   Nostrand Company, 1963.
Kessen, William, and Kuhlman, Clementina, eds. *Thought in the Young Child*.
   Chicago: The University of Chicago Press, 1962.
*Phillips, John L., Jr. *The Origins of Intellect: Piaget's Theory*. San Francisco: W. H.
   Freeman and Co., 1975.
Piaget, Jean. *The Construction of Reality in the Child*, trans. by Margaret Cook. New
   York: Basic Books, 1954.
_____. *The Language and Thought of the Child*, trans. by Marjorie Gabain.
   New York: World Publishing, 1971.
_____ and Inhelder, Barbel. *The Growth of Logical Thinking from Childhood
   to Adolescence*, trans. by Anne Parsons and Stanley Milgram. New York: Basic
   Books, 1958.
Sund, Robert B. *Piaget for Educators*. Columbus, Ohio: Charles E. Merrill Co.,
   1976.
Wadsworth, Barry J. *Piaget's Theory of Cognitive Development*. New York: David
   McKay Co., 1971.
*These works contain complete bibliographies on Piaget.

4

Religious Thinking in Adolescence

John H. Peatling

The topic of this chapter involves two very complex words: *religious* and *thinking*. To understand what the term *religious thinking* might mean calls for a small amount of logic, just as to know what it has meant during the 1960s and 1970s requires some historical information.

It can be said that *religious* and *thinking* have three and only three relationships. First, they can be equivalent. Second, they can be distinctly different from each other. Third, they can share something in common.

If readers will recall the set theory they learned long ago in elementary school, they will be able to visualize three sets of circles. First, the circles overlap so much that the set looks just like one circle (A equals B). Second, the circles do not overlap at all (A does not equal B). Third, one set exhibits an overlap, but some of each circle is outside the overlap. (Some is A and not B; some is B and not A; and some is both A and B.)

Therefore, one of the first things that must be said about religious thinking is that it has not been used to affirm that thinking and the religious are synonyms. Neither has it been used to affirm that thinking and the religious are separate and unrelated. Rather, it has been used to affirm that the terms exhibit some overlap. What is beginning to be suggested in the late 1970s is that conceptual clarity requires yet further distinctions within this one-of-three possible relations.[1]

The discussion up to now should help us to avoid some wrongheaded notions. Religious thinking has never affirmed that religion (or the religious life) is simply a matter of thinking. Whatever religion may be, there is some overplus that is not thinking. Similarly, whatever thinking may be, there is something about it that is not religion. This, of course, does not mean that thinking is nonreligious or antireligious, but simply that it is areligious. The study of religious thinking, then, is both a religious endeavor and an endeavor that involves categories, ideas, methods, and procedures that are other than religious.

However, while the otherness of both terms is a necessary affirmation, that must not blind a religious person to the fundamentally positive affirmation that thinking and the religious are related via intersection. (In the union of A and B there is some which is both A and B.) There is some thinking that is applied to, used in the service of, or is a part of whatever we call religion or the religious. Therefore, religious thinking is a way of addressing some but not all of the reality of the religious life known experientially to many, many persons. It can help one understand not only others but also something of his own self. Most particularly, a study of religious thinking can help one be realistic about what seems to be involved in the lengthy process of growing a human being. It can help us see that this human being is capable of becoming a religious person but does not always become one.

This may be enough conceptual mapping to enable a reader to sense the importance of the topic as well as to recognize that there are some inevitable limitations to it. Salvation does not occur through cognition; for Christians, it comes through faith in Jesus the Christ as an evidence of God's love for all humankind. Still, those who have a saving faith find, as generations before them have found, that, out of either near despair or celebratory joy, they tend to think about their religious beliefs.

One expression of that tendency to think is theology. Another is what came to be known during the 1960s and 1970s as the study of religious thinking. However, theology and the study of religious thinking are different enterprises. Both share logic as a basic tool. But the study of religious thinking requires research. And up to the early part of 1977 it had generated much empirical research. Its conceptual roots are in developmental psychology and in Jean Piaget's study of how we come to know (what he called genetic epistemology).

Although theologians might blanch at the thought (and psychologists might not be too happy with it either!), religious thinking may be regarded as the empirical underside to the theological coin. If religious thinking is the empirical flip side of theology, its generality means that it does not demand adherence to a particular theology. It is useful with theological positions that can range from the conservative to the liberal. Thus, no religious person should fear the study of religious thinking.

Maximally, if God's grace abounds, such a study can lead to no more surprising state than the Johannine Christ suggests when he promises to lead us "into all the truth" (John 16:13, RSV). Minimally, such a study can lead to no more than a state sages have pointed toward with the advice to know ourselves. Hopefully, this exposition of religious thinking will occupy some intermediate ground, although the author would be remarkably rewarded if the Johannine promise should prove to be moved forward by anything that he has written.

Religious Thinking: What It Has Meant

As near as the author knows, the words religious thinking were first put together by Ronald J. Goldman sometime in the very early 1960s. At that time, Goldman was working on a doctorate in psychology at the University of Birmingham in the United Kingdom. His doctoral adviser, Professor E. A. Peel, encouraged Goldman to apply Piaget's work to the problem of the religious development of children and adolescents. This he did.

The results of his doing that led not only to his doctoral degree in 1962 but also to two books and a surprisingly long-lasting effect upon religious education in the United Kingdom. In many ways, there is no better way to understand Goldman than to read his books. *Religious Thinking from Childhood to Adolescence* (1964) is based solidly upon his 1962 dissertation.[2] *Readiness for Religion* (1965) is an extended venture in inferring educational practice from the results of his doctoral research.[3] Although one can now regard both works as quite germinal, honesty and friendship impel the author to acknowledge a considerable intellectual debt to Goldman.

Goldman was remarkably clear about what he was doing. He specifically said that he was interested in studying the effect of the development of thinking upon a series of topics of presumed religious value. As he wrote in *Religious Thinking from Childhood to Adolescence*, he used the compound religious thinking as "a shortened form of expressing the activity of thinking directed toward religion, not a term meaning a separate rationality" (RTFCTA, p. 4).[4] He was interested in thinking *per se* and, particularly, thinking "directed toward religion" (that is, the intersection of thinking and the religious). As a psychologist, Goldman's interest was in what is called cognition. As a Piagetian, he was interested in cognitive development through a sequence of stages identified by Jean Piaget. As one concerned for the intersection of thinking and the religious, he was concerned with how cognitive development affected an individual's understanding of religion. As both an educator and an educational psychologist, he was particularly interested in how thinking's intersection with the religious affected a student's understanding of religion in the religious education classes which, in the United Kingdom, were organized around a locally agreed syllabus.

When Goldman began his research, those agreed syllabi were heavily weighted in favor of a sequential study of the Bible, with only minimal attention to whether the students could understand the material. In addition, the schools had a state mandate to include a worship service in the school day, so he was also interested in the students' understanding of worship, prayer, and the Scripture passages used in those services.[5]

Goldman undertook a careful investigation of his topic. He stayed close to the method Piaget had used in his early studies, a rigorous procedure called a clinical interview. He developed three projective pictures and a series of standard questions about them. He also developed a series of standard questions about three biblical stories, which challenged students to think about their meaning. The three miracle stories are Moses and the burning bush, the crossing of the Red Sea, and the temptation of Jesus by the devil.[6] Goldman constructed a stratified representative sample of two hundred students in ten age levels: he had ten boys and ten girls in each age level from six years of age through fifteen years of age. He interviewed each student in his sample and reported that each interview took about eighty minutes.

Goldman methodology has been appreciatively reviewed by North American psychologists and, minimally, should be regarded as an excellent example of a clinical interview.[7] For technical reasons, although many questions were asked, Goldman's developmental analysis of the effect of Piagetian levels of thinking upon students' religious understandings made use of responses to only five questions. Three questions concerned the story of Moses and the burning bush; one question concerned the story of the crossing of the Red Sea; and one question concerned the story of Jesus' temptation by the devil.[8] Goldman was quite open: "They were chosen because the discussion of each question with each child revealed the possibilities of checking the child's mode of thinking by Piagetian methods" (RTFCTA, p. 51). The result of his analysis was that he found evidence to substantiate Piaget's position that "there is a continuum of thinking which follows an 'operational' sequence" (RTFCTA, p. 62).

While Goldman clearly specified that different children would move along Piaget's continuum of thinking at different rates, he also identified evidence for three of Piaget's four periods: a so-called *pre-operational* (or intuitive) stage, a so-called *concrete operational* stage, and a so-called *formal or abstract operational* stage. (The sensorimotor period was not studied.) Goldman suggested that mental age was the best indicator of when a child was likely to achieve thinking at one or another of these three stages. He found that the children who were interviewed achieved the concrete operational stage of thinking between six years six months and eight years ten months of mental age. The achievement of the formal or abstract operational stage did not come until between thirteen years five months and fourteen years two months of mental age. As he recognized, this later "boundary" is much later than Piaget had reported for his studies of Swiss children.

In *Readiness for Religion* (1965) Goldman ventured a usefully daring summary of his research by presenting a three-step diagram of a sequence of religious thinking (RFR, p. 196). He equated the level of pre-operational thinking with what he called pre-religious thought. He called the level of concrete operational thinking subreligious thought. He suggested that only the level of late concrete operational thinking and the level of formal or abstract operational thinking deserved to be called personal religious thought. In many ways, since that diagram was first published in 1965, those three terms have generated far more heat than light.

Religious educators have been particularly challenged by the idea that children were *not* religious thinkers until as late as eleven years of age. However, by 1977, one should be able to recognize that regardless of the labels one may choose to attach to the various stages in a Piagetian continuum of cognitive abilities, the research (Goldman's and that of the author and his colleagues) lends support to the fact that cognitive level and religion interact in a describable, discernible way to affect one's understanding of religion, its practices, and its scriptures. If one can understand that, it may be possible to let Goldman's 1965 phrases stand as simple clues (or even as hypotheses!) to a reality that the religiously committed person doing education must recognize and, then, work with. Those clues are both a limitation and a challenge. Without killing hope, they require rigor!

One of the influential suggestions that Goldman made in *Readiness for Religion* was that a formal, structured religious education curriculum should not begin until between seven and nine years of age and, then, should start with what he called life themes (RFR, pp. 110–111). As an educator, Goldman was concerned with building a conceptual base for the obviously religious topics in such a curriculum. So he suggested postponing either the rigor or the sequence of a normal academic study of religious history, fact, or theology until well into adolescence (that is, until formal or abstract operational thinking was more likely). Implicitly, he allowed one to infer that much of what had been tried with younger children was really the challenging stuff of adolescent and adult religious education. Although not everyone will agree with Goldman, we must admit that those suggestions are clearly no more than (a) the informed insights of a researcher working out from his study in the early 1960s or (b) the considered judgment of a trained educator acutely aware of the cognitive development of children and adolescents. Fifteen years after Goldman's dissertation was accepted at the

University of Birmingham, religious educators have more research data available than they did; and the implications for adolescents are becoming clearer and clearer. Moreover, much of that subsequent research has been done by the author and his colleagues in the United States with student populations five to fifteen times the size of Goldman's original study of two hundred children in the United Kingdom.

Religious Thinking: What It Now Means

In the same year in which *Religious Thinking from Childhood to Adolescence* was published (1964), the author brought Goldman to the department of Christian education of the Episcopal church for a one-day consultation. Thus began a relation that lasted across the 1960s and into the 1970s. At Goldman's suggestion, the author and his co-workers in the department of Christian education began the lengthy and expensive process of initiating a North American replication of Goldman's study with a large, representative sample of children and adolescents. The desire to study a large sample of students in the United States of America, in itself, led to the translation of Goldman's clinical interview schedule into a paper-and-pencil test that could be administered locally. Even in the affluent society, no one could imagine sending highly trained interviewers all over the United States. Also, it became increasingly evident that, if one were to deal with large numbers of responses, it was imperative to shift from coded records of interviews to pretest criterion-referenced records. Finally, while Goldman's work indicated that the projective pictures were a rich source of information, they did not speak directly to the question of religious thinking with anything like the precision of the questions and responses associated with the three biblical miracle stories. Essentially, what happened during the mid-1960s was that religious thinking became operationally defined so as to be useful in additional research.

Religious thinking itself was explicitly recognized to be shorthand for the effect of the Piagetian sequence of levels of thinking upon how one thought about the religious. Further, consideration of Piaget's own work made it clear that any stage of thinking was a dominant tendency, not an all-or-nothing affair! It was also evident that both the rate of movement through the Piagetian sequence and the level of achievement varied from person to person and from subject matter to subject matter. Goldman himself had suggested that the sheer complexity of religious language accounted for much of the chronological lag in achieving formal or abstract operational thinking directed toward religion. These ideas and some technical problems with psychological measurement led the author and his associates to more narrowly define religious thinking. Our operational definition is that most of the time religious thinking is the preference for one or another Piagetian type of thinking—especially when a person is presented with a puzzling religious story that implicitly invites one's interpretation.

The stories chosen for assessing that kind of religious thinking were the same three stories Goldman had used, but the format was shifted to that of a multiple-choice test. For each of four questions per story, four possible answers were identified from the actual responses of North American Sunday School students (who had been queried in much the same way Goldman had done). Each of those four possible answers per question was referenced to a different one of Piaget's levels of thinking, using criteria suggested by Piaget or Goldman.[9] Then a student was asked to check which answer in each set of four possible answers he or she most agreed with and which he or she least agreed with. These responses left two possible answers unchecked. In this way, each student created a three-place rank order on four items. Across twelve such sets of a question and four possible answers, an individual would create a uniquely complex pattern of personal preferences for four levels of thinking. Thus, each student would not only exhibit a distinct pattern of preference for a type of religious thinking but would also receive a distinct scale score on one of four basic scales of religious thinking.[10]

In addition to the three stories used by Goldman, there had been added (1) a moral puzzle story from Piaget's early book on *The Moral Judgment of the Child* (1932); [11] (2) Mathis' Environmental Participation Index, a sixty-four-item checklist to assess socioeconomic class; [12] and (3) a series of questions from the University of Michigan's *Youth in Transition* study (1967), which probed the religious behavior and commitment of respondents.[13]

With the cooperation of the National Association of Episcopal Schools, a random sample of classes within each of the nine grade levels from four through twelve was drawn. Between late November 1969 and the end of February 1970, teachers in some ninety-one schools administered the author's instrument *Thinking About the Bible* to just under two thousand students. The basic data processing consumed a fair part of 1970. Then the processed data was read onto magnetic tape, and a computer analyzed it according to programs from the University of California's biomedical computer programs package. This computer analysis took up what remained of 1970 and about two-thirds of 1971. The actual printouts were many, and it took the author two more years to complete writing up the interpretation of his study of religious thinking as a 695-page dissertation for the School of Education of New York University.[14]

However, in 1971 news of *Thinking About the Bible* spread, and two studies were mounted using it. The United Methodist Church's publishing house used it as part of a prepublication test of the then new Adult Bible study materials with a national sample of 3,289 adults. That study proved that adults did not object to the instrument and, in fact, found it quite stimulating. As one would expect, the adults tended to prefer abstract levels of thinking on a Piagetian continuum more so than had the children and adolescents in the author's original study.[15]

A second study in 1971 involved a close working relationship with Dr. Charles W. Laabs of Concordia Teacher's College in River Forest, Illinois, who drew a sample of 988 students from schools affiliated with the Lutheran Church-Missouri Synod in northern Illinois. The study indicated that the Lutheran students moved through the same sequence of levels of thinking as the Episcopalian students, although they tended to do so at a noticeably slower rate. While the same progression was found in both studies, obviously the two student populations were different in how fast and how far they moved.[16]

In 1974 Dr. Kalevi Tamminen, professor of religious education in the Faculty of Theology at the University of Helsinki, translated *Thinking About the Bible* into Finnish and included it in an extensive study mounted by the Institute of Practical Theology. In that study, 1,374 Finnish children and adolescents in the Finnish grade levels equivalent to North American grade levels four through twelve, plus ninety-six second-year students in the Faculty of Theology, were studied. This Finnish study gave clear evidence that religious thinking, as it is assessed by *Thinking About the Bible,* is neither a North American nor an English-speaking phenomenon. Evidence for each of the levels of thinking found earlier by Laabs and Peatling was found in the Finnish data. The Finnish theology students and the United Methodist adult Bible students seemed more alike than dissimilar in their thinking. Thus, it is probable that religious thinking is a reflection of a fundamental, inescapable human process of cognitive development.[17]

Religious Thinking: the Religious Education of Adolescents

The results of all of these studies clearly suggest that religious thinking tends to develop toward a level of formal or abstract operational thinking (that is, a level of thinking in which one assumes objectivity toward oneself and ideas, uses propositional logic, and is able to envision a range of alternatives). Moreover, both Tamminen's and Peatling's studies lend support to a thesis of Professor E. A. Peel that adolescence is a period in which noticeable growth occurs in the ability to think.[18] This finding denies the facile idea that adolescents really are adults who are held in school until the job market is ready for them. It suggests that adolescents are still cognitively developing humans. All educators need to be aware that adolescence is most probably a period of cognitive growth toward adult levels of thinking. Adults are distinguished from adolescents, in terms of religious thinking, by their preference for abstractions, their increased ability to deal with them, and the decreased likelihood that they will get caught in the sheer concrete specificities of a situation. Adolescents approach this pattern, but have not yet arrived at a thoroughly adult level of thinking.

This view of adolescent thinking is also supported by data the author has for a select sample of 107 adult religious educators in their twenties, thirties, forties, and fifties. The sample is quite ecumenical; its participants came from Protestant, Roman Catholic,

Anglican, and Eastern Orthodox churches and several Jewish synagogues. Moreover, their average scores on the scales of religious thinking generated by *Thinking About the Bible* tend to be in excess of those for the high school students in any of the other studies.[19] Logically, psychologically, and developmentally, Professor Peel's thesis seems to be true. Therefore, those who assume the work of religious education should *expect* adolescents to change their thinking across the years of junior and senior high school. For example: [20]

1. Some questions will become very important for early adolescents, and they will press them quite hard. Then they will seem to resolve those questions and, perhaps, move on to others. But in a few years, those same questions will come up again—only this time they will be asked from a new, more advanced cognitive level. The old answer no longer satisfies the growing thinker, and a new answer needs to be found.

2. Probably decisions that are made in early adolescence will, in a sense, come unglued. They will be questioned. When this happens, a middle or late adolescent is looking for a cognitively advanced reason to maintain the earlier commitment. Cognitively, the old must continuously be built into the new. If this does not happen, earlier good reasons may all too easily be discarded as too childish.

Basically, adolescence is a period of cognitive transition. The ways of thinking children prefer (largely, they prefer to think on a concrete operational level) are changing into the beginnings of the ways adults prefer to think (on a formal or abstract operational level). Anyone working with adolescents must, then, understand that their religious thinking is in transition. However, all of the studies during the 1960s and 1970s indicate the direction in which thinking is changing during adolescence. Thus, the most practical advice anyone can give is to expect adolescent boys and girls to change in how they think and to be prepared to think along with them at increasingly formal or abstract levels. Doing that may be not only all one can do; it may well be the most effective way to help an adolescent grow into adulthood as a still religious person.

The author's original study of Episcopalian students indicated that they went through four discernible levels along the way to becoming a high school graduate. Those levels were associated with school grade levels and may be of help to the reader in understanding adolescence as a period of growth. Therefore, they are listed below.

10, 11 yrs. 1. *Grades 4 and 5.* This level includes a lot of changing and growing, but it clearly marks the beginning of a transition from the concrete operational thinking of childhood. The religious thinking of students at this level tends to be very concrete: They will take an all-too-literal interpretation, albeit often a tolerably logical one, given *only* the situational specifics. They will probably do better with history as fact than they will with history as the expression of meaning. Metaphors, allegories, and some analogies may be difficult for them. However, one must continuously check to see just where in their cognitive development they are.

12, 13 2. *Grades 6 and 7.* This level includes slightly less change and is a further step in the transition from concrete operational to formal or abstract operational thinking. These students' religious thinking still tends to be quite concrete, but now the attractiveness of a next level of thinking probably is recognized. This group is hard to characterize, for they will probably show moments of next–level thinking without actually consistently preferring the formal or abstract operational level. Some will begin to be able to appreciate metaphor, allegory, and analogy. One must, however, continually check to know where their thinking is, and one should not expect too much consistency in thinking from them.

14, 15 3. *Grades 8 and 9.* Adolescents in this level are reasonably alike in their thinking. This is the first level where there is evidence for most (but not all!) students' preferring an early form of formal or abstract operational thinking. These students will probably be able to start to understand history as the expression of meaning, and they will have begun to be able to appreciate metaphor, allegory, and analogy. However, because this level is but a first step, one must still check carefully just how they are thinking, although their consistency will probably show a marked improvement.

16, 17, 18 4. *Grades 10, 11, and 12.* Not only are the youth in this level reasonably alike in their thinking; they are noticeably more likely to consistently prefer to use formal or abstract operational thinking. These students are quite likely to understand that meanings are often expressed in and through the simple facts of history. They quite probably can appreciate metaphors, analogies, and allegories. They may even be creative in creating contemporary ones on their own. At this level of religious thinking, some intellectual rigor can be appreciated. The sequential study of the Bible, the exploration of either a theology or a set of theological themes, and the investigation of the complexities of translating principles into actions can be a challenge rather than an example of asking far too much far too early from a growing person.[21] Still, it is important to check the actual level of thinking of any group of adolescents, for they are growing cognitively. Listening carefully and thinking along with them remains an important strategy in working with these adolescents.

One may wonder what is left for adult cognitive growth. Actually, a great deal. The author's select sample of adult religious educators indicates a growth spurt during the late twenties to a plateau that lasts throughout the thirties and early forties. Another growth spurt during the late forties moves to an advanced plateau that lasts throughout the fifties and (perhaps) well into the sixties. During these decades of adult life, preference for formal or abstract operational thinking becomes stronger and stronger until, sometime around the early fifties, adults exhibit a preference pattern for the types of religious thinking that exactly match the sequence of types on a Piagetian continuum of operational thinking.[22]

Still, one may well ask, "What does that mean?"

Although the study of adult religious thinking is just beginning, it is probable that what we do know involves the fundamental affirmation that adults can mature into:

1. A growing appreciation of Paul's poignant sense of the ambiguity of the religious life (Rom. 7:15–20);

2. A realistic appreciation of what it means to be saved by grace alone (Rom. 3:21–25; Eph. 2:4–10);

3. A paradoxically humbling ennoblement as one identifies ever more closely with Peter's commission to "feed my lambs" (John 21:15–18);

4. A growing awareness that the busy disciples on the road to Emmaus are distinct examples of persons like ourselves (Luke 24:13–16).

Each of these insights requires an objectivity toward oneself and one's ideas, an ability to abstract oneself from the concrete specificities of a situation and to identify meaning within, through, or underneath one's personal historical facts. Each of these insights is a mark of maturity in the Christian life.

What the research data suggests is simple: Such maturity comes slowly across decades of living. Adolescents are moving toward that maturity, but one should not expect them to do more than move toward it. Some will reach it sooner than others, of course, but (in sheerly Pauline terms) that fact is no more than a "gift," which exists for the health of the whole (1 Cor. 12:7). It certainly is no sign of any spiritual superiority!

Moreover, as adults increasingly prefer formal or abstract operational thinking, there may come a profound appreciation of what it means to regard thinking and the religious as related by intersection. The relation of intersection insures a mystery in the religious that is not thinking: God, while approachable, always remains the Other to his creatures. It probably takes adult-level religious thinking, for example, to either understand or to find strength in the theological truism that while we depend upon God, he does not depend upon us. It is toward such a possibility that adolescents grow as they tend toward more and more formal or abstract operational thinking. Like many things in God's creation, that result is not inevitable. But that possibility means that those who work with cognitively growing adolescents can be filled with hope.

Notes

1. Dr. Leslie Francis' creatively critical paper, "The Humpty Dumpty Phenomenon in Research on Religious Thinking," delivered at the second Lancaster Colloquium on the Psychology of Religion (Jan. 8-9, 1977) suggested a threefold distinction: thinking about religion; thinking religiously; and thinking in religious categories.

2. Goldman, Ronald J. *Religious Thinking from Childhood to Adolescence* (London: Routledge and Kegan Paul, 1964; New York: Seabury Press, 1968). This work is referenced in the text as *RTFCTA*.

3. Goldman, Ronald J. *Readiness for Religion: a Basis for Developmental Religious Education.* (London: Routledge and Kegan Paul, 1965; New York: Seabury Press,

1968). This work is referenced in the text as *RFR*.

4. Although this denial of a separate religious rationality may seem to be unexceptionable in the late 1970s, the author can recall the severe shock experienced by some of his colleagues in the department of Christian education of the Episcopal church in 1964 when Goldman made this point quite explicitly during a one-day consultation.

5. As of 1977, the state-supported schools in England are still governed by the parliamentary Education Act of 1944, which made religious education a state-mandated school subject in all schools.

6. Goldman reported that he used in preliminary interviews the stories of (1) Moses and the burning bush, (2) the crossing of the Red Sea, (3) the call of the child Samuel, (4) King Ahab and Naboth's vineyard, (5) Jesus in the Temple as a boy, (6) the healing of blind Bartimaeus, (7) the temptations of Jesus, and (8) the resurrection appearance on the road to Emmaus. See *RTFCTA*, p. 37.

7. See the reviews by the North Americans David Elkind and Bernard Spilka, as well as that by the Belgian Andre Godin, in Merton P. Strommen, ed., *Research on Religious Development: a Comprehensive Handbook* (New York: Hawthorne Books, Inc., 1971).

8. The five questions Goldman used in his developmental analysis are listed in *RTFCTA*, p. 51 (English and American editions).

9. In addition to criteria for Piaget's basic sequence of (1) pre-operational, (2) concrete operational, and (3) formal operational levels of thinking, the author added criteria suggested by Goldman for an advanced formal operational level of thinking. That suggestion was contained in a mimeographed summary of his dissertation that Goldman published privately in 1962 while teaching at The University, Reading, England.

10. The four basic scales of religious thinking generated by the author's instrument, *Thinking About the Bible,* are called: (1) *Very Concrete,* which is referenced to criteria for pre-operational and early concrete operational thinking; (2) *Concrete,* which is referenced to criteria for concrete operational thinking; (3) *Abstract,* which is referenced to the criteria for formal operational thinking; and (4) *Very Abstract,* which is referenced to Goldman's criteria for an advanced level of formal operational thinking.

11. See Jean Piaget, *The Moral Judgment of the Child* (New York: Crowell-Collier Publishing Company, 1932/1962).

12. The basic reference for Mathis' EPI is H. Mathis, "Environment, Aptitude, and Race." Master's thesis, Wayne State University, 1966.

13. See J. G. Bachman et al., *Youth in Transition* 1 (Ann Arbor, Michigan: University of Michigan, Institute for Social Research, 1967).

14. Peatling, John H. *The Incidence of Concrete and Abstract Religious Thinking in the Interpretation of Three Bible Stories by Pupils Enrolled in Grades Four Through Twelve in Selected Schools in The Episcopal Church in the United States of America.* Doctoral dissertation, New York University, 1973.

15. See John H. Peatling, Charles W. Laabs, and Thomas B. Newton, "Cognitive Development: a Three-Sample Comparison of Means on the Peatling Scale of Reli-

gious Thinking," *Character Potential: a Record of Research* 7, no. 3 (August, 1975), pp. 159-162.

16. See John H. Peatling and Charles W. Laabs, "Cognitive Development of Pupils in Grades Four Through Twelve: A Comparative Study of Lutheran and Episcopalian Children and Youth," *Character Potential: a Record of Research* 7, no. 2 (March 1975): 107-115.

17. See Kalevi Tamminen, "Research Concerning the Development of Religious Thinking in Finnish Students: a Report of Results" and John H. Peatling, "Finn and American: Reflections on a Comparison," *Character Potential: a Record of Research* 7, no. 4 (April 1976): 206-225.

18. See E. A. Peel, "Intellectual Growth During Adolescence," *Educational Review* 17, no. 3 (June 1965): 169-180. Also see E. A. Peel, "A Study of the Differences in the Judgments of Adolescent Pupils," *The British Journal of Educational Psychology* 36, part I (February 1966).

19. See Table 11, Comparison of Student and Adult Religious Thinking (Total Abstract) Scale Means by Age-level Groupings in John H. Peatling, *Signs of Structure and Signs of Dissonance: Adult Responses to a Piagetian Moral Puzzle* (Schenectady, New York: The Author, 1976), p. 51.

20. In these two examples the author, like Goldman, offers an informed and knowledgeable inference from his research data on adolescent levels of religious thinking to adolescent cognitive behavior. The reader should be aware of the exact nature of these examples as inferences, for the empirical research to describe adolescent questioning and its relation to earlier decisions (as a function of level of religious thinking) still needs to be done.

21. The author is consciously echoing Goldman's thesis that a weakness of Christian education is "a direct result of trying to teach too much (and too much which is inappropriate) at too early an age." (See RFR, p. 65.)

22. See John H. Peatling, "Continuing Development of a Sense of Justice," *Vocational Guidance Quarterly* (June, 1977).

Bibliography

Goldman, Ronald J. *Religious Thinking from Childhood to Adolescence*. New York: The Seabury Press, 1968.

Goldman, Ronald J. *Readiness for Religion*. New York: The Seabury Press, 1968.

Peatling, John H. "Cognitive Development in Pupils in Grades Four Through Twelve: the Incidence of Concrete and Abstract Religious Thinking in American Children." *Character Potential: a Record of Research* 7 (October 1974): 52-61.

Peatling, John H., and Laabs, Charles W. "Cognitive Development of Pupils in Grades Four Through Twelve: a Comparative Study of Lutheran and Episcopalian Children and Youth." *Character Potential: a Record of Research* 7 (March 1975): 107-115.

Peatling, John H., Laabs, Charles W., and Newton, Thomas B. "Cognitive Development: a Three-Sample Comparison of Means on the Peatling Scale of Religious Thinking." *Character Potential: a Record of Research* 7 (August 1975): 159-162.

Peatling, John H. "Finn and American: Reflections on a Comparison." *Character Potential: a Record of Research* 7 (April 1976): 220-225.

Peatling, John H. "On Beyond Goldman: Religious Thinking and the 1970s." *Learning for Living* (Summer 1977).

Tamminen, Kalevi. "Research Concerning the Development of Religious Thinking in Finnish Students: a Report of Results." *Character Potential: a Record of Research* 7 (April 1976): 206-219.

5

Moral Development in Adolescence
Margaret Webster

Some adults would say, "It's about time we considered the moral development of youth!" Older generations have frequently tended to accuse youth of introducing a new morality or of having no morals.

Youth themselves claim that they are trying to discover what morality is, whose values are best, what the right decisions are in a world of many choices. They are aware of different standards in the home, the church, the peer group, and society as a whole. In the midst of such confusion, they ask, "How does one make moral judgments, and how can one live morally?"

In recent years Lawrence Kohlberg has contributed greatly to the understanding of the moral development of persons. Consideration of his work can help those who work with youth understand where youth may be in this development. However, since any youth group is likely to include persons at a variety of stages of development, it is important to look at the total scope of Kohlberg's contribution.

Kohlberg—the Man and His Work

Heinz, hoping to save the life of his wife, who was dying of cancer, tried in vain to raise sufficient money to purchase a new, promising drug that had been discovered by the druggist in their small European village. He also failed to persuade the druggist to give him credit toward the purchase. Desperate, Heinz broke into the store one night and stole the drug. Should Heinz have done this? If he was caught, should the judge send him to jail? If Heinz' wife was suffering unbearably and pleaded with the doctor to give her sufficient painkiller to end her life, should the doctor agree? Should a judge punish the doctor if he did so?

Using stories and questions like those of the Heinz dilemma,

Lawrence Kohlberg has spent much of his adult life studying the development of moral judgment in children and adults. Kohlberg, who was born in Bronxville, New York, in 1927, developed during a three-year period as a United States Merchant Marine a keen interest in ethics and psychology. His subsequent university studies focused in these areas, and in 1958 he received a doctor of philosophy degree in psychology from the University of Chicago. His thesis title was "The Development of Modes of Moral Thinking and Choice in the Years Ten to Sixteen."

Kohlberg is now professor of education and social psychology at Harvard University, where he has continued his interest in moral development and has explored the implications of his theory as a basis for moral education.

Other Studies of Moral Development

Among several theories of moral development, the one theory that Kohlberg believed to hold some promise for the understanding of moral development was that of Jean Piaget. Among the many aspects of cognitive development studied by Piaget was the development of moral judgment (1932). Piaget had concluded that the child's cognitive structures influenced his perception of experience and therefore of morality. He delineated two stages of moral development. One he described as a heteronomous stage (before seven or eight years) during which the child views morality as obedience to unchangeable rules fixed by respected authorities, with disobedience leading to imminent retributive justice. The second he identified as an autonomous stage in which responsibility shifts to the self; rules are the result of mutual agreement with peers; and justice is distributive.

Recognizing the merits of Piaget's cognitive developmental approach but also the limitations of a two-stage theory to explain variations in thinking for persons over age eight, Kohlberg undertook his own research and constructed his theoretical framework.

Kohlberg's Research

The original sample for Kohlberg's research was a group of seventy-five boys aged ten, thirteen, and sixteen. He has now followed these boys in a longitudinal study, testing them at three-year intervals from early adolescence into adulthood. He and others have replicated his original research in cross-sectional studies in the United States, Canada, Great Britain, Taiwan, Turkey, Malaysia, and Mexico.

In his research, Kohlberg used ten dilemmas similar to the Heinz dilemma with related questions. With younger children he always had interviews; with older children, youth, and adults he used oral interviews or written responses.

His interviews took the form of the semiclinical method used by Piaget—that is, though there were some fixed questions, the interviewer was also free to pursue the subject's own direction of thinking. Interviews were taped and transcribed for analysis.

To aid in the analyzing of protocols from interviews and written responses, Kohlberg and others have developed scoring guides. In this way, assessment of moral reasoning on a more uniform basis is possible.

Findings from this research led Kohlberg to formulate his theory of the development of moral judgment. Similar research by J. Rest, E. V. Sullivan, E. Turiel, and others has given support for the theory.

The Development of Moral Judgment

Definition of the Moral

For Kohlberg "the term 'moral' refers to moral judgments or decisions based on moral judgments . . . . We define morality in terms of the formal character of a moral judgment or a moral point of view, rather than in terms of its content." [1] "Moral judgments are judgments about the right and the good of action . . . . Moral judgments tend to be universal, inclusive, consistent, and grounded on objective, impersonal, or ideal grounds." [2]

The highest stages of moral judgment are "principled." By moral principle he means "a universal mode of choosing . . . a general guide to choice rather than a rule of action." [3]

Kohlberg indicates that for him the highest moral principle is justice. "Our major and most controversial claim is that the only 'true' moral principle is justice." [4]

It is evident that Kohlberg rejects the understanding of morality as a code of ethics, a "bag of virtues," or a set of relativistic values. His assumption is "that there are in fact universal ethical values and principles." [5] To be moral, then, is to think morally, to apply one's cognitive abilities to moral issues. While moral judgment has its *affective* aspect, "the quality . . . of affects in moral judgment is determined by its *cognitive-structural* development, a development which is part and parcel with the general development of the child's conceptions of a moral order." [6] "It is this emphasis on the distinctive form (as opposed to content) of . . . moral thought which allows us to call all men moral philosophers." [7]

Stages of Moral Development

As moral philosophers, people develop through stages of moral reasoning. Kohlberg describes three developmental levels, each with two stages: [8]

Preconventional Level: The child is concerned with the consequences of action or with the power of those who enforce the rules that govern his action.

Stage 1. Punishment and Obedience Orientation: Judgments regarding behavior are made in relation to fear of punishment, with unquestioning deference to superior power.

Stage 2. Instrumental Relativist Orientation: Judgments are determined by the usefulness of their consequences to the individual. "It is right if it is good for me." Occasionally the needs of others are considered, but from the point of view that reciprocity is a matter of "You scratch my back and I'll scratch yours."

Conventional Level: The expectations and rules of the individual's family, group, or nation become important. Personal conformity to and societal maintenance of law and order are paramount concerns.

Stage 3. Interpersonal Concordance or "Good Boy—Nice Girl" Orientation: Judgments regarding good behavior involve that which pleases or helps others (especially family or peers) and is approved by them.

Stage 4. Law and Order Orientation: Judgments are made in relation to authority, fixed rules, and the maintenance of the social order. Doing one's duty, showing respect for authority, and maintaining the social order are important.

Postconventional Level: There is a thrust toward autonomous moral principles that have universal validity and application.

Stage 5. Social-Contract Legalistic Orientation: Judgments are made in relation to what is best for the greatest number of people and may involve the changing of society's laws.

Stage 6. Universal Ethical-Principle Orientation: Judgments are based upon self-chosen ethical principles that appeal to comprehensiveness, universality, consistency, and justice.

While Kohlberg's work focused on these six stages in the development of moral reasoning, it should be noted that more recently he has tentatively proposed the possibility of two additional stages. He indicates that, in his work with persons in reform and penal institutions, he has discovered what appears to be a stage 0, with only rudimentary and undifferentiated moral thinking. He also sees the possibility of a stage 7, "meaning of life" orientation, in which such questions as "Why be moral?" are considered religious or metaphysical questions.[9]

Occasionally Kohlberg also discovered, with some young people—particularly with some college youth—what appeared to be stage 2 arguments but with much more sophistication in language and content. His theory does not allow for regression. He finally concluded that some people, in transition from stage 4 conventional thinking to the more autonomous stage 5 thinking, appear temporarily to use relativistic arguments in the transitional process. This type of transitional argument he now calls stage 4½ or 5 (2).

The Meaning of Stage

As in other cognitive developmental theories, the stages of moral development are *structured wholes*, total ways of thinking regarding moral issues. The construct stage implies a state in which the cognitive structures are qualitatively different from those of other stages. The stages are culturally universal, occur in an invariant sequence, and have a hierarchical relationship with each stage building on the previous ones.

Kohlberg has elaborated on his description of stage thinking in regard to twenty-eight basic aspects of morality which he believes to be found in any culture. These universal aspects of morality include the value of human life and motives for engaging in moral action, duty, responsibility.[10]

Developmental Transition

Development occurs partially as a result of the individual's internal reorganization of cognitive structures and partially from the interaction of the individual with the environment. The individual is active in this process, so that development is "self-constructed and self-regulated."[11] Kohlberg speaks of "cognitive conflict," which leads to "internal cognitive reorganization."[12]

Stage mixture is frequently seen as an indication of movement from one stage to the next. For instance, a person who is using chiefly stage 3 arguments may still retain some stage 2 thinking and may, on occasion, introduce some stage 4 ideas. Such a person is likely to be involved in a transitional process from one stage to the next; that person, however, will rarely be able to use arguments from more than one stage below or one above those of the dominant stage.[13]

As a stimulus to development, Kohlberg stresses the importance of opportunities for the person to take roles or role-play and to participate in family, peer group, and school communities.[14]

Persons pass through the stages at varying speeds and may become fixated in any stage of development. Kohlberg suggests that stages 5 and 6 "are still minority stages in the adult American population, even though stage 5 constitutes the public morality of the Constitution and the Supreme Court."[15] Probably "only 5 percent reach the highest moral stage."[16]

Moral Judgment and Moral Action

The work of Kohlberg has been primarily in regard to moral judgment, moral thinking, and moral reasoning. At the lower stages of development in moral judgment, moral action does not necessarily correspond with moral reasoning. However, Kohlberg points out that at the higher stages there is greater consistency between moral judgment and moral action. "Moral maturity," he says, is "the capacity to make decisions and judgments which are moral (that is, based on internal principles) and to act in accordance with such judgments." [17]

Moral Development: The Aim of Moral Education

In several of his articles Kohlberg has dealt with the implications of his theory of the development of moral judgment for moral education. He points out that, consciously or unconsciously, the school is inevitably involved in moral education. He refutes the idea that the educator's primary task is the transmission of information and of rules and values collected from the past.[18] Instead, Kohlberg states that "the goal of moral education is the stimulation of the 'natural' development of the individual child's own moral judgment and capacities, thus allowing him to use his own moral judgment to control his behavior." [19]

Consistent with his emphasis on peer-group participation as a stimulus for development, he stresses the importance of the classroom in providing this participation. A climate of freedom, cooperation, and justice in the school and classroom will, he believes, help to foster development.

As the chief means of stimulating development he proposes that, in moral education discussions, students be confronted with arguments at a level 1 stage higher than that in which they are presently functioning. This means that teachers need to be at least generally aware of the developmental stage or stages in which students are located. It also suggests that, for effective communication, there should be a match between the teacher's level and the child's. The teacher should be located in or utilizing arguments typical of one stage above that of the most advanced pupil.

Kohlberg and Religious Education

Kohlberg does not see religion as a motivating force in moral development. He states that there is fallacy in "the notion that basic moral principles are dependent upon a particular religion, or any religion at all. We have found no important differences in development of moral thinking between Catholics, Protestants, Jews,

Buddhists, Moslems, and atheists. Children's moral values in the religious area seem to go through the same stages as their general moral values." [20]

He does, however, recognize that "with regard to the *content* of moral beliefs, religious differences exist." He goes on to say:

> Formal religious education has no specifically important or unique role to play in moral development as opposed to the role of the public school and the family in this area. The primary purpose of religious education in our society is not to develop moral character but rather to develop religious beliefs and sentiments. The teaching of religious beliefs requires a teaching of their moral aspects as well as their theological aspects, since all religions stress an associated moral code. On the whole, however, the mark of success of such teaching is that it helps the child to make his religious and his moral beliefs and sentiments an integrated whole. [21]

A Critique of Kohlberg's Theory

Following this survey of Kohlberg's work and thinking, we should endeavor now to assess his contribution to an understanding of moral development. It is apparent that there are both strengths and weaknesses in his theory.

There is undoubtedly merit in his placement of moral development firmly within a cognitive-structural framework. In a society that holds such a variety of value systems, persons must apply their own cognitive abilities to judgments concerning moral issues. His emphasis on rational decision making and personal choice in moral development is a healthy antidote to the encouragement of blind acceptance and internalization of society's values. As persons use their cognitive abilities and develop through the various stages, they become increasingly autonomous, free and responsible individuals capable of moral decisions and moral behavior.

Kohlberg's careful description and analysis of stages of moral reasoning and stage transition have provided valuable insights for those who wish to understand the thinking of children, youth, and adults regarding moral issues. His research has been replicated in sufficient places and by sufficient people to confirm its validity. A developmental orientation such as his is helpful to educators, who need to be aware of the type of discussion of which students are capable and the type of discussion that might stimulate further development.

For persons who are prepared to undertake in-depth study of moral development and the assessment of moral reasoning, Kohlberg's instrument for discerning stages of moral judgment (related to the ten dilemmas) is a most useful tool. It has been used with good success to analyze the moral reasoning of children, youth, and adults, and to discover development of reasoning that may result from moral education classes and discussions.

With Kohlberg's theory, however, as with other developmental theories, caution needs to be exercised to ensure that stage analyses do not become person labels, which may imply disapproval of some thinking and therefore of some persons. We ought not to speak of a stage 2 person but rather of the stage 2 thinking, which a person may be using. It must be remembered that in most cases people make the best type of moral judgment of which they are capable at the time. Also, in most cases they have the potential for other viewpoints, which they will utilize as they are able. Kohlberg's theory is useful in helping us to understand where people are in their development and where they may be moving; his theory is not to be used to evaluate, judge, and condemn people.

One problem that many scholars find in Kohlberg's work is his inconsistency in regard to the relationship of form and content in moral reasoning. Within a single article contradictions occur. For instance, in his 1971 paper on "Stages of Moral Development" he indicates: "We define morality in terms of the formal character of a moral judgment or a moral point of view, rather than in terms of its content." [22] Then, a few pages later, he says: "Our conception of moral principle implies that one cannot ultimately separate form and content in moral analysis." [23] In considerations of the adequacy of reasoning within the various stages, questions arise as to whether it is the quality of reasoning or the nature of the content of such reasoning or a combination of both that is being examined. Similarly in some places where he stresses the primacy of the principle of justice he appears to have in mind a content-free "moral resolution of competing claims." [24] In other places justice appears to include such content as reciprocity and equality in human relations, liberty, and sympathy. While Kohlberg appears to prefer emphasis on moral reasoning rather than content, it would seem that the content of such reasoning is of importance also. He fails to deal adequately with the relationship.

A closely related problem arises for those concerned about religion and morality. Kohlberg minimizes the contribution of religion to moral development. As noted above, he has made some reference to the religious content of moral beliefs. But the place he gives to religious influences in regard to the development and the content of religious thinking seems most inadequate, especially to those persons who have recognized the importance of religious motivation in relation to many of their own ethical decisions. Much more work needs to be done regarding the relationship of religious influences on moral development.

In spite of the inadequacy of Kohlberg's treatment of the relationship between religion and moral development, a number of persons concerned with religious development have found inspiration from Kohlberg's theory of moral development. The present writer undertook research to discover whether persons think of God as judge in the same way that they think of the judge in the Heinz dilemma. In an exploratory study such thinking was evident and appeared to influence the individual's total idea of God. Edward Everding, Clarence Snelling, and Mary Wilcox have examined the influence of a person's social perspective, as seen in the various Kohlberg stages, on the person's interpretation of biblical material. James Fowler, drawing heavily on the work of Kohlberg as well as on insights from Piaget and Erikson, has developed a theory of faith development. In each of these studies implications for religious education have been explored.

Thus, while there are limitations in Kohlberg's work, religious education is indebted to him for his contribution to an understanding of how persons think about moral issues at various stages of development and how such development can be stimulated. Religious educators are also indebted to Kohlberg for the seminal nature of his work, which has led to additional studies specifically in the area of religious development.

Youth in Kohlberg's Developmental Stages

What, then, has Kohlberg to contribute specifically to our understanding of youth? The answer to that question is not easy to discover. Kohlberg has helped in the understanding of the way persons develop in their moral reasoning capacity; but he has not suggested age specifications for his developmental stages. He has indicated that persons develop at their own speed through the stages and may become fixated within any stage. Taken seriously, these claims could mean that a youth might be located in any stage from 1 to 6 and that any group of youth might include persons located in many stages.

In seeking a clue regarding the probable stage location of a majority of youth, the work of Edmund Sullivan, a co-director of the Moral Education Project undertaken by the Ontario Institute for Studies in Education, is helpful. In preparation for experimental moral education classes in elementary and secondary schools, several samples of children and youth (aged nine to eighteen) were tested with Kohlberg's moral judgment questionnaire. The younger children (nine- and ten-year-olds) responded chiefly with preconventional stage 1 and 2 judgments. At eleven years, stage 3 responses appeared more frequently; by age twelve most stage 1 responses had disappeared; and by age fifteen stage 3 thinking was the predominant mode. Between fifteen and eighteen years stage 3 thinking remained the most common, but stage 4 thinking appeared more frequently; and occasional evidence of stage 5 thinking emerged. No stage 6 thinking was apparent in the sample.[25]

If one can generalize from this sample (and generalization is accompanied by the possibility of error in many individual cases), it might be implied that thinking related to moral judgments tends to develop somewhat as follows:

Elementary school children: Thinking is predominantly in preconventional stages 1 and 2.

Junior high school youth: This is a transitional period with thinking moving from preconventional to conventional levels.

Senior high school youth: The predominant mode of thinking is in the conventional stages 3 and/or 4, with the possibility of some postconventional stage 5 thinking beginning to appear during the later years.

Adults: Thinking may be conventional or postconventional. The prerequisites for the more rarely found stage 6 thinking are probably both a good deal of formal cognitive ability plus considerable maturity and experience with adult life issues.

This probably means, then, that most youth are making moral judgments at the stage 3 or 4 levels. Some may exhibit remnants of stage 2 thinking. A few may begin to give evidence of stage 5 thinking. Those who work with youth, then, should have a clear understanding of the nature of reasoning within stages 3 and 4, to be aware of the present thinking of the youth, and also an understanding of stage 5 reasoning, toward which youth may be moving. Some further elaboration of stages 3, 4, and 5 reasoning is therefore provided below.

Stage 3: Interpersonal Concordance or "Good-Boy, Nice-Girl" Orientation

The person who has attained stage 3 thinking has left behind the more egocentric, relativistic, and hedonistic thinking of the preconventional level and is now concerned with moral judgments in relation to "my family, my group, my local church." Moral decisions are based on what these groups, which entail personal involvement, believe to be right and on what will help and please the other persons who belong to the groups. Other families, other groups, other churches may be somewhat suspect; their moral judgments may indeed be quite wrong. Behavior now is judged by intention; "he means well" begins to appear.

To the Heinz dilemma the person with stage 3 thinking may reply: "Heinz should have done this because he loved his wife very much and this was the only way he could save her. So he was forced to do it . . . . The judge should let him go free because the judge should understand that the stealing of the drug was for a good cause and that it was the poor man's only solution. What else could he have done?" (Response of a sixteen-year-old girl.)

In regard to any religious content of thinking, persons using stage 3 reasoning are likely to think of God as a kind, loving Father or friend who is concerned about the covenant relationship with his children, watches over them always, and is ready to forgive them in a fair, impartial way. The church for them should always be a loving, caring community to which they may be loyal. The good thing to do is that which the church approves; the good thing to avoid is that which the church disapproves.

Into the somewhat pleasant, rose-colored world of stage 3, however, conflict may intrude. That which pleases my peer group may not please my family or my church and vice versa. The judgments of others outside my group may appear to have validity also. As persons come increasingly into contact with other families, other groups, other churches, such conflicts may increase. The person facing such conflict may retreat into fixation in a stage 3 position or move forward to stage 4 thinking.

Stage 4: Law and Order Orientation

In stage 4 authority moves to a broader grouping—society, the nation. Now "my country" is right; "my country" is the best in the world. The person now recognizes that, if society is to survive, order is important. Laws and regulations have been established to maintain this order. It is a citizen's duty to abide by the laws, respect authority, and report wrongdoing.

In regard to the Heinz dilemma the person with stage 4 thinking says: "No, Heinz should not have done that. He was breaking the law. It was his duty to help his wife but also his duty not to break the law about stealing. He should have found some other way to help her . . . . The judge would have to punish him. If everybody broke laws like that, we would have chaos." (Response of a seventeen-year-old boy.)

This type of thinking leads to thought of God as a lawgiver (the Ten Commandments) whose chief concern is that people keep his laws. He will judge people accordingly. The church then has responsibility for teaching God's laws and admonishing people to live by them. The church and/or the Bible becomes the final authority in relation to moral judgment and action. The law of God as recorded in the Bible and proclaimed by the church demands unquestioning obedience.

But even the security of loyalty to a law-and-order society may be shaken. Older youth may become aware of corruption within a nation's legislative structure; they may discover that a particular set of laws is not adequate to deal with a specific situation; they may see one so-called Christian nation at war with another. Recognition of such inadequacies in legal authority may lead to movement to a stage 5 type of thinking.

Stage 5: Social-Contract Legalistic Orientation

As one moves into stage 5 thinking he begins to gain the ability to look objectively at his own society and laws in a more autonomous fashion. There is an attempt to discover some universal principles that one can adopt to guide decision and action. Utilitarian concerns (the greatest good for the greatest number) become important. It is now recognized that laws are important for the functioning of society but that they are made by mutual agreement to provide for concern for the greatest number. Laws can be changed when it is expedient to revise them.

The Heinz dilemma for the person with stage 5 thinking raises the question of the value of human life as opposed to any law regarding theft: "For Heinz there will be a real moral dilemma. He would not wish to violate the legal code that prohibits theft, but he would value even more the life of a human being. For this reason he would steal the drug and be willing to accept the consequences of his action." (Response of man age twenty-six.)

The religious content of thinking at stage 5 represents God as giving freedom and responsibility to every individual. People within the stage are now able better to understand the teachings of Jesus such as "You have heard that it was said . . . . But I say to you" (Matt. 5:38–39, RSV).

This does not mean that persons at this stage reject all of the church's teaching but that they begin to comprehend why certain things are taught. They then accept or reject these things for themselves. They begin to reach the maturity mentioned in Ephesians 4:13: "Until we all attain to the unity of faith and of the knowledge of the Son of God, to mature manhood, to the measure of the stature of the fullness of Christ" (RSV).

The Church and Youth Development

Finally, what has Kohlberg to say to those who carry leadership responsibility for youth in the church? A study of Kohlberg's theory of moral development raises many issues for the consideration of those concerned with the religious education of youth. Only three of these will be mentioned here.

1. *Know youth.* If the church is to work effectively with youth, it must seek to know them and their thinking, including their thinking in relation to moral judgments. Those concerned with youth must be ready to respect them as persons and to listen with similar respect to their thinking. Kohlberg's theory will help in the understanding of the thinking of youth and the direction in which we hope their development will go.

2. *Know the goals and objectives* of the church in relation to the religious education of youth. If the goal of a church is merely to have its youth absorb the traditional body of biblical and doctrinal teaching and maintain the status quo of the congregation, then it can use narrative, indoctrinative methods of transmitting its heritage to youth.

If, on the other hand, the goal is, like Kohlberg's aim in regard to moral education, to stimulate the development of the capacities and judgment of youth to the place where youth make their own response and decisions, methods to stimulate thought and development must be found.

3. *Know the leaders of youth.* The leader's level of development in moral and religious thinking seems bound to influence the level of discussion and thinking that takes place in any youth group. An authoritarian, conventional-thinking leader is not likely to help youth move to an autonomous stage of thinking and acting. Nor will such a leader be able to comprehend the thinking of some youth who may be far beyond the development of the leader. Such lack of understanding may mean that youth will become discouraged and leave the youth group and the church.

A church's knowledge of its youth, its establishment of appropriate goals and objectives for religious education, and its selection and training of suitable leaders will do much to provide the stimulation which will help youth in their development of moral judgment and, indeed, in the development of faith.

Notes

1. Lawrence Kohlberg, "Stages of Moral Development as a Basis for Moral Education," *Moral Education*, ed. C. M. Beck, B. S. Crittenden, and E. V. Sullivan (Toronto: University of Toronto Press, 1971), p. 55.

2. Ibid., p. 56.

3. Ibid., p. 58.

4. Ibid., p. 62.

5. Ibid., p. 32.

6. Ibid., p. 45.

7. Ibid., p. 36.

8. Ibid., pp. 86-88.

9. Lawrence Kohlberg, The Ethical Life, the Contemplative Life, and Ultimate Religion. Unpublished lecture, 1970.

10. Kohlberg, "Stages of Moral Development as a Basis for Moral Education," p. 88.

11. E. Turiel, "Stage Transition in Moral Development," *Second Handbook on Teaching*, ed. R. M. Travers (Chicago: Rand McNally and Co., 1973), p. 732.

12. Kohlberg, "Stages of Moral Development as a Basis for Moral Education," p. 49.

13. Ibid., p. 38.

14. Lawrence Kohlberg, "Moral Education in the Schools: a Developmental View," *School Review* 1 (1966, 1974): 17; "Stages of Moral Development as a Basis for Moral Education," p. 50.

15. Lawrence Kohlberg, "Moral and Religious Education and the Public Schools: a Developmental View," *Religion and Public Education*, ed. T. R. Sizer (New York: Houghton Mifflin Company, 1967), p. 170.

16. Lawrence Kohlberg, "Development as the Aim of Education," *Harvard Educational Review*, 1972, p. 486.

17. Lawrence Kohlberg, "Development of Moral Character and Moral Ideology," *Review of Child Development*, ed. M. L. Hoffman and L. W. Hoffman (New York: Russell Sage Foundation, 1964), p. 425.

18. Kohlberg, "Development as the Aim of Education," p. 453.

19. Kohlberg, "Stages of Moral Development as a Basis for Moral Education," p. 71.

20. Ibid., p. 39.

21. Kohlberg, "Moral and Religious Education and the Public Schools: a Developmental View," pp. 180-181.

22. Kohlberg, "Stages of Moral Development as a Basis for Moral Education," p. 55.

23. Ibid., p. 60.   24. Ibid., p. 63.

25. E. V. Sullivan, *Moral Learning: Some Findings, Issues, and Questions* (New York: Paulist Press, 1975), pp. 14-17.

Bibliography

Hartshorne, H., and May, M. A. *Studies in the Nature of Character.* 3 vols. New York: Macmillan Co., 1928, 1929, 1930.

Everding, H. E., Snelling, C. H., and Wilcox, M. M. Report of a Research Project on Kohlberg's Theory of Moral Development and Biblical Interpretation. Unpublished paper, 1975.

Fowler, J. W., III. "Toward a Developmental Perspective on Faith." *Religious Education* 69 (1974); 2, 207-219.

Kohlberg, Lawrence. "Moral Development and Identification." *The Sixty-second Yearbook of the National Society for the Study of Education (Child Psychology),* 1963.

Kohlberg, Lawrence. "Development of Moral Character and Moral Ideology." *Review of Child Development Research.* Edited by M. L. Hoffman and L. W. Hoffman. New York: Russell Sage Foundation, 1964.

Kohlberg, Lawrence. Moral Education in the Schools: a Developmental View." *School Review* 1 (1966, 1974): i-30.

Kohlberg, Lawrence. "Moral and Religious Education and the Public Schools: a Developmental View." *Religion and Public Education.* Edited by T. R. Sizer. New York: Houghton Mifflin Company, 1967.

Kohlberg, Lawrence. The Ethical Life, the Contemplative Life, and Ultimate Religion. Unpublished lecture, 1970.

Kohlberg, Lawrence. "Stages of Moral Development as a Basis for Moral Education." *Moral Education.* Edited by C. M. Beck, B. S. Crittenden, E. V. Sullivan. Toronto: University of Toronto Press, 1971.

Kohlberg, Lawrence, and Mayer, R. "Development as the Aim of Education." *Harvard Educational Review,* 1972, pp. 449-497.

Piaget, Jean. *The Moral Judgment of the Child.* Translated by M. Gabain. London: Rutledge and Kegan Paul, Ltd., 1968.

Sullivan, E. V. *Moral Learning: Some Findings, Issues, and Questions.* New York: Paulist Press, 1975.

Turiel, E. "Stage Transition in Moral Development." *Second Handbook on Teaching.* Edited by R. M. Travers. Chicago: Rand McNally and Co., 1973.

Webster, C. M. Towards a Cognitive Developmental Approach in Religious Education: a Study of Developmental Stages in Certain Aspects of Religious Thinking (with emphasis on the perception of God as judge). Unpublished doctoral dissertation, University of Toronto, 1975.

6

Counseling with Youth

Stanley J. Watson

Most young people live in a pressure-cooker environment consisting of a whirlwind of social activities, school assignments, and family schedules. In a driving effort to meet these demands, many of them remain personally dissatisfied. This unmet hunger leads them to experiment with drugs, astrology, therapy fads, and Eastern religious cults. It is not unusual to poll a youth group and find them declaring that their greatest problem is too many assignments. They may go on to assert that their greatest need is for more things to do!

The answer to this paradox appears to be that, although they are engaged in many activities, they do not find them particularly rewarding. It might be observed that at this stage in life one finds it nearly impossible to find contentment because some major needs are suspended and cry out for fulfillment. Teenagers could hardly be expected to have resolved their tensions concerning a life's vocation or to have channeled their sex drives into a happy, satisfying love life. Neither could they be expected to have arrived at a state of mature Christian faith that has resulted in a healthy value system and synthesized the diverse teachings of the Hebrew-Christian traditions and the secular scientific concepts they absorb in the public educational system.

Teenage Dilemmas

Even in their day-by-day decisions young people must choose options and take serious risks.

Gloria felt that she could not live without Jim. She described him as a warm, caring human being. He was handsome, personable, and easy going with many friends at school and in the community. But Jim got into trouble with the law. An undercover policeman identified him as a distributor in a marijuana ring in the high school.

Gloria was with him when he was arrested. Jim was tried and sent to jail. Gloria was given a suspended sentence because she and Jim were able to convince the judge that she was not involved. She was assigned to a professional counselor for a series of sessions with regular reports to her parole officer.

Joe is the smallest member of his gang and has the wit and energy often associated with a person of his stature. His friends love to have him around to see what he will dream up next. His teachers and church leaders find his charm hard to resist and, in the words of one, "let him get away with murder." But one day he was taken to the mental health clinic because his stash of marijuana had been located, along with a handful of medicine bottles containing an assortment of minor tranquilizers and amphetamines. Joe's parents placed him under the care of a psychologist, and he is still being seen regularly.

Louise was persuaded to spend a Saturday night in a fraternity house. She is a very pretty girl who is mildly retarded. Because her parents were so deeply embarrassed when the affair became public knowledge, they sought no help.

Lonny reacted with his fists when his father tried to respond to his verbal abuse. His mother finally called the sheriff's office. When the local deputy had him under restraint, he was taken to the mental health center and diagnosed as schizophrenic.

Larry has come to realize that he is homosexual and is struggling with the question of whether he should tell his parents. He is undecided whether he should seek professional help and has grave doubts that he can or needs to be helped.

Diane, a shy, retiring girl, somewhat obese, with a beautiful complexion and lovely brown eyes, has no ambitions and very few friends. Although her grades were low, she graduated from high school last year. But she has almost become a recluse in her room. Her mother and father are very concerned but have no idea where to turn. She went to a therapist over a period of time but refused to accept another one when he left the community.

Do these cases sound extreme and their numbers few? They are not. The persons and incidents are very real; most of them exist in a single, small community; and all of these cases, along with many others, are in the files of one counselor. The majority of these young people are members of churches and are regular in attendance.

Areas of Counseling

Although there are many Larrys, Dianes, Louises, and Joes, most teenagers fall in the normal category.

Bill, an intelligent, hard-working young man, is concerned with keeping his grade average high and with locating a college that will prepare him to enter medical school.

Judy, a vivacious, personable junior, has an abundance of energy and is planning to enter the seminary to prepare for a ministry in youth or children's education on a church staff. But she can't decide whether to combine her vocational plans with a decision to marry.

Russ and Debby have gone steady since the eighth grade. During the last two years their relationship has become more intimate, and two months ago they began having sexual relations. Russ tries to deny his feelings of guilt, but finds himself unable to go back to the previous relationship. Debby cannot deny Russ, and her need for emotional intimacy is as great as his. Both feel tense and fear they will be discovered and confronted by their parents. They feel guilty because their church teaches that premarital sex is a sin. Apart, they suffer with their negative feelings; together, they share their pain and comfort each other with rationalizations and emotional support. They cannot decide whether to continue their present relationship, to discuss their dilemma with their parents, or to get married secretly.

The general areas of counseling fall into two categories: vocational-educational and personal-social. The first relates to what to do in life; the second deals with how to live a life. Schools are designed to prepare an individual to become educated and to get ready for a vocation. Homes and churches are presumed to be responsible for teaching adolescents how to live successfully. Unfortunately, in a society in transition, the limitations of the basic institutions are evident. They become obsolete and out of step or, for many reasons, fail to accomplish their tasks. The task definition for the school has been altogether too narrow, it appears. The young person is a complete entity; and while he is getting an education and preparing at school for a vocation, he is also formulating a basic philosophy and developing a life-style. The educator who adopts a secular stance in order not to influence the students religiously has only succeeded in modeling for them a secular point of view.

Personal-social problems are generally expressed in social conduct and relationships between the sexes.

Developmental Tasks of Adolescents

Consider the broader demands for personal adjustment outlined by Robert J. Havighurst in his developmental tasks for adolescents.[1] In previous generations a young person identified himself by his life's work, his sex, his religion, and his socioeconomic status. No longer are teenagers involved directly in helping the family economically. In the main they will bypass manual labor in order to develop a technical skill that will allow them to enter into the automated world of today or to prepare for a profession. From an era when work was valued and children a blessing, they are growing up in a world in which the moral value of work has greatly decreased and children are generally viewed as liabilities rather than assets.

Apart, then, from the traditional ways of self-identification, one must go about the formation of identity without reference to vocation. Also, there are strong trends toward eliminating sex as an important aspect of identity. The youth is pressured to lay aside religious concepts and to ignore socioeconomic status. With due consideration for the dangers of discrimination, is it any wonder that the youth of this era, more than those of previous generations, suffers from identity diffusion of crisis proportions? (See chapter 1.)

In spite of the cultural changes today, society, family, and the individual himself require that certain developmental tasks be completed in order for the youth to be considered a functioning adult. It is in the struggles of youth to accomplish these tasks that they encounter problems. The counselor should be familiar with the tasks and goals one must pursue in reaching maturity. In summary form, the tasks are as follows:

1. Every adolescent must learn to view girls as women and boys as men. He must also learn how to work with his own and the opposite sex for the good of all. Equally important is the need to

learn how to control personal feelings and to develop the ability to exert leadership without dominating.

2. The adolescent must accept and feel comfortable with his or her masculine or feminine social role. While the traditional role concepts are changing, one's basic self-concept demands a clear sexual identity and social role.

3. The adolescent must adapt to his own body and learn to use it effectively. This task will require that he accept its shape, its strong points, and its limitations, and that he observe the rules of good health, including proper nourishment, regular exercise, and a sensible schedule of sleep.

4. The young person must also develop enough autonomy to become relatively free from an emotional dependence upon his parents. This does not mean that his affection for them will decrease; indeed, it may well increase. Affection derives from a mutual respect between parents and their young people as autonomous individuals of different generations.

5. Youth is the time to develop a positive view of marriage and family life. This involves attitudes toward children and the development of skills in parental effectiveness and in home management.

6. The young person must prepare himself for a career in a highly complex industrial world. His ability to formulate a viable vocational goal and to organize his life to meet its educational requirements will have a great influence upon his view of himself and his place in society.

7. The adolescent will acquire a set of moral values and develop an ethical system of one kind or another. For good or for ill, he will formulate an idealogy which may or may not be effective in guiding him to cope with moral problems and to make ethical decisions. (See chapter 5.)

8. During teenage years an individual develops personal responsibility. At this time he determines the degree of his adherence to the values of his society and the level of his own involvement.

Later in life the youth will reevaluate, revise, and adjust to the demands of each task; but much of the spadework is done during the teen years. In a few cases dramatic changes occur later in life, but in the vast majority of cases the views and conduct of the adolescent, with further refinement and amplification, remain constant throughout life.

Coping Skills for Daily Living

The coping skills a youth develops in seeking to fulfill his developmental tasks are determined by several factors. Such factors as mental ability, physical appearance, emotional maturity, and social competence are significant. They in turn are determined by his genetic heritage, the modeling of parents and other significant adults, and the prevailing social values of his peers. From the pressures built up by society and self to accomplish tasks, a set of attitudes begins to emerge. The degree to which these attitudes correspond with his conduct will vary greatly from person to person.

1. Sexual feelings, sexual relations, and attitudes toward sex are a constant source of problems. Such problems evolve around questions about masturbation, dating, premarital sex, and postmarital sexual adjustment.

2. The use of drugs, alcohol, and tobacco can be a source of problems for youth. They may have resolved the question of whether to participate and to have determined frequency and amounts, only to discover that some of the side effects and social results are counterproductive. Often the young person will seek help in coping with the results while at the same time denying the cause-and-effect sequence of his habits. The greatest damage from the use of drugs may be their interference with his accomplishment of the developmental tasks.

3. Other social patterns, such as gambling and cheating in school, may come in for social, group, and individual evaluation.

4. The forms of recreation can influence youth development and are generally a source of conflict with parents.

5. The process by which one may gain popularity or notoriety is a ripe area for breeding problems that call for counseling.

Counseling of adolescents in the area of religion has to do with personal spiritual growth and covers such subjects as conversion, prayer, worship, temptation, and personal commitment. For example, many young people have made professions of faith at an early age, but later have questioned their earlier decision. After personal introspection and counseling, some decide that they did not have a valid experience. At this point they generally make a public profession of faith and are baptized. Others come to the conclusion that they sincerely responded to God in faith at their earlier maturity level. They decide generally to make a public rededication at their near-adult maturity level. (See chapter 7.)

Principles and Procedures in Counseling Youth

Good counseling can only come about when the counselor and young person develop an atmosphere in which both feel comfortable. The purpose of a counseling interview is neither simply to answer a problem nor to find a solution. Its purpose, instead, is to develop a skill on the part of the counselee by which he may be able to learn how to resolve his own problems. The counseling atmosphere must have at least three elements.

Positive regard. The counselor is primarily responsible for developing interpersonal relationships with the young person that leave no doubt in his mind that he is welcome and that the counselor is not assuming a parent relationship to him. The counselee must be seen as a person who has the ability to resolve his own problems and to take a positive direction in his own self-development. The positive regard of the counselor is expressed through his eyes, the tone of his voice, and the expression of warmth toward the young person throughout each session.

Empathy. As a young person begins to express his feelings and deal with his problem, the counselor begins to identify with him and feel the tensions and anxieties that have built up as a result of his problem. Emotionally and even mentally, the counselor feels that he almost stands in his counselee's shoes.

Confidential nature of the material. By clear statement the counselor should let it be known that whatever transpires is private and that the information belonging to the counselee will not be divulged without his permission.

Youth workers sometimes express a certain amount of bewilderment over the fact that they are not often called upon for counseling with youth. Close attention to the atmosphere of counseling may hold the answer. If only one of the elements is missing, the possibility for counseling in an effective manner is destroyed. The person who is too busy to empathize, who is too preoccupied to give positive regard and acceptance, or who carelessly reveals information that has been given in private will find that young people can be unforgiving and that their relationship can be quickly terminated.

The Counseling Interview

Attention. The counselor must give careful attention to the counselee. At the same time he is listening to what the counselee says, he will need to observe his body motions and give close attention to his eyes and facial muscles. This requires a great deal of skill in listening. The fact is that some young people have never had an adult to give complete and undivided attention to what they had to say.

Permission. The counselor must allow a young person to express himself without reservation. In many cases learning the information he shares will be like looking into a person's innermost thoughts. The teenager is not guarded and is not passing judgment upon what he says, but is giving and sharing all that he has discovered in the secrets of his own mind and feelings. For this reason, anything goes. This means that the counselor will not judge, will not show shock, and will not argue. Judgments or arguments can destroy or terminate counseling in the early stages of the session.

Respect. The feelings of the young person should be respected and in many cases will need to be clarified. This means that much of the time, the feelings come out in the form of expressions that are emotional and confused. Clarification for the young person as well as the counselor is helpful at this point. A statement like "If I understand, what you are saying is _____" or "You are saying that you feel _____" is helpful. At no time should the counselor express a negative response indicating that the young person should not feel the way he says he feels. His feelings must be respected, whatever they are. Only after delving into his emotional responses to situations and people can he truly know the effect they are having upon himself.

Problem Solving. Identify the problem with regard to the cause.

This often calls for probing or opening with questions in which the young person gives more and more information. Layers of feelings and responses are laid bare until the cause is discovered. The fact that a person has identified the cause of the problem does not mean, however, that the problem is solved. Problem solving requires a consideration of alternatives. This means that there are occasions when the young person has misinterpreted or has based his assumptions and responses on faulty logic. It is surprising how many adults carry inadequate or immature thinking throughout their lives and have not used their rational ability to describe and analyze their problems. Another alternative is referral if the problem seems too great. At no point should the counselor indicate that this is a procedure by which he can rid himself of the time and trouble it takes to do counseling. In each case it should be mutually decided that someone else has more of the skill or information needed for the young person in his dilemma.

In considering alternatives by which a person can make decisions, the counselor should introduce Christian considerations, including faith in God and prayer if the time and the response of the person is appropriate.

A proven way of handling alternative possibilities is the pro-con method of decision making. In this very simple approach the counselor leads the counselee to consider the factors that would be in favor of one of the alternatives chosen for consideration and all of the factors that would be against it. One method of doing this is to write the problem at the top of a sheet of paper, and on one side factors for and on the other side those against. By this means a person can readily see the factors that would be in favor of that solution and, in contrast, the factors that would be against it.

Technique. The technique of responding to the young person is to listen carefully and to reflect. Reflection means that the counselor will continue to indicate to the young person that he is reading his feelings. This is somewhat like holding up a mirror in which he can see his own reactions to the problem.

Background Information. The counselor will attempt to gain as much information about the young person as possible. A part of the session can be well spent in asking questions and in discovering background information.

Many times a young person will approach the counselor with superficial problems. These pseudo problems are intended to find out how well the counselor can handle something that is not really significant to the counselee. After the period of testing, he will then share what is really uppermost in his mind.

Young people who are conditioned to quick remedies and television shows in which the problem is solved in thirty minutes or one hour come to the counselor expecting an immediate and simple solution. It may take a while for them to realize that there are no easy answers and no shortcuts to personal growth. The counselor himself is sometimes tempted to find simple solutions. This reveals itself in his attempt to give advice, to preach. We need to remind ourselves constantly that the young person is not here to answer one problem, but rather to develop the skill of problem solving.

Indeed, in the process of counseling the young person will find that he will go over the same material time and again, puzzling, seeking answers, and trying to understand. This calls for patience on the part of the counselor and persistence on the part of the young person.

Structuring. The temptation will often arise for the counselor to spend too much time in a counseling session. While going over an hour or even up to an hour and a half is acceptable under critical circumstances, to go far beyond an hour and a half is likely to be counterproductive. The counselor will need to explain to the counselee exactly the amount of time that he has available. It should be at a time when both are free to devote their undivided attention to the counseling process. Much of the time is spent in allowing the young person to ventilate. This means that he will freely express his feelings and frustrations. The counselor will find himself coping with expressions of anger and, on some occasions, tears.

During the process of counseling, projection often occurs. The young person will become angry at the counselor, as he may have been in the habit of becoming angry at other adults in his life. He may blame the counselor for things which are not his fault. In many cases, he is unable to determine just why he became so angry with this adult who is making every effort to help him with his problem.

On the other extreme, he is apt to become very emotionally attached to the counselor. This is normal and should be handled with maturity, consideration, and thoughtfulness. In cases where the counselee is of the opposite sex, it is especially important that the counselor be able to relate in a way that will maintain the respect of the individual without encouraging the deepening of dependency.

The final goal of the counseling process should be kept in mind at all times. Self-understanding and self-acceptance are vital to the youth's ability to understand and deal with his problems. More importantly, his sense of self-esteem will determine the measure and level of his growth and maturity.

Terminating. Eventually the young person becomes comfortable enough with his decision to become independent from the counselor. At this time the counselor can make the young person feel free to return for other sessions if the need arises.

Referring. The counselor would be well advised to refer the young person to someone else when the circumstances call for it.

Certainly if the counselee shows symptoms of mental illness, professional help should be found. This is a sensitive but critical move. Usually the advice and support of a professional would be required before such a transfer can be made. Symptoms of mental illness appear in abnormal ways of thinking and acting by the counselee.

1. He may hear voices that no one else can hear.

2. He may see people or things that simply do not exist.

3. He may become very withdrawn and not respond to people or events around him.

4. He may reverse his way of expressing himself. For example, a quiet person, when ill, may become extremely happy and boisterous. Or a peaceful person may become angry and aggressive.

5. He may become confused and unable to know where he is or who people are, including himself.

6. He may offer grandiose schemes or claim to be a famous or well-known person.

7. He may feel that everyone is plotting against him and that others are trying to hurt or kill him.

8. He may complain of bad odors or a foul taste in his mouth.

9. He may think that his body has changed its form; that some of his parts, such as his head, arms, or legs, are not connected to his trunk; or that he is coming completely apart.

10. He may repeat acts in a ritualistic way, such as washing hands or turning around in a prescribed way before seating himself.

11. He may laugh at nothing and fail to laugh at what others consider funny.

12. His eating habits may change radically. He may refuse food.

13. He may not sleep but spend the nights and days in restless movement.

14. His language may become nonsensical, consisting of garbled sounds or meaningless words and phrases.

15. He may appear to have no feelings at all. He may appear sad and listless.

16. He may become suspicious of and angry at the people closest to him. Normal people show many of these symptoms in mild forms. The mentally ill or psychotic person experiences them to a much greater degree.

The neurotic young person may also need referral. The most obvious difference between him and the psychotic person is the degree of insight. The psychotic is so preoccupied with the extreme activity going on inside his brain that he relates primarily to a very private and individual world. He does not consider himself insane but thinks that other people simply do not understand his world. The neurotic, on the other hand, is excruciatingly aware of his suffering and cries out for relief. He seeks to relate to the real world, only to find that the experience is painful and exhausting. The counselor can do much to help the neurotic. He may find, however, that his expertise and patience have reached their limits and that he must call upon someone else whose training and experience would contribute to his efforts.

Referral skill requires that a counselor know the resources available in a community. For example, a knowledge of the mental health programs and personnel in the area would be needed.

Other problem areas call for further information about community resources.

Who will help a youth find a summer job?

Who can help him discover his abilities and interests in regard to a life's vocation?

Who can help a transient youth with food and lodging?

Who will help a youth on drugs or who shows signs of alcoholism?

Who can help when a youth's relations with his parents have deteriorated and the problem is beyond the skill of the counselor?

Who can help a youth who needs instruction on clothes and grooming?

Who can help a youth in trouble with the law, who is unable to hire a lawyer?

Who will give tests and treatment to a youth who suspects that he has veneral disease?

Who can help youth (girls and boys) involved in pregnancy when parental help is not adequate?

Records

Good records are important in counseling. While they may serve to jog the memory, they are valuable in evaluating the problem and in organizing the procedure of counseling. The following guidelines are suggested.

Background Information. An information sheet should be filled out on each counselee. The counselor can fill out the sheet in preparation for or after the first session, or he can have the young person do so. This sheet should have the date and the person's name, age, sex, address, and telephone number. It should also record his school grade and/or place of employment and duties. It should include his family size, socioeconomic status, a description of the parents and siblings, and the position of the young person in his family. Other pertinent information, such as medical history and difficulties at school, at home, or in the community is also needed.

Present Problem. A concise statement of why the young person came for counseling can help to clarify the need and set the pattern for counseling.

Problem List. In addition to the problem for which counseling was initiated, one will generally find a number of other problems. For example, if a youth is having problems with his teachers, his grades might be affecting his elegibility for sports; or he might be at odds with his girl friend. Other symptoms might also appear, such as a tendency to drink or smoke marijuana as an escape. Also, he should be questioned and observed for evidences of any physical problems or a poor regimen as to rest, nourishment, and exercise.

Progress Notes. A record of each session should be kept in the form of notes. Several systems are available such as verbatim, anecdotal, or a brief summary. One of the simplest and best approaches is to analyze each problem that was dealt with in a simple outline as follows:

SUBJECTIVE: A paragraph is written in which the counselor reports how the youth sees himself in relation to the particular problem.

OBJECTIVE: This paragraph contains a description of how others, including the counselor, see the young person in regard to the problem.

ANALYSIS: This paragraph consists of a description of the dynamics of the problem with whatever interpretative insights the counselor may bring to bear upon them.

PROCEDURE: Finally, the counselor describes the steps that he plans to follow in helping the young person cope with his problem.

After a counseling relationship has been terminated, a final summary should be placed in the young person's file and should contain a brief history and the reason for termination.

Personal Factors in Counseling

Nearly every counselor will concede that the most important counseling tool he owns is himself. Techniques are important and skills are essential, but personal adjustment is more significant in achieving success.

Emotionally, the counselor must be well adjusted and relatively free of wide swings from elation to depression. His ability to respond warmly to his counselee must be balanced by good judgment, moral fiber, and the ability to remain loyal to personal commitments. Too many Christian counselors have become emotionally and sexually involved with vulnerable persons who have come for help. Nearly always the intention of the counselor was good, but the fact remains that he was not personally prepared for the task. He must learn to accept as a matter of course the transference of love and affection, of hatred and suspicion. It is not easy to become the target for anger or the object of love and remain stable and balanced while maintaining a caring relationship. The counselor must do this successfully, however, if he is to counsel at all.

Socially, the counselor must remain open, approachable, and available. He is expected to establish times and places he may be seen and to let the youth know how he can be reached when the need is especially urgent. His attitude of friendliness does more to declare his availability than any other kind of communication.

The counselor's willingness to hear any and every kind of problem and to respect the young person regardless of how he is handling it is essential to establishing rapport. Young people equate moral judgment as rejection and respond with anger and withdrawal. Acceptance of the person, on the other hand, does not signify approval of his actions.

The development of tolerance requires a reassessment of one's biases and a willingness to make philosophical and emotional adjustments in depth. Consider, for example, the areas of counseling in which the counselor might have emotional hang-ups. The religiously oriented are likely to find sex to be a most difficult subject. At the same time, this is a most troublesome area to youth. They are physically mature and capable of mating, but not ready for marriage. The sex drive is at its peak; and, to many young people, there appears to be no socially approved sexual outlet. The counselor must be prepared to deal with the youth who masturbates, the one who is promiscuous, and the homosexual, as well as those concerned with the usual moral issues surrounding dating.

In the realm of religion, the counselor may be called upon to counsel some who espouse one of the Oriental methods of meditation or those who are obsessed with the charismatic movement and speak in tongues. He may be approached by the youth who is certain that he has committed the unpardonable sin or one who is psychotic and is under the care of a therapist. In each case he is expected to relate to the person with Christian care and professional skill. If he fails in either of these, let it be at the point of professional skill.

A healthy interest in other persons and a concern for their welfare is the Christian basis for counseling. A preoccupation with morbid details evidences unresolved problems on the part of the counselor and detracts from his ability to deal with the real issues at hand. Experience in counseling will convince the counselor that very few things are unique enough to surprise him; and sooner or later he develops the ability to see even bizarre things in their true perspective. At the same time he will need to become even more sensitive to the cry of the counselee for help.

An assessment of each counselee includes a knowledge and an understanding of the characteristics of his age level. Excellent work has been done on age-level traits by such men as Havighurst, Erikson, and Gesell. The writings of these men and others should be researched for an understanding of developmental tasks, age-level characteristics, and studies of their behavior patterns. The counselor must be aware of the unique personality of each young person as well as the traits he holds in common with his age-mates.

The counselor is able to inspire courage and optimism in young people to the degree that he reflects those qualities in his own life. Probably the most pressing need of young people is for encouragement and hope. Consequently, it would be difficult to overestimate the power to bless that the counselor holds in his hands.

Finally, the counselor must possess the willingness, the time, and the emotional energy required to counsel. He must often sacrifice his personal preferences in the interest of troubled youth. Only time will reveal the strength of his influence, however, should he choose to devote himself to the development of a skillful ministry of counseling with members of the oncoming generation of Christian young people.

Note

1. Robert J. Havighurst, *Developmental Tasks and Education* (New York: David McKay Co., 1973), pp. 43-82.

Bibliography

Erikson, Erik H. *Identity, Youth, and Crisis*. New York: W. W. Norton and Co., 1968.

Havighurst, Robert J. *Developmental Tasks and Education*. New York: David McKay Co., 1972.

Irwin, Paul B. *The Care and Counseling of Youth in the Church*. Philadelphia: Fortress Press, 1975.

Maston, T. B., and Pinson, William M., Jr. *Right or Wrong?* Nashville: Broadman Press, 1971.

Narramore, Clyde M. *Counseling Youth*. Grand Rapids: Zondervan Press, 1966.

Strommen, Merton P. *Five Cries of Youth*. New York: Harper and Row, 1974.

7

Youth and the Affirmation of Faith

G. Temp Sparkman

Identity is the major task of adolescence, but the most important decision that youth will make is the affirmation of faith. People of faith have long believed that apart from understanding our relationship to God, there can be no complete self-understanding. Leading theologians through the years have expressed such a conviction, suggesting that the life of faith is the fully human existence, the complete life. This chapter is built on the assumption that the affirmation of faith is closely related to the dynamics of the identity quest.

The term *affirmation of faith* has a special meaning in this discussion. It is not exactly the same thing as what is meant by persons who use such phrases as profession of faith, conversion, confirmation, or accepting Jesus. It includes all of these, but it is broader than any one of them.

Affirmation of faith involves two elements: an appraisal of the heritage and a declaration of personal faith. Thus it incorporates both the dynamics of the profession of faith, as practiced in evangelical churches, and something of the assumptions behind confirmation, as practiced in liturgical churches. My hope is that, regardless of the theological viewpoint from which you come, you will see that these two elements make up the ideal way for children to come to a self-assumed faith.

The Dimensions of Affirmation

Before examining the two basic elements in the affirmation of faith, let us look at some dimensions of affirmation. Apart from the substance of the affirmation of faith, what can be said about affirmation itself?

For one thing, affirmation is voluntary. It is the result of personal response. To affirm is to say yes to something or someone. To affirm is to respond favorably to something we have encountered or experienced. No one can affirm something for us, for we alone can will something for ourselves. Others can want something for us and can attempt to force or influence us toward that something. But only we can affirm that something for ourselves.

From early childhood the individual will develops, and we become more independent as we gain ego strength. We become persons in the fullest sense when we are capable, to a reasonable degree, of making choices on our own. Of course, we can never become completely independent of others. That would be undesirable even if it were possible. And there is a sense in which we are more aware of dependence on God as we grow older. So we are not talking here about a person who has an overexaggerated sense of independence, but about one with an identity strong enough to make a decision and to assume personal responsibility for it.

A second dimension of affirmation is that the power to affirm is a gift of God. The God who made us also chose out of his own autonomy to make us free beings—free to follow, free to go our own way, free to love, free to reject. To be sure, our autonomous choices are not without their consequences; but they are free and unencumbered.

This leads to a third dimension—namely that, while free, we are influenced by others. How many of us could explain our own personal faith apart from the influence of Christian men and women who brought us up in the faith? These influences have varied from loving to coercive, but their power cannot be denied. No doubt some of our decisions have been in response to an overbearing influence of a parent, a teacher, a pastor, or a friend. However, the more fulfilling and long-lasting decisions are those made out of the loving influence of sympathetic adults who have surrounded us with religious nurture.

Another aspect of affirmation is that it cannot be the automatic result of educational process. There is much that education can do for us, much that it can prepare us for, much that it can lead us toward. However, education stops short of making decisions for us. Just as others cannot make choices for us, neither can the educational process make choices for us. It can lead to but cannot affirm faith in Jesus Christ. Faith is much too personal for the educational process to be able to assure that we will appropriate it for ourselves.

A final dimension of affirmation is that it is radical but not necessarily cataclysmic. When we affirm faith we are doing something radical—that is to say, something that will affect our lives totally. From medical experience we know that radical surgery means surgery that is going to have a pervasive effect as well as an inherent aspect of high risk. The affirmation of faith is that way. It cannot be a mere formalized response to education or the result of having attained a certain age. No, it is far more radical, for it influences all of our other decisions and relationships.

Two Elements in the Affirmation of Faith

We know that the affirmation of faith is approached according to various theologies. Some churches baptize their children when they are infants and then confirm them in the faith at some time in late childhood or in the youth years. Other churches do not baptize their children until the children make professions of faith. Such profession and baptism may happen at various ages during childhood or youth, or they may not occur until adulthood.

The position of this chapter is that the affirmation of faith is a far richer experience than can be explained simply by the terms *profession of faith* or *confirmation*. Both of these terms do, of course, have their own deep meanings. The following discussion attempts to explain those meanings and to blend them into a single term, *affirmation of faith*.

An affirmation of faith has two complementary, inseparable elements—an appraisal of the heritage and a declaration of faith. Both elements are essential if the youth is to experience the full meaning of affirming faith. If one element is taken seriously and the other lightly, the youth will have a distorted understanding of what it means to take up the faith for oneself.

Element 1: the Heritage Appraisal

The affirmation of faith includes an appraisal of the heritage in which youth have been nurtured. This appraisal is a journey back through childhood in an attempt to remember what the church has already done for youth. It is looking back over the teachings that formed their early education. It is an attempt to get in touch with the feelings that surrounded the warm environment in which they were nurtured.

This journey that is necessary in making an appraisal of the heritage will be different from church to church, but its aim is the same. In the liturgical churches the appraisal is a reminder to youth of the baptismal vows made in their behalf in infancy. It may also be a reminder of the time in childhood when they first took communion. In such churches this aspect is already provided in the confirmation rite, during which youth are asked to accept the pledges made in their behalf when they were too young to do so for themselves.

In the evangelical tradition there are no infant baptismal rites. However, an increasing number of churches are sponsoring what are generally known as dedication services. In such services the parents are reminded of the privileges and responsibilities of parenthood, and the church is challenged to surround the child with love and right teaching. Youth who have been a part of such services can be told what was said and done in their behalf. Where no services of this kind have been provided, youth can be told of the other things that have been done for them to ensure that they would grow up in the faith.

In all cases this backward look can include a review of some of the central teachings of the church, the kind of worship the church has celebrated, and some of the activities the church has sponsored. Some of those persons who taught the youth during childhood can be brought to these heritage appraisal sessions. This personal experience might evoke more help for the appraisal than would doctrines, the worship, and the activities.

The journey into the past is not, however, all there is to the process of appraising the heritage. Of equal importance is a study of the basic doctrines and character of the church. Regardless of the rites and teachings that made up their childhood experience, youth are now ready for a new level of exposure to the church's teachings. Their new cognitive ability (see chapter 3) will make it possible for them to grasp deeper meanings, and the search for identity (see chapter 1) will cause them to recognize subtleties that childhood experience did not include.

Some of the themes to be studied are God, the life and work of Jesus Christ, the meaning and mission of the church, and the meaning of sin, faith, and commitment.

Such a study may take several directions, but the most fruitful will begin with how youth presently understand these themes. Since it is a personal faith that we are aiming toward, it is only right that we begin by reviewing what the youth understand rather than by telling them what they are supposed to believe. The author once approached such a study by leading the youth to formulate a confession of faith. We began by looking at some historic creeds and confessions, then began working on our own. We produced a very meaningful statement of faith.

While the focus of the sessions will be on what the youth believe, leaders will likely teach the youth some aspects of these doctrines and themes. It does become important to teach youth about beliefs that they themselves might not personally hold to. This is a realistic practice because the faith belongs to a community of believers, and that community takes on a certain theological character. It would be deceptive to allow youth to look at their heritage without telling them the entire story.

Most denominational publishing houses have curriculum materials that can be used in the appraisal of the heritage. These materials can be utilized as they are or adapted to fit a particular situation. Enterprising leaders can create their own sessions.

The hope for all of this remembering and this discussion of doctrine and character is that our youth will affirm the heritage. There is no more fulfilling moment for parents than when their children say, "This heritage is mine. What you have been doing for me I wish to continue in." At such a high point parents and teachers are rewarded for their faithful instruction and patient guidance.

Affirming the heritage, however, does not constitute the whole of an affirmation of faith. Besides looking at the heritage and affirming it, there is also an element of having personal faith in Jesus Christ that transcends the heritage. This element is the declaration of personal faith. Let us describe and analyze such a declaration.

Element 2: the Declaration of Personal Faith

The affirmation of faith is made complete when the declaration of personal faith is joined with the appraisal of the heritage.

The heritage has been looked at; the doctrine of the church has been reexamined; and youth have chosen to continue in that heritage and with the church family which holds that doctrine. But this much, while indispensable, does not amount to personal faith. Therefore, something more is needed. Beyond the identification with what has been done in their behalf, youth have to assume the faith for themselves. In the liturgical tradition youth have to take the baptismal vows upon themselves, not merely accept them ceremoniously.

This declaration is in a sense only one in a long series, although, as we shall see, it is unique in adolescent experience. Interwoven throughout the education and nurture of children has been the necessity of some personal decisions about the meaning of Jesus Christ, about commitment to some Christian causes, and about ethical alternatives. In these decisions children are trusting and committing and choosing rightly. When children pray in times of fear, they are trusting. When they join in some worthy project or minister to someone, they are committing themselves to the Christ. When in the face of an ethical dilemma they choose rightly, they are doing what Christians do.

Yet, these decisions added together do not constitute the full meaning of a declaration of personal faith. This full meaning has waited upon adolescence. This personal decision, made sometime during the youth years, has an existential involvement and a futuristic element not fully present in the early, more intuitive and concrete decisions. More of selfhood is involved, and more of a future commitment is possible at this time. To see what this "more" is, we will need to return to earlier discussions. Inhelder and Piaget (see chapter 3) suggested that one of the distinguishing characteristics of adolescence over childhood is the adoption of a life plan, a kind of model that turns the adolescent toward adulthood. In their thought the life plan is one of the elements responsible for the development of formal reasoning. It is more than a vocational choice and certainly more complex than childhood fantasies about certain careers. This notion of a life plan has roots in the writing of a German psychologist, Eduard Spranger, who believed it to involve a very idealistic life philosophy and emphasis on the future.[1]

Chapter 1 focused on the search for identity as the major task of adolescence. We saw in that discussion that the adolescent ego is trying to find a new strength, based in some balance between the negative and positive forces that pull on it. When these pulls are brought under control there is a fidelity, an inner resonance that gives the youth a base from which to handle experience. When the pulls are not mastered, there is confusion of identity; and the youth are left without anchorage. Of course, life cannot be fully mastered at so young an age, but it is possible for enough of a stability to be established to mark a flowering identity that is going to hold under fairly normal conditions. The identity is always subject to threats that it cannot handle, as witnessed in the breakup of stable personalities during divorce, death in the family, or other crises.

This discussion is not to say that personality identity and religious identity are the same. It does, however, raise the perplexing question as to whether the personality identity can be truly complete without the religious dimension. For our purposes we are more concerned with whether religious identity is possible apart from the dynamics of personality identity in adolescence. Can a person face seriously the challenges of a personal declaration of faith apart from the questions of selfhood that make up the identity quest?

It is the author's belief that the very pulls of the identity crisis are the mix out of which personal faith is most likely to be born. As youth face the deepest questions of selfhood, they are at last prepared to face also the meaning that faith brings to personality. The unity sought in the identity struggle seems elusive, and youth look for a unifying reality. They can find that reality in what the church has told them about Jesus Christ and themselves.

In the liturgical tradition the youth have always been told that they are a part of the church and are children of God because of their baptism. Now, at this disruptive time in their experience, they sense a discrepancy between who the church has told them they are and what they feel about their relation to God. For all of their feeling about being children of God, there still exists an obscuring of that relationship; and it cannot be seen so clearly. In this tradition this process reveals the awful face of sin. Though they are children of God, they feel some measure of alienation from the Father.

In the evangelical tradition youth have been told since early childhood that they are sinners and outside the family of God. Now in the identity crisis they see the same face of sin, the same one the youth of the liturgical tradition see. While they had been told all along that they were sinners, their consciousness of sinfulness was vague and foreboding. Now, in their youth years, they can understand what was meant.

Regardless of the tradition out of which the youth have come, regardless of the beauty and integrity of the heritage, the condition is the same. For the first time youth see that the unity they are seeking is elusive. It is here that the elusiveness and the alienation are interpreted as the result of sin. Sin is seen not merely as that which can be reduced to a listing of sins, faults, or wrongdoings, but as an obscuring, disintegrating force working against the distinctiveness of the image of God in which all have been created.

Youth come to a time when they sense that more is wrong in their existence than history, doctrine, worship, or community ethos and ethic can solve.

This is not the first time youth have heard of sin, for it has been talked about in many settings in the church and home. It is, however, the first time in life that they have been able to grasp the full meaning of sin and to make some personal decision about sinfulness and the meaning of Jesus Christ. It is not the first time youth have heard of Jesus Christ, for they have heard much about him as Savior—in the hymns, prayers, and preaching of the church. And while they remember having followed the teachings of Jesus as best they could, it is the first time that they can grasp fully the real import of the redemptive work of the Christ.

This new ability is what was discussed in chapter 3 concerning cognitive processes. You will remember that the child was characterized as a concrete-bound thinker, unable to perform formal operations or to manipulate data abstractly, apart from concrete experience. In that chapter a new kind of thinker was characterized as one who could understand abstractions, do second-order thinking, and think about thought. The concept of sinfulness is an abstraction, a generalization. To be sure, sin itself is very concrete; but sinfulness is an abstraction. It cannot be explained merely by adding up all of the concrete instances of sin that one can imagine.

To limit our understanding of sinfulness to one or more concrete sins and to hold persons responsible for those would mean that preschool children would be responsible for sin. And to hold to sinfulness as an accumulation of sins would raise the question as to when a person has accumulated enough sins to be considered sinful and therefore responsible. This leaves us with a concept of sin that has to be generalized from concrete instances. We have already employed such terms as alienation, obscurity, disunity, disintegration.

The understanding of such a concept requires a formal thinker who can look at the fact and fruit of sin and perceive a condition, an uncontrollable force, an awry dimension of personhood. Such a level of thinking is an adolescent, not a childhood, realization. This can be illustrated by what some children said when they were asked, "What is sin?" A six-year-old said, "A sin is what gets you into more trouble than you know what to do with." A seven-year-old introduced the idea that there are degrees of mistakes and that sin is the worst degree: "A sin is a really bad mistake. When you make a little mistake, your parents punish you. But when you make a sin, God punishes you. And I bet he can really spank." A nine-year-old suggested that there are degrees of sin: "A sin is when you disrespect the law of God. There are big sins and little sins. Like when you beat up your sisters . . . that's a middle-sized one." Ronald Goldman found that only from the age of twelve years, eight months, and up was there an understanding of "evil as a propensity within every person." A girl aged thirteen, four months said of the devil, "It's the evil spirit in us all." [2]

The great hope we have for our youth is that they will see themselves as inextricably bound up in the defection common to all persons, realize that the work of Jesus Christ is to show them the way out of that sin, and declare personal faith in him. In some theological families this experience is called conversion. In other families it is known as confirmation. In some cases it might be thought of as one of many conversion experiences already had and yet to come, but pivotal and giving more of a direction to a person's life.

To be a genuine declaration it must, however, go beyond a mere emotional experience, a repeating of baptismal promises, a character-setting decision, or an automatic culmination of an educational process. It must be a deliberate, self-made declaration that what Jesus did is now being personally appropriated. It is thus emotional; it does relate to earlier pledges; it does affect the character; and it speaks well of education. But it is more than any or all of these.

Summary

The youth has examined the heritage of faith and has said, "This heritage is mine. What you have been doing for me I wish to continue in." The youth has struggled with identity questions, has sensed an alienation from the God who makes things whole, and has said, "I confess my sinfulness and Jesus Christ as Savior"—or, as in some communions, "The vows made for me in baptism I now make my own."

Since such a decision will not be made immediately upon turning from childhood to youth or will not be a scheduled ceremony at which time all youth are expected to make a declaration, we who work with youth will need to be patient. This will not be easy, for there are times when events in the identity crisis seem to be working against an affirmation of faith. What looks like a flowering faith one day suddenly appears gone the next. Our anxiety during such times can be relieved only if we remember that we are witnessing an identity being born and that, just as in natural birth, there is some pain and risk.

To be sure, we cannot be detached from the travail, for much is at stake—the future of our children in the faith. Still, it is a personal decision, and there is nothing that we can do except what we have already done. We can continue to model and interpret the meaning of faith and support our youth as they find what that means for them.

The question comes: What about those youth who come to us without a background in the faith? Obviously these youth have no heritage to appraise; thus, the first element of the affirmation will be missing. But the second element, the declaration of personal faith, does not depend upon the first. Rather, it follows the person's own development and understanding of sin and belief. Once such youth come under our influence, however, they begin to understand the kind of faith community they have come to. Thus the meaning of a faith heritage will begin to be developed and will continue.

Your Own View of This Issue

This chapter is the author's view of what is involved in a genuine affirmation of faith. Those of you who want to develop your own statement are referred to several resources that will be of assistance.

First, the issue probably has been debated within your denomination within the last twenty years. Your education and curriculum board will have papers and bibliographies of such discussions. In addition, some denominations have prepared materials that state an ideal for the movement of religious experience from infancy to adolescence.

Second, numerous books, booklets, and articles are available. See the journal *Religious Education*, published in New Haven, Connecticut, issues for September-October 1963 and July-August 1965. William E. Hull has an unpublished paper, "The Child and the Church." The dynamics of the religious experience of youth can be studied in *Adolescent Religion* by Charles W. Stewart (Abingdon). Lutheran publishing houses have a booklet, "Affirmation of the Baptismal Covenant." *The Nurture and Evangelism of Children* by Gideon G. Yoder (Herald) includes a chapter on adolescent experience.

Third, look at the bibliographies for chapters 1—5 of this book. Also, examine firsthand the research mentioned in chapter 4. Many have attempted to formulate a view of the affirmation of faith without listening seriously to what human development specialists have to say. Because it is persons that we are dealing with, psychology is of utmost importance.

Fourth, a study of psychology is not sufficient. The theology of sin and belief, of Christology and personhood are of special significance. See the works of the major theologians and your denomination's articles or confessions of faith. In addition, it is probable that your denominational education and curriculum board has a statement of theological assumptions that underlie the preparation of curriculum materials.

Fifth, every resource will have a blind spot—some dimension missing, some reality seemingly distorted or ignored. This is where your own discipline of thinking will become important. Considering thoughtfully all of the information at hand, how will you put it all together? That is the question. If you attempt to create your own view, I hope that it will be as rewarding to you as it has been to me and that it will send you down as many exciting roads, still with miles to be traveled on each before the final destination can be seen or reached.

Notes

1. Quoted by Rolf E. Muuss, *Theories of Adolescence* (Westminster, Maryland: Random House, 1966), p. 50.

2. Ronald Goldman, *Religious Thinking from Childhood to Adolescence* (New York: The Seabury Press, 1968), p. 174.

8

Involving Youth in Worship and Learning
William R. Cromer, Jr.

The water of life and true worship are linked by the Gospel writer in John 4:7–26. Physical thirst requires continuous attention. Even so, thirsty souls must return again and again to the living water, like a panting hart searching for a water brook. Those who seek with all their being to worship God "in spirit and in truth" discover that their need for worship is matched by God's affirmative action: "But the hour cometh, and now is, when the true worshippers shall worship the Father in spirit and in truth: for the Father seeketh such to worship him" (v. 23, KJV).

The Father seeks youth to worship him.

Worship: a Definition

The record of early Christian worship (begun before the record was written) is found chiefly in Acts and the epistles, with some suggestions in Revelation. W. D. Maxwell has pointed out that four factors were prominent in these experiences of worship: worship practices learned in synagogue and Temple, the *agape* or love feast, the Lord's Supper, and prophesying or speaking in tongues. By A.D. 150 only the synagogue feature of Scripture reading and exposition "in a setting of praise and prayer" and the Supper remained.[1]

To define worship in a way agreeable to everyone would prove difficult. Nevertheless, its meaning needs clarification. First, *worship* is the English form of *worthship* and is derived from the Anglo-Saxon *weorthscipe*, meaning a state of worth or worthiness. Second, a working definition of Christian worship: Worship is the response of confession, adoration, praise, offering, and service to God through Jesus Christ, his Son.

Acts of Worship: It is *how* worship is to be accomplished that seems most often to divide Christians, especially adults and youth.

The distinctive character of meaningful worship for youth is that the *means* that may elicit a worship response are often different because youth are different developmentally and by social conditioning. For example, the editor of a religious paper objected to the music at an evangelism conference, while a young person testified that it "really spoke to me." There are those who legitimately feel as Browning:

> I then, in ignorance and weakness,
> Taking God's help, have attained to think
>   My heart does best to receive in meekness
> That mode of worship, as most to his mind,
> Where earthly aids being cast behind,
> His All in All appears serene
> With the thinnest human veil between.[2]

Others agree with Marilee Zdenek and Marge Champion, who believe that worship should utilize all forms of art, spontaneous movement and expression, emotion, multimedia, and so forth. These authors even propose that such an approach is scripturally based.[3] A still more innovative example is the programmed creativity of folk-rock worship experiences for youth—experiences that rarely fail to puzzle some adults.

QUESTIONS: *What do you feel is lacking in the suggested definition? How does your church view the nature of worship? (A conversation with two or three members could prove revealing.) Do your church youth appear to have a particular concept of worship? What is it? Is the concept of worship in your church reflected in practice?*

Worship: a Model

Soren Kierkegaard (1813-1855), Danish philosopher-theologian, left us a penetrating suggestion about worship that merits study.[4] He observed that worshipers went to church to sit and participate in the experience as they would the theater. They were the spectators, there to watch the preacher and choir, who were the main performers. God filled the role (if present at all) of a remote prompter. The entire transaction seemed one-way, from actors to spectators; only the actors were presumed to have any direct reference to God. The relationship might be pictured as follows:

Kierkegaard declared that true worship was quite different from going to a concert or play. Worshipers are not to be *passive*, receiving the word of the Lord revealed only and uniquely through a spokesman. Instead, worshipers are the prime actors whose diverse actions are a "performance" that affirms their devotion and praise to God. God is not a hidden prompter but rather the *audience*. Clergy and choir are *prompters* who remind, suggest, and assist the worshipers. This model might be diagrammed thus:

One significance of such a model is that it changes the focus of *responsibility* for worship. No longer is the preacher or leader solely responsible for the experience. The worshiper becomes responsible for his own worship. No longer is he free to blame or credit others; he must face his own actions and develop his own acts of confession, adoration, praise, offering, and service. Worshipers must become involved or their actions cannot be "in spirit and in truth."

QUESTIONS: *What changes would you make in worship experiences in your church in order to implement Kierkegaard's model? Would it mean changes in what your church is not doing for/with youth? What worship aids are available but not now being used with your youth group?*

Involving Youth in Worship

A bumper sticker I spotted some time ago read: "God is not dead. He just doesn't want to get involved." Effective worship will demand that youth get involved if they are to find ways to express

joy/
  thanksgiving/
    sorrow/
      disappointment/
       prejudice/
        hate/
         anger/
          celebration/
           compassion/
            hope/
             confession/
              other concerns.

Some youth are comfortable with structured worship services planned by the church staff. Having grown up with a traditional pattern, they accept it without reservation. The fellowship of peers, mingling with the opposite sex, familiar seating area, music perceived as being religious, and attractive platform personalities serve their particular pattern of needs. Small changes in the structure or content of worship might be perceived as novelty. A good source of meaningful planning suggestions for enriching their worship is John T. Wayland's *Planning Congregational Worship Services.*[5]

However, after studying 7,050 church youth Merton Strommen concluded: "An enigma for youth is why gatherings to celebrate their faith, such as Sunday morning worship, are often dull. Many find inspiration totally lacking in this function of their church family."[6]

For what are these who feel an absence of excitement and celebration in worship searching? Are there ways the church may assist them to experience the holy and transcendent in "here-and-now" categories that are valid?

Creative, Contemporary: The collection of structured responses to these questions have been loosely called creative or contemporary worship. Creative and contemporary, unfortunately, have come to mean everything from a changed order of service to the bizarre. In an effort to be more precise, James L. Christensen has suggested these characteristics of creative or contemporary worship.

1. It attempts to meet people where they are in scientific understanding, with a vocabulary that expresses faith in terms relevant to the twentieth-century mind . . . . Contemporary worship strives to use contemporary thought forms and urban language.
2. It attempts to recapture the spirit of celebration, expressing joy in what the Holy Spirit has done and is doing in the world. Themes of worship focus on the new life and victory in Christ's love and hope.
3. It is oriented to the needs of persons rather than the needs of the institution. Some traditional worship services have seemed tantamount to a rally, encouraging support and loyalty to the organization . . . . It focuses upon where God intersects humanity in everyday happenings.
4. It strives to involve the worshiper, both bodily and mentally.
5. It is characterized by focus upon life and the social applications of faith, in contrast to the other-worldly emphasis.[7]

QUESTIONS: *What means have you used to learn about youth needs in worship? In what ways are the developmental needs of youth important to their worship? Do you agree with Christensen's ideas on contemporary worship? How do they apply to youth in worship?*

Preliminary Considerations

"But do our kids really want that kind of experience?" A basic principle is to avoid assuming you know what youth want and will respond to in worship. Ask them! This can be done in at least two ways.

First, youth may serve as part of a churchwide study group on worship. David Randolph holds that "In virtually every case when significant progress is made to more meaningful worship there is a small group in the church that made an intensive study of the meaning of worship." [8] He urges that such study include both those who do and do not attend worship services and that it become part of a cycle of study, data-gathering, creation of resources, designing of services, worship, evaluation, study, and so forth. Wilfred M. Bailey has printed some results of this process for a marriage ceremony, a funeral, and a baptismal service in one church.[9]

A second technique is to utilize a worship inventory that provides data on youth attitudes, preferences, and desires. Such data could help in planning and evaluating youth worship experiences as well as in assisting the church staff in planning worship for the entire congregation. A suggested inventory follows.

YOUTH WORSHIP INVENTORY

Age _____ Sex _____ Church member? _____ How long? _____

1. The high point of the worship service for me is:

    ____ morning prayer   ____ special music

    ____ Scripture reading   ____ sermon

    ____ invitation   ____ congregational singing

                                                 ____ other.

2. Which of the following type of worship service would you prefer:

    ____ very formal   ____ restrained, but not too formal

    ____ more spontaneous and less structured   ____ very informal, unstructured

3. I prefer a sermon that:

    ____ is highly evangelistic

    ____ relates Scripture to everyday problems

    ____ is based on personal illustrations from the pastor

    ____ explains a Scripture passage

    ____ is based on real youth experiences.

4. How long do you believe a sermon should be? _____

5. Which type of music do you prefer in a worship service? (Underline.)
    old familiar hymns; new catchy tunes; folk music; choir anthems; solo.

6. Do you feel that dramatic presentations help you to worship?
    yes _____ no _____ sometimes _____

7. Do announcements detract from worship? _____

8. If you could, what one thing would you change in the worship service of your church? _____

9. What do you feel should be the strongest note or theme in a worship service? (Underline.)
    laughter; thanksgiving; joy; assurance; hope; seriousness; commitment.

10. Would you prefer to have regular Youth Worship Services separate from adults?
    yes ____ no ____ occasionally ____

11. When new elements are introduced in a worship service (guitars instead of organ, dialogue instead of sermon, drama, or any change from the regular service), what is your reaction?

12. Do you like sermons that are obviously directed toward youth (sex, dating, vocation, and so forth)? _____ What subjects would you like to hear discussed? _____

13. Would you like for the pastor to preach occasionally on topics suggested by youth in your church? _____

14. Do adults in your church encourage youth to participate in the leadership of worship services? _____

15. What is your favorite song for use in worship? _____

16. Consider the meaning of the words of the following songs, and number them in order of their significance for you in worship.

___ In the Garden	___ One in the Spirit
___ Here Is My Life	___ Holy, Holy, Holy
___ How Great Thou Art	___ A Mighty Fortress
___ Room at the Cross	___ Jesus, the Very Thought of Thee

17. Listed below are a few of the many types of music used in worship today. Circle the types most significant to you and explain why.

    a. Major works, such as Handel's *Messiah*
    b. Formal anthems, such as settings of scriptural texts
    c. Folk musicals, such as *Good News*
    d. Anthems that are hymn arrangements
    e. Gospel songs, such as "Love Lifted Me"
    f. Choruses, such as "Sweet, Sweet Spirit"
    g. Spirituals, such as "He's Got the Whole World in His Hand"

18. What do you usually do during the morning worship service? ____

_____

19. The greatest problem I am facing just now is _____.

20. What do you do in order to help you worship in private (Bible reading, prayer, meditation, and so forth)? _____

21. When I listen to the preaching, I am:

    ___ a. interested most of the time
    ___ b. bored most of the time because
            ___ I usually don't listen
            ___ the sermon is not relevant to me most of the time
            ___ I'd rather be somewhere else
            ___ I honestly don't understand what's being said most of the time.
    Other:

22. The offering is part of the worship service because:

    ___ the church needs the money to pay bills
    ___ it is my obligation to give
    ___ the Bible says we should give
    ___ it gives me opportunity to give something of myself to God.

23. When other people lead in prayer, I:
    ___ listen to the words and participate silently in the prayer to make it mine also
    ___ feel close to God and enjoy the experience
    ___ think of other things
    ___ think about the prayer but don't know what to do or what to concentrate on.
    Other:

24. When I participate in the Lord's Supper, I:
    ___ understand its meaning
    ___ consider it routine; I don't really understand it
    ___ enjoy the reverent atmosphere
    ___ feel the presence of Christ in a special way.
    Other:

25. When the Bible is read in a worship service, I:
    ___ don't pay much attention
    ___ listen for the meaning of the passage
    ___ read along silently in personal or pew Bible
    ___ consider it a meaningful part of the worship for me.
    Other comments:
    I read the Bible for private worship: ___ never
                                            ___ sometimes
                                            ___ on a regular basis.

26. Meaningful characteristics of worship for me are:
    ___ service to others   ___ talking about religion
    ___ feeling forgiven   with friends
    ___ praising God   ___ speaking to God
    ___ being quiet   ___ listening to God
    ___ praying   ___ singing
    ___ going forward during   ___ giving money
        the invitation   ___ listening to the preacher
    ___ being with friends   ___ other.

27. I really feel God's presence most when (consider *any* time—public or private):

Once you have discovered youth attitudes, another principle is to avoid using worship experiences to *justify* an activity you have already decided to promote. It is patently unacceptable to use worship as a means to a predetermined end. The emotions of youth have sometimes been prostituted in this way by professional and amateur religious hucksters. Simply put, don't use worship to manipulate persons for your purposes.

A third principle is that the success or failure of worship cannot be determined by whether or not a predetermined activity results. Success is not to be measured in terms of the activity the *leader* desires. For example, he may wish a tithing commitment when the worshiper needs to give his commitment "to do justly, and to love mercy" (Mic. 6:8) or to repent of prejudice.

Planning for Youth Worship Experiences

A basic assumption in all youth education is that there is need for adult guidance in the process. Thus, caring adults are needed to assist youth in planning for their worship experiences. This helping process involves several considerations.

1. Objective-theme-reason for the experience. Determination should be made of the focus of the experience, including whether it is to be built around a sermon or whether a sermon is to grow out of the theme. How is this theme or objective to be expressed and developed?

2. Consider carefully the composition of the youth audience/group. Significant factors include age, sophistication, prejudices, recent events in the immediate situation, theological climate of the community and church, and pastoral leadership.

3. Consider the length and character of the responsible adult's relationship to the group. Closeness may permit dealing with their personal concerns in worship but make their personal, open response more difficult. Personal distance, if accompanied by respect, may even make response easier. (This is a factor in Billy Graham crusades, where personal distance seems to facilitate response.) Still another factor is age, since there is a tendency to choose vehicles for worship that suit the adult's age rather than teenagers.

4. Consider available leadership resources: reading, drama, music, media, speaking, art. It is better to do *less* through use of youth than always to bring outsiders to do a great deal *for* youth. Youth become involved and grow through participation.

5. Consider physical factors that may affect worship. These include group size; setting and atmosphere; seating arrangements;

musical instruments available; physical comfort; lighting; materials such as hymnals and bulletins. John Burke reports that some youth choir members even ask, "Why do we have to wear robes which cover up our individuality when the church teaches the worth of the individual, and when society does everything to remove the individuality and to establish a mass culture?" [10]

6. Consider specific (and perhaps even unusual) ways to involve group members in participation: litany, liturgy, dialogues, music, responsive readings, prayers, directed meditation, or sharing through written or artistic symbols.

7. Consider the impact of symbolism and ritual with this particular youth group. What is likely to be the impact upon them—not the adult? The leader should not force his symbols on youth. He may discover they have a negative effect. For example, some youth groups would respond negatively to the presence of a cross and candles on a covered table as the visual focus for worship.

8. Consider specific methods or activities through which youth may express in action their essentially emotional responses. "What can I *do* in response to this experience?" is a question deserving of an answer.

Selected Resources: In addition to sources cited in the chapter, see the bibliography at the end of this chapter for ideas that can enrich worship experiences for youth.

Learning as the Mode

Teaching-learning was deeply imbedded in the tradition of Israel. The *shema* of Deuteronomy 6:4–9 was a classic description of family responsibility for ensuring learning. The rabbi was an educator as well as an interpreter of Scripture. So serious was the rabbis' view of learning that they posited a question: "What does God do in the fourth quarter of the day?" Reply: "He sits and instructs the school children." [11] One rabbi said: "Perish the sanctuary [place of worship], but let the children go to school." [12] Let the church burn down, but save the place of learning, the synagogue school. Learning was even more important than worship!

Jesus stressed the importance of learning. Indeed, his whole life and ministry suggest that rabbi or teacher was his chief role for most of his followers.

What is the implication of this? It is simply that of all the processes for transmitting a religious heritage (indoctrination, force, sacraments, slavery), the Christian faith rests primarily upon the process of teaching and learning. Learning is the mode for both communication and survival among men of God's revelation in Jesus Christ.

Learning: a Definition

Psychologists, researchers, and laymen all wish they knew more about the nature of the learning process. Education and selfhood, as Roger Shinn observes, are still a mystery. Perhaps the most that can be said about learning is to identify several processes through which it occurs, suggest some basic theories, and propose a definition.

Processes: The chief processes through which learning occurs are *rote conditioning* (which includes even subconscious responses), resulting from experiences of pleasure/pain; *identification* with peers and family; *trial-and-success* (problem-solving, exploration, discovery, testing); and *insight* (discovering clues that enable one to see new connections and a new synthesis and to find a solution). Jesse Ziegler has also suggested *sublimation*—when it serves to prevent primitive sexual drives from interfering with the learning process.[13]

Theories: Learning theories are both numerous and complex. It is not within the purposes of this chapter to critique them. However, the bibliography at the end of this chapter should provide some helpful references for further study.

Additional reading might include the writings of Jean Piaget, Lawrence Kohlberg, Jerome Bruner, and Sidney Simon.

Definition: Learning is technically an intervening variable used as an explanatory concept to account for the relatively permanent changes in behavior that occur as a function of experience. It is the inference of these variables that we call "learning."

A more workable definition is that learning represents changes in perceiving and behaving as a result of experience. It is the difference, the change, that constitutes learning. It involves changes in cognition (knowledge, knowing), motivation (learning to like or dislike), group identification (belonging to or alienation from a culture), and voluntary control of the bodily muscles (speech, motion, self-control).

Teaching, then, becomes arranging the conditions necessary to learning and learning how to learn. The learner becomes responsible for his own learning, and his decision in each experience conditions his future learning potential. Jesus clearly described this aspect of personal responsibility in Luke 8:18, about which Frank Stagg comments:

> Jesus insisted that the hearer is responsible for how he hears. Verse 10 does not mean that God determines who may understand and who may not. The difference is in the condition of the hearers. It has to do with attitude. The conclusion to the parable is a warning that how one hears determines whether his capacity for hearing increases or decreases. . . . The consequence of refusing to hear is the loss of ability to hear.[14]

To expect that intentional learning will occur in a youth group or anywhere else solely because a teacher or leader is present (even if he is prepared) is a church tradition that needs demythologizing! The learner's attitude and preparation are always 51 percent of any successful teaching-learning transaction. That is the main purpose of printed curriculum materials: They are aids to the *intentional* learnings of youth.

Specific study and learning programs for church youth are commonly designed for intentional, cognitive learning experiences. They usually involve classrooms, printed curricula, learning aids, planning, and infrequent evaluation. These tend to be viewed as the sole or chief provisions for teaching and learning. It should be recognized, however, that learning is of three types (cognitive, psychomotor, and affective) and occurs in many ways, in a variety of contexts. For example, significant learning results from activities such as sports, camping, mission tours, music, drama, crafts, hobbies, travel, creative writing, photography, and art. One ministry of the church is to help youth discover and develop skills that not only bring satisfaction but that also may provide some income and even an occupational career. This type of learning may not always yield to the use of classroom agenda but will result primarily from participatory experiences. (Denominational publishing houses have materials which provide guidance in these areas.)

Leaders should encourage youth to develop creativity by providing incentive and technique. Ross Snyder's ideas for "processing lived moments into culture," "phenomenologizing," and "theologizing about existence" through the use of art, documentary imaging, and haiku are deserving of study and experimentation for this purpose.[15]

Youth ministry projects may also involve youth in learning about other groups, finance and fund-raising, tutoring, ministering to senior adults, service projects, learning about political power, dealing with bureaucracies, and so forth.[16]

Sunday School as a Learning Context

The popular assumption regarding youth Sunday School seems to be: "There is some bad news and some good news. The bad news is that most youth Sunday School classes experience only exposition and lecture and are therefore dull and uninteresting. The good news is that some other youth classes are creative, exciting, and always interesting discovery experiences which, if duplicated by others, would cause youth to crowd into classrooms." Neither of these statements is totally true.

The assumption that expository teaching is always dull and uninteresting is refuted by the recollections of most students. There *are* persons whose knowledge, speech, and communication skills make such a learning experience very exciting. Also, certain special knowledge about Bible interpretation as well as mature experience may most immediately be available through a teacher. Nevertheless, this approach does tend to overlook the learner's need to be self-active and the fact that few Sunday School teachers are so gifted as to pull that off. This probably explains why helpful how-to books are rare, if not nonexistent.

Harvard psychologist Jerome S. Bruner has given new significance to the concept of learning as essentially a process of discovery.[17] Confronted with a problem or need, the learner discovers a solution through purposeful seeking. This concept has become popularized as "creative," "inductive," and "interest-centered" teaching and learning.

The discovery or creative approach to teaching is usually basic to viewing youth Sunday School experiences as a total period, organized around a central truth or theme. Thus, whether working as a large group or in small groups, youth Sunday School needs no time segmented as class or teaching time. The total experience is one of active learning through discovery and creativity. All methods and resources for learning are encouraged and employed: art, music, dramatic improvisation, gaming, role-playing, case study, and group techniques.

Involvement of Youth

Youth are most readily involved in learning that meets their needs. Strommen reported that church youth's most intense feelings of need are loneliness (or self-hatred), parental alienation, anger over social injustice, prejudice, and a need for "identifying with a personal God and a believing community." [18] One survey of selected church youth indicated that their major concerns were determining God's will for their lives, relationships with parents, school problems, vocational decisions, and loneliness. These findings suggest possible topics for study, but final choices should be based upon needs of a specific youth group.

"Don't lets:" In a leader's efforts to gain youth involvement in learning, the factor over which he has greatest control is *himself*. Therefore, here is a list of "don't lets" for youth leaders.

1. Don't let the thoughts and suggestions in printed curriculum materials become a substitute for your own thinking and creativity. Curriculum materials are based upon developmental needs, not immediate needs. Immediate needs must be met by the individual leader in a specific youth group.

2. Don't let initial lack of deep interest by youth in Bible study discourage you. Most leaders confront the same problem. Plan learning procedures that begin with an awareness of the level of youth interest and attempt to create a need for learning.

3. Don't let a lack of familiarity with new methods and processes prevent you from experimenting with them. Try them!

4. Don't let the classroom become the sole location or context for the teaching-learning transaction.

5. Don't let things like appearance, equipment, and arrangement

of chairs within a room or other location prevent the "Sonshine" from coming through. Change to facilitate learning goals.

6. Don't let the frothiness of group process, games, and sharing shroud the need for exploring substantive issues and the usually hard discipline of Bible study.

7. Don't let your learning goals and personal interests interfere with the development and adoption by youth learners of their own goals.

Modeling: The leader who seeks youth involvement must first be involved in study and learning. Youth must see their leaders as persons for whom the Bible is functionally, as well as devotionally, the most important book in life. Youth leaders must know and even memorize portions of Scripture as a regular part of their growth and involvement. Appropriate use should be made of Scripture in conversation, not for show but as a symbol of its place in life. Pastoral leaders can help youth become involved in learning by *using* the Bible in preaching and worship.

Planning: There are no substitutes for planning for youth involvement in learning. Not even Bible knowledge and charisma will suffice. Leaders must plan study units so as to deal carefully with a flow of requirements: unit goals, specific session aims, printed resources, human resources, learning aids, and evaluation. Study leaders need two to three hours of planning for each study-learning unit and additional planning for specific sessions. All leaders must themselves become involved in learning through such planning.

Plans must be implemented to create an effective learning environment. Rather than a bare room and hard chairs, utilize meaningful posters; place the study theme on butcher paper on the wall; provide chalkboards, maps, resource materials, tables for writing, and Bible commentaries to achieve an atmosphere of *intention* for learning. A commonly accepted truth is that persons learn best when all their senses are employed in the task. Plan to reinforce learning by using all of the learner's receptors: sight, sound, feeling, and so forth.

Resources: Each major denomination has its own curriculum materials, special helps, and a wide variety of interesting and valuable support materials for youth learning experiences. Independent religious publishers, not willing to be left out, have added their own brands of such materials. (See resources at end of chapter.)

As with any learning materials, the judgment, discretion, and abilities of adult leaders must be exercised in the use of these resources.

A CREATIVE BIBLE STUDY

Youth Need: Strommen and others report that youth feel lonely, alienated, and even friendless.
Title: "The Care and Feeding of Friends" or "You Got a Friend"
Bible Material: Philemon

INTRODUCTION

Provide necessary materials such as felt, burlap, glue, felt-tipped pens, and butcher paper, asking that groups of youth compose and construct banners on the theme of friendship or friends. A suggestion that the banners might be kept for later display may increase the seriousness of group efforts. They could be included as part of a larger plan for competition.

While the groups work, play background recordings (not too loud) of pop songs dealing with friendship. Leaders will want to examine the texts of such songs before using them, since some pop songs are not acceptable for use as background music.

GROUP REPORTS

1. Ask each group to report by commenting on what they were trying to say through their banner(s).
2. While seated, the groups may be given copies of the words to the songs used as background music. (Remember that copyright laws must be observed.) Give only one song to each group. Ask the group to study and discuss the words, considering what these lyrics say about friendship. Then ask groups to share their observations with the entire group.

BIBLE STUDY

Leader: These lyrics are among those representing man's ways of expressing his desire and need for friendship. I wonder how they compare with examples of friends in the Bible.

One particular book in the Bible is about friendship. It is actually a kind of short story. But it reveals some things about friendship that are very important. (Youth may be provided with a duplicated copy of Philemon, or plans may be made for each to have a Bible.)

The book is called Philemon and has three principal characters: Paul, Philemon, and Onesimus. (Ask someone to give the essential facts of the story.)

Philemon: Resident of Colossae, owns slave Onesimus. By Roman law he has absolute authority over the person and life of his slave. Onesimus has run away and is going to Rome. Philemon had become a Christian through Paul's earlier preaching in Asia Minor (v. 19), and his home is now a meeting place for a Christian congregation (v. 2).

Paul: Is under house arrest in Rome (about A.D. 61-63), has won Onesimus to faith in Christ. He now persuades Onesimus to return to Philemon. Writes letter to be carried by Onesimus to Philemon, for purpose of achieving reconciliation. This is the book of Philemon.

DISCUSSION QUESTIONS

1. What do verses 4–7 say about friendship?

2. What is the exact appeal and request made by Paul in verses 8–14? Do you think Paul's request is justified? Why? (Note play on words in v. 11.) Is Paul using Philemon?

3. Was Paul a good friend to Onesimus? To Philemon? Why do you think so?

4. What is an ideal friend like? What would an ideal friend do? (Discuss the ideas of the song lyrics.)

5. Judged against such an ideal, how would you evaluate the friendship in our youth group—on a scale of one (perfect) to ten (terrible)?

6. What, if anything, could improve friendship within our youth group?

INTROSPECTION

With bowed heads, ask youth to consider their own friendliness, confess failures, resolve to befriend one new person in group, or to make any other commitments they wish to as the pianist plays softly "What a Friend We Have in Jesus" or another appropriate theme on friendship.

Conclusion

Let it be said that the single most important influence upon youth learning is the life lived by the congregation. In the final analysis, the whole church is the teacher of the Christian faith and its practice—not just certain members elected as teachers. The church's most powerful vehicle for teaching and involving youth in learning is congregational life, which is consistent with proclamation. Failure here is suicide.

Notes

1. W. D. Maxwell, *An Outline of Christian Worship* (London: Oxford University Press, 1939), pp. 1ff.
2. "Christmas-Eve," st. xxii, quoted in *Interpreter's Bible*, 8, p. 528.
3. Marilee Zdenek and Marge Champion, *Catch the New Wind* (Waco: Word Books, 1972), pp. 15-37.
4. Soren Kierkegaard, *Purity of Heart Is To Will One Thing* (New York: Harper and Brothers, 1948), pp. 180-181.
5. John T. Wayland, *Planning Congregational Worship Services* (Nashville: Broadman Press, 1971).
6. Merton P. Strommen, *Five Cries of Youth* (New York: Harper and Row, Publishers, 1974), p. 124.
7. James L. Christensen, *Contemporary Worship Services* (Old Tappan, New Jersey: Fleming H. Revell, 1971), pp. 9-11.
8. David James Randolph, *God's Party: A Guide to New Forms of Worship* (Nashville: Abingdon Press, 1975), p. 115.
9. Wilfred M. Bailey, *Awakened Worship: Involving Laymen in Creative Worship* (Nashville: Abingdon Press, 1972), pp. 133-146.
10. John Burke, "It's Time For a Resurrection," *The Choral Journal* (December 1973), p. 8.
11. Lewis J. Sherrill, *The Rise of Christian Education* (New York: The Macmillan Co., 1950), p. 50.
12. William Barclay, *Train Up a Child* (Philadelphia: The Westminster Press, 1959), p. 1.
13. Jesse H. Ziegler, *Psychology and the Teaching Church* (New York: Abingdon Press, 1962), pp. 40-43.
14. Ross Snyder, *Young People and Their Culture* (Nashville: Abingdon Press, 1969).
15. Frank Stagg, *Studies in Luke's Gospel* (Nashville: Convention Press, 1967), p. 65.
16. Several such projects are described in Corbett, Janice M., and Johnson, Curtis E., *It's Happening with Youth* (New York: Harper & Row, Publishers, 1972).
17. Jerome S. Bruner, *The Process of Education* (New York: Random House, Inc., 1960) and *Toward a Theory of Instruction* (Cambridge, Mass.: Belknap Press, 1966).
18. Strommen, *loc. cit.*, p. 92.

Bibliography   *

Benson, Dennis. *The Rock Generation*. Nashville: Abingdon Press. 1976.

Billups, Ann. *Discussion Starters for Youth Groups*. Valley Forge: Judson Press. 1966.

_____ . *Discussion Starters for Youth Groups: Series Two*. Valley Forge: Judson Press. 1969.

_____ . *Discussion Starters for Youth Groups: Series Three*. Valley Forge: Judson Press. 1976.

Boehlke, Robert R. *Theories of Learning in Christian Education*. Philadelphia: Westminster Press. 1963.

Brown, John. New Ways in Worship for Youth. Valley Forge: Judson Press. 1969.

Christensen, James L. *Creative Ways to Worship*. Old Tappan, New Jersey: Fleming H. Revell Co. 1974.

Habel, Norman C. *Interrobang*. Philadelphia: Fortress Press. 1969.

Hester, Richard L. *God's Reconciling Love*. Nashville: Convention Press. 1963.

Hilgard, Ernest R., ed. *Theories of Learning and Instruction*. Chicago: University of Chicago Press. 1964.

Keith-Lucas, Alan. *This Difficult Business of Helping*. Richmond: John Knox Press. 1965.

Killinger, John, ed. *The 11 O'Clock News and Other Experimental Sermons*. Nashville: Abingdon Press. 1975.

Olsson, Karl A. *Find Yourself in the Bible*. Minneapolis: Augsburg. 1974.

Pate, Billie. "Youth and Celebrative Worship Experiences." Nashville: Sunday School Board of the Southern Baptist Convention. 1972.

Randolph, David James. *Ventures in Worship*, Vols. 1-3. Nashville: Abingdon Press. 1972.

Respond (four volumes). Valley Forge: Judson Press. 1971, 1972, 1973, 1975.

Ridenour, Fritz. *How to Be a Christian Without Being Religious*. Glendale: Regal Books. 1967. Paperback edition by Tyndale House Publishers available.

Stone, Nathan. *Bread*. Nashville: Convention Press. 1975.

Taylor, Marvin J., ed. *Foundations for Christian Education in an Era of Change* (pp. 54-67 by James E. Loder). Nashville: Abingdon Press. 1976.

Watts, Richard G. *Straight Talk About Death with Young People*. Philadelphia: Westminster Press. 1975.

Weber, Hans-Ruedi. *Salty Christians*. New York: Seabury Press, Inc. 1963.

Westerhoff, John H., ed. *Colloquy on Christian Education*. Hyattsville: Pilgrims Press. 1972.

Youth Bible Survey Series (seven volumes). Nashville: Convention Press. 1974, 1975, 1976.

9

Involving Youth in Mission and Witnessing
Dan Boling

The Christian experience was never meant to be kept secret. Sharing that experience vitalizes the Christian life. Youth need to learn to witness in order that they can grow and mature in their faith.

A close connection exists between witnessing and mission. Witnessing is part of the mission of the church, and the church should be on mission to witness. This chapter is designed to help you involve youth in mission and witnessing.

What Is Mission and Witnessing?

Youth can become confused with terms such as *mission* and *witnessing*. We need to define these terms.

Mission is a word that we are used to hearing in the plural. We think in terms of home missions and foreign missions. Youth come to think of missions only as something that you give to in a financial way. Especially is this true where youth are encouraged to give to missions offerings. Youth can also come to think of missions only as something a person does as a life's vocation. Most youth consider becoming a foreign missionary at one time in their life if they are active in the church.

Mission, however, is basic to the Christian faith. It is the divine plan to get the good news of God's salvation to the world. The word comes from the Latin word *mittere*, "to send." The noun form is *missio*. While Latin is not the language of the New Testament, the Latin derivation corresponds to the Anglo-Saxon word meaning "sending." The Hebrew *shalach*, the Greek *apostello*, and the English *send* all translate the same passages.[1] Such usage would indicate that the concept of mission is basically thought of as sending.

Mission should be thought of as an event and an idea. Jesus

139

described himself on mission and the sending of his followers as
being on mission in John 20:21: "As my Father hath sent me, even
so send I you" (KJV). This is mission as event. Jesus had earlier
described this event as an idea. He had prayed, "As thou hast sent
me into the world, even so have I also sent them in the world" (John
17:18). God's purpose in sending Jesus was for the purpose of
accomplishing salvation (Rom. 8:1–3). God's purpose in sending his
followers on mission is that they might give witness to the saving
work of Christ in their lives. Mission and witnessing, therefore, are
closely connected.

Witness is a word that basically means giving testimony to God's
nature and to his work in the world. Youth think of witnessing
basically as proclamation. We are told in the Great Commission to
be witnesses (Acts 1:8). Proclamation is witnessing, but the concept
of witnessing is much more inclusive. It is possible to witness
through one's deeds. Jesus referred to his work as a witness (John
15:27; 10:25). Ministry, therefore, is a witness to the work of God, as
is proclamation. As youth do the work of ministry and service, they
are witnesses; but there is a danger in thinking that just living a good
life is all there is to being a witness.

Proclamation is expressed in two New Testament words. The first
is *kerusso*, "to herald." Another is *euaggelizo*, "to preach the gospel." The first means to tell the bare facts of the gospel, and the
latter is the work we translate as evangelism. Youth need to realize
that they are to proclaim the message of salvation, but the gospel is
never proclaimed in a vacuum. The gospel is always proclaimed in a
meaningful context of ministry.

Jesus expressed this connection between mission and proclamation as he quoted the prophecy of Isaiah 61 in Luke 4:17–21. In this
passage proclamation is mentioned three times, but always in the
context of ministry. Jesus was on mission to proclaim, to heal, to set
people free, to help people see, and to announce his coming. The
ministry of proclamation is a mission, and to be a follower of Jesus is
to share in his mission.

Mission and witness have been described so far in a theological
context, and such an understanding is necessary for the person who
seeks to involve youth in these important ministries of the Christian

life. A problem can arise, however, in the ambiguity of the terms as they are used in a theological discussion, in contrast to the practical way they are used in the life of the church. Some would, by way of definition, include everything that the church does under the heading of mission. Others would include all that the church does under the term *evangelism* or *witnessing*. To do so opens a youth program to the danger of broadening these terms so much that they become meaningless. Difficulty can arise in getting youth involved in mission and witness if the terms are too broad. Thus the terms need to be defined in a more narrow way.

Witnessing for the remainder of this chapter will be used to describe sharing in a group or sharing in a one-to-one encounter of one's faith. Witnessing always extends to persons beyond a fellowship of believers and is a vital part of a mission trip. The purpose of witnessing is to influence persons to respond to Jesus Christ and to join a fellowship of believers, the church. While the life of the witness is directly connected to the effectiveness of the witness, witnessing is more than living the Christian life. Witnessing is the verbal proclamation of how Christ has made life meaningful in one's own life and the telling of what purpose Christ had in coming into the world.

The term *mission* will be used from this point to describe an event that is an organized group activity directed beyond the fellowship of the church. It may be but does not necessarily need to be directed toward bringing persons into the church. It is mission for the sake of the needs of persons. It includes proclamation by telling, but it also includes proclamation by doing. The latter is referred to by some as mission action.

Youth involved in experiences of witnessing and mission find the real meaning of what it means to be in Christ. Workers with youth need to consider the many ways that youth can be involved in this important part of the Christian life.

Why Involve Youth in Witnessing and Mission?

Witnessing and mission have been discussed as inherent in the very nature of being a follower of Jesus. Youth need to be involved in witnessing and mission for what it does for Christ and what it does for them. Other reasons are discussed below.

1. Witnessing and mission help youth fulfill biblical directives. Youth cannot attend church or youth group activities without being confronted with the command of Jesus recorded in Acts 1:8, "Ye shall be witnesses." Lawrence Richards describes a survey made among three thousand youth in evangelical churches. Ninety-five percent of the respondents indicated they ought to witness.[2] The four reasons most often given for failing to witness were fear, lack of know-how, lack of relationship with a lost person, and a feeling of aloneness in the witnessing task. The latter refers to youth who felt they would be the only persons in their peer group who would witness.

Many feel guilty because they do not witness. Probably the majority of Christians in our churches have not had a one-to-one verbal encounter with a nonbeliever once in their lives. Helping youth to learn to witness helps them get rid of a great deal of guilt.

2. Faith is kept vibrant when it is shared. Jesus was concerned that his followers experience discipleship as giving meaning and fullness to life. He instructed his disciples to be busy bearing fruit, for in so doing they would find joy (John 15:11). Joy found in sharing the good news helps make a stagnant Christian experience become vibrant.

Youth years are a time of questioning. Most youth will have some doubts as to their own Christian experience. Doubts left alone tend to be like festering sores. Although they scab over, beneath the surface the infection has a possibility of spreading to other areas of the body. Doubt in the Christian life, when left alone, can cause faith to become stagnant. As youth get involved in witness, they get away from abstractions. Abstractions and doubts are not as significant when one is facing a real human being with a real need.

3. Youth grow in Christian maturity as they share the Christian life. Youth will feel a compulsion to give witness to their Christian experience because the Bible says they should witness. It is only in sharing, however, that they find out that a compulsion to share is not a good enough reason to witness. Sharing must result from a loving concern for those with whom you share.

Rosalind Rinker describes her first attempts to witness as a youth.

She did not want to be branded as "not a good Christian." Beginning with a mechanical approach (learning all the answers to excuses people would give), she quickly saw there was much more to witnessing. She came to realize that she needed God to teach her to love people as he loved people.[3] In her witnessing attempts, her own experience with God grew, as did her effectiveness.

Youth in your church need to grow in their Christian experience. As they relate their testimony to others, they begin to discover weaknesses and strengths of their Christian life. Weaknesses, once identified, can be strengthened by study in the biblical faith and by affirmation from members of the body of Christ. Strengths that you already have tend to be affirmed in other Christian experiences.

4. Youth are effective in reaching out. Youth are effective in witnessing, and their mission efforts make a real impact upon the people and communities to whom they minister.

Merton P. Strommen of the Youth Research Center in Minneapolis, Minnesota, describes a research project of training youth to reach youth. The project was entitled "Youth Reaching Youth," and its ultimate purpose was to alter the behavior and life-style of youth by means of the friendship and concern of other youth.

While the above project was complex and multifaceted, the results showed that college-age youth surpass professional trainers in reaching out to high school youth and that high school youth can effectively train others their age.[4] Strommen's project does show that youth can be taught to reach out to alienated youth and that when they do, they have a reasonable degree of effectiveness.

5. Non-Christian youth need to receive a witness. In considering why youth need to be involved in witnessing and mission, we must never forget the reason Christ came into the world. Jesus said, "For the Son of man is come to seek and save that which was lost" (Luke 19:10). The Old Testament injunction "Remember now thy Creator in the days of thy youth" (Eccl. 12:1) well points up how youth are responsive to religious influence during this period of their lives. Many studies show that the youth years are the most productive years for Christian conversion.[5]

Christian youth, properly trained, have the best opportunity to reach non-Christian youth for Christ. They go to school together;

they are aware of the needs of each other; and they know how to communicate with each other. Who better can give witness to non-Christian youth than Christian youth?

6. Our complex society calls for mission action. Not only do youth need to know about Christ, but there are many others in our society who need to receive the benefits of the good news. Jesus came "to seek and to save the lost," but he also came to heal persons of their physical and emotional pain. He was concerned also for those who were hungry and in need of feeding.

Youth need to be involved in mission action because people have many needs in our complex society. Youth, with all of their enthusiasm, can bring warmth to those who are cold, love to those who are lonely, and hope to those who are hopeless.

7. Mission outreach puts faith in action. One young girl said after a mission trip, "I never realized that Christianity was something you do." Getting involved in her youth group's mission trip helped her see that the truths learned in church were to be used in life. Involving youth in witnessing and mission will allow them to grow as they put their faith into action.

Involving Youth in Witnessing

Youth will find a real sense of fulfillment as they are involved in witnessing. A barrier to their involvement, however, is that while most Christians are impressed by witnessing testimonies, they cannot identify themselves as being so bold. Below are some suggestions to help involve youth in witnessing.

1. Involve youth as a group in witnessing. Studies show that younger youth, those who are twelve to fourteen, do not like to stand apart from their peer group. Even older youth do not feel sure enough of their identity to do certain things apart from a group. It is best, therefore, to involve youth in witnessing as a group project.

A group project in witnessing does not mean that a whole group approaches one person in a witnessing encounter. Probably the most effective witnessing is accomplished by two or three people approaching one person. Youth do not want to feel as if they are the only one among their peers who is training to witness. Enlist a group of youth to train together.

2. Challenge youth to witness by using biblical motivation. Motivation is both intrinsic and extrinsic. Youth who have committed themselves to Christ want to please their Lord. Desire to please is intrinsic motivation. Passages from the Bible, extrinsic motivation, stimulate youth to witness about Jesus and his message.

In using biblical motivation, however, the youth worker should avoid some past abuses. Seek to find passages that motivate out of a sense of love rather than out of guilt or fear. In the past, some youth in the church have feared the loss of their own salvation from a failure to witness. These fears come from misinterpretation of such passages as John 15. Jesus described himself as the vine and his followers as the branches. The term *bear fruit* is sometimes used to tell Christians that they need to win people to Christ. Actually, the Holy Spirit does the winning. Jesus' instruction in this passage was that Christians should produce love for people. We do that as we abide in him. When unbelievers come in contact with a loving fellowship of believers, the Holy Spirit can use that environment to win the lost to Jesus.

Passages that emphasize the joy of witnessing should be used with youth (John 15:11; Acts 2:41–47; 5:41–42). Youth need to see that they will have power to witness (John 15:26–27; Acts 1:8) and that when they witness there will be results (Acts 2:41; 8:26–39). Important to youth is the fact that they do not witness alone (Acts 5:32).

3. Training helps youth be effective in witnessing. Once you motivate youth to witness, they must not be expected to witness without knowing how. Plan some type of group training experience to help them learn some simple witnessing techniques.

Pick a training program that includes a lab experience. Two examples of such labs are W.I.N. (Witness Involvement Now) training or a W.O.W. (Win Our World) clinic. Both provide an opportunity for an actual witnessing encounter as part of the training experience.

4. Help youth overcome fear of witnessing. Fear in witnessing is everybody's hang-up. Paul told us that the source of fear is not God. "For God hath not given us the spirit of fear; but of power, and of love, and of a sound mind" (2 Tim. 1:7). Fear can incapacitate youth, keeping them from what they would like to do.

Types of fear youth experience are fear in not knowing how to witness, fear of a lack of ability to witness, fear of driving their friends away from Christ and themselves, fear of ridicule, and fear of failure.

At the first training session, discuss the fear of witnessing. Let youth know they will have some fear. A trainer who is open about his own fear can lead the group to ask God for help in overcoming fear. Love for those to whom you witness helps overcome this fear.

5. Reinforce youth in their common sense. Some training programs approach witnessing in a way similar to what Rosalind Rinker first experienced. These programs teach people to be ready to answer all of the questions that could possibly be asked in a witnessing encounter. Such approaches tend to give all sorts of hints about what to do before, during, and after a witnessing attempt.

Pick an approach that trains youth to use a small booklet or tract in witnessing. Give them some training in how to use the booklet, but encourage them to use common sense in knowing what to do.

6. Youth need to experience modeling in witnessing. Do not expect youth to do witnessing on their own. Help them begin the sharing life by showing them how to witness. Modeling is a dynamic teaching method and is more difficult than merely telling youth how to witness. Provide youth with people who model witnessing. An effective model knows when to turn to his youth partner and say, "Why don't you share what Christ means to you?"

7. Allow youth to share the results of their witnessing. Keep in mind that all witnessing does not result in someone's coming to know Jesus in personal faith. If a youth has witnessed to his own faith, he has been successful and needs to feel so. Youth need to share with others that they have followed the commissioning of Jesus in being a witness.

Sharing the witnessing experience can take place as the conclusion to a lab night, or it can be a special time set aside during a mission trip. At the discretion of the youth worker, youth can be invited to participate in regular worship services of the church by giving testimonies about witnessing experiences. Youth are sometimes embarrassed before a large group, however; and they may not want to stand apart from the youth group.

Involving Youth in Mission

Youth will respond to opportunities to be involved in mission, whether they be in their local community or on a trip away from home. Here are some principles to remember when involving youth in mission.

1. Let youth help plan their mission. Youth, developmentally, are ready to assume leadership roles. They like to express their ideas and to have their ideas affirmed. Lead youth to see the need for mission, but challenge them to be actively involved in planning mission outreach.

A word of caution: Too many adult planners will stifle youth's ideas. Freedom to express these ideas helps youth to mature and increases their involvement in the project. Youth can help pick the site for the mission, set objectives to be reached, plan for financing the mission, and enlist other youth to go.

2. Youth can help finance their mission. Various kinds of mission outreach programs call for differing financing. Projects to raise money for needs on the mission can involve youth in the mission project even before it begins. A mission trip should pay its own way as far as possible and not be a burden to those you are going to help.

A youth group should first check with its church as to whether there are any bylaws against raising funds for a mission project. If there are no objections, youth can raise funds by car washes, bottle drives, rent-a-youth days, garage sales, and other fund-raising projects.

3. Prepare youth for what to expect while on mission. If the mission takes youth to a different section of their city or to another community, help them to know about cultural differences. Lead them to adopt rules of dress and action that will not violate any cultural morés encountered or cause any danger to youth group members.

Prepare the youth to perform specific tasks. If they are expected to teach in backyard Bible schools, they will need training in the use of curriculum materials. If group members will be expected to do housekeeping chores, youth should know they are expected to do their part.

4. Keep youth from overextending themselves in mission action. Youth, with limited experience, tend to adopt higher goals than they can achieve. It is imperative that they feel a degree of success in what they attempt to do. Short-term projects are better for youth than long-term.

Youth are more effective with younger age groups than equals or elders. Bible clubs with younger children may be the best type of project for beginning efforts.

Realism in adopting financial goals keeps youth from trying to do more than they are able. Be careful not to dampen their enthusiasm and optimism.

5. Take advantage of talents in your youth group. Youth are more likely to be involved in mission outreach if you will plan to use their particular talents. Youth feel left out of a mission trip if the whole effort revolves around a musical performance and they themselves do not sing. Plan to take advantage of skills of art, publicity, teaching, organization, electronics, and just plain hard work.

6. Provide youth with adequate adult leadership for their mission outreach. While it would be possible to have too many adults involved, supply enough adult leadership to insure success. The principle holds true in preparation for mission and while on the mission. Adults can give youth supervision, whether it be in teaching preschoolers a Vacation Bible School lesson or in putting a roof on a house.

7. Youth need recognition for their involvement in mission. Recognition reinforces youth in their commitment to be involved in the ministry of Christ. It also serves as an enlistment device for other mission projects.

Publicity should be given to the church while youth are planning their mission action project. News of the project promotes church awareness to lend support to the effort and encourages youth in their mission. While the mission is in process, the church should be encouraged to pray for the mission and to lend support when they can. Closely following the completion of the mission effort, recognition should be given to the youth in some regular gathering of the church.

Types of Witnessing Activities

Workers with youth can find many and varied activities in which to involve youth in witnessing. A partial list of witnessing activities follows.

Win Our World (W.O.W.)—a seminar designed to train youth in the verbalizing of their Christian experience. W.O.W. materials are available from the Home Mission Board, Evangelism Department, 1350 Spring Street, NW, Atlanta, Georgia 30309.

"E" Groups—groups of youth that meet for one night a week for twelve weeks. The "E" stands for evangelism, and those who join commit themselves to train to witness. They agree to witness at least once a week by the time of the fifth meeting. These experiences are shared in weekly meetings and evaluated.

Touch Ministry—a program where youth workers plan regular visits to high school and junior high school campuses. The workers develop friendships that later become witnessing opportunities. Christian youth help make vital contacts on campus.

Youth Discipleship Training—a program to help committed youth to develop a quiet time, to grow in Bible study, and to learn to help another youth in a one-to-one relationship.

Joy Explosion—can be a party at someone's home, a beach party, a retreat, or some informal activity. Non-Christian youth are invited for fun, followed with the sharing of testimonies by Christian youth and their leaders.

Youth Rallies—large gatherings of youth with activities that include group competition, singing, drama, and other activities that attract youth. Youth are encouraged to bring non-Christian friends, and time is given to sharing of their faith.

Youth-led Revivals—week-long or weekend revival meetings. College students are used to preach, lead singing, direct fellowships, and lead seminars. High school and junior high youth do the planning, publicity, and visitation. Youth-led revivals are led by youth but are for the entire church family.

Canvassing—training a youth group to take a religious census. Information gained is used in follow-up by the church, and the census form leads into a witnessing opportunity at each home.

Musicals—youth musicals are an effective way to launch an evangelistic ministry into shopping centers, parks, beaches, and high school assemblies. Singers can mill around with the audience after each performance and share their personal testimonies.

Performing Groups—singing or instrumental groups with an evangelistic thrust.

Resort Witnessing—planned witnessing opportunities for youth in resort areas such as beaches, ski areas, and national parks. Christian youth engage other youth in conversation, which leads to sharing the faith.

Church Bus Evangelism—the use of youth as bus captains and workers on church bus ministry routes. Youth develop a loving relationship with their riders, which leads to witnessing opportunities.

Youth Outreach—planned visitation for youth. Going in groups of two or three, church youth can reach out to non-Christian youth. Variations of this form of outreach are witnessing in homes, picking up youth as part of a human scavenger hunt, or inviting youth to an informal party, where sharing will take place.

Types of Mission Activities

Youth on mission can vary from a group going down the block to a group going to a foreign country. Their purpose is to minister in the name of Christ. Here are some ideas for mission involvement.

Backyard Bible Clubs—the gathering of children by youth for an hour or two of activities. The curriculum is similar to Vacation Bible School, which includes a Bible story, handicraft projects, and refreshments.

Ministry to the Aging—raking leaves, mowing grass, delivering hot meals, aiding with grocery shopping, and running errands are ways youth can minister to the aging.

Crisis Closet—collection of clothing and groceries from church members to establish a closet or room in the church. Supplies from the crisis closet are used to help needy families.

Institutional Ministries—ministry in children's homes, hospitals, jails, and retirement homes. Youth can lead worship services, read stories and articles, write letters, sing, and lead recreation.

Tutoring—done by youth in institutional settings—for example, in children's homes or in a deprived area of the community. Youth, who have had time to excel in a school subject, usually are more effective in tutoring persons younger than themselves.

Literacy Teaching—older youth using the Laubach Literacy method, which they can do effectively. Social agencies will help in finding people to teach.

Day Camping—a camping program at a local park or recreation area. Youth serve as counselors.

Mission Vacation Bible School—youth helping with the VBS program as a mission of their church or as part of a mission trip.

Work Trips—a mission venture with work as its object. Youth have painted church buildings, cleaned up yards of needy people, repainted houses of people on welfare, been involved in new church construction, and been part of disaster teams that go in and clean up debris.

"Hot Line"—selected youth are trained to monitor telephones as part of a crisis ministry, such as helping runaways.

Summary of This Chapter

Youth want to be involved in the life of the church. Vital to the life of the church are mission and witnessing. Youth are effective when they are trained, inspired, and given an opportunity to go on mission and to witness. Involvement in these tasks helps youth share the ministry of Jesus and helps make vibrant their own personal growth in the Christian life.

Notes

1. Francis M. DuBose, "From 'Missions' to 'Mission,'" *The Commission,* July 1969, p. 8.

2. Lawrence O. Richards, *Youth Ministry* (Grand Rapids: Zondervan Press, 1972), pp. 279-280.

3. Rosalind Rinker, *You Can Witness with Confidence* (Grand Rapids: Zondervan Press, 1962), p. 20.

4. Merton P. Strommen, "Project Youth: Training Youth to Reach Youth," *Charac-*

ter Potential: a Record of Research 1, no. 4 (February 1974): 180.

   5. Ted W. Engstrom, "The Challenge of Today's Youth," *Youth and the Church*, ed. Roy G. Irving and Roy B. Zuck (Chicago: Moody Press, 1968), p. 14.

Bibliography

Acteens Mission Action Projects Guide. Birmingham: Woman's Missionary Union, 1970.

Corbett, Janice M., and Johnson, Curtis E. *It's Happening with Youth.* New York: Harper and Row, 1972.

DuBose, Francis M. "From 'Missions' to 'Mission.'" *The Commission*, July 1969, pp. 8-9.

Ideas for Youth Outreach 1, 2, and 3. Nashville: Convention Press, 1970, 1971, 1972.

May, Helen. *Impactivity: Youth Program Resources.* Nashville: Broadman Press, 1974.

Richards, Lawrence O. *Youth Ministry.* Grand Rapids: Zondervan Press, 1972.

Rinker, Rosalind. *You Can Witness with Confidence.* Grand Rapids: Zondervan Press, 1962.

Strommen, Merton P. "Project Youth: Training Youth to Reach Youth." *Character Potential: a Record of Research* 6, no. 4 (February 1974).

THE
OVER
flowing
LIFE

It Can Be Yours

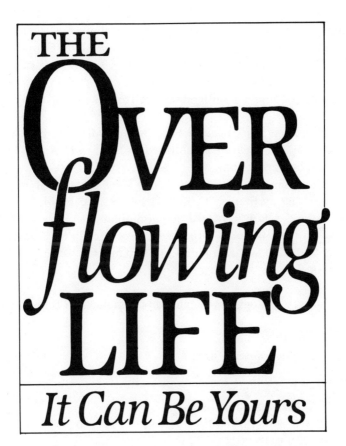

THE Over flowing LIFE

It Can Be Yours

Stanley C. Baldwin

Fleming H. Revell Company
Old Tappan, New Jersey

BV
4501.2
B38183
1987

Library of Congress Cataloging-in-Publication Data

Baldwin, Stanley C.
    The overflowing life.

    Bibliography: p.
    1. Christian life—1960–   . I. Title.
BV4501.2.B38183   1987   248.4   87-13001
ISBN 0-8007-1548-9

Copyright © 1987 by Stanley C. Baldwin
Published by the Fleming H. Revell Company
Old Tappan, New Jersey 07675
Printed in the United States of America

CONTENTS

Contents

TO GOD

PART
I

The Reality
of the
Overflowing Life

ONE

If You Knew
the Gift
of God

"If you knew the gift of God and who it is that asks you for a drink, you would have asked him and he would have given you living water."

John 4:10

A lot of people feel jinxed. They suffer from a Charlie Brown syndrome. Like the kid in the famous cartoon strip "Peanuts," they just know that life is not going to work out for them. However much Lucy promises otherwise, when Charlie Brown goes to kick the football, Lucy will move it. He will kick thin air and end up on his caboose.

For people who really are Charlie Browns, however, it's not funny. They have a serious problem. Not surprisingly, therefore, people do some strange things to try to shake a jinx.

Some hope that adjusting their lives by astrological signs will give them an edge. Others seek help in biorhythms, hypnosis, good-luck charms, or religious ritual.

Jesus met one woman who might well have thought herself jinxed, since her life had never gone right: The woman at the well, who had lived with six men. She must have felt jinxed—at least as far as men were concerned. Nevertheless, she was not excluded from God's offer of an overflowing life. Jesus told her, "If you knew the gift of God and who it is that asks you for a drink, you would have asked him and he would have given you living water" (John 4:10).

Exactly what is this living *water* that Jesus Christ, the Son of God, offers to messed-up people? What is it that she would surely have asked for, had she known its nature and the identity of the one offering it?

We get a hint as to the nature of this gift of God when we read, a few verses later, "Whoever drinks the water I give him will never thirst. Indeed, the water I give him will become in him a spring of water welling up to eternal life" (John 4:14).

Notice here that the gift "will become *in* him" an inexhaustible and life-giving spring of water.

Just as the Charlie Browns of this world know that life is not going to work for them, so you can know that it will for you. Something deep within you can assure you of that.

That something deep within you will be the Spirit of God. It's true! The gift of God—the well of living water within us—is the Spirit of God.

We might say, then, that the gift of God *is God,* just as a gift of money is money and a gift of land is land. God's gift to those who receive it is *Himself.* He is both the giver and the gift.

That's why this gift is so glorious! That's why we can properly call it the overflowing life. When God, who is the source of all life, dwells within us by His Spirit, things change for us. We can no longer be jinxed.

Recently I had occasion to watch an old Shirley Temple movie, *The Little Princess.* Shirley Temple played an abused little girl in a children's home, who refuses to believe that her missing war-hero father has died in battle. Daily she fulfills her demeaning duties at the home and then slips away to search for her father among the wounded soldiers in a nearby military hospital. For the audience, the most exquisite moments of pain come when father and daughter cross paths several times without either knowing it. They seem about to go their separate ways forever. "If they only knew!" our hearts cry.

Most of the characters in the movie think the little princess is holding on to false hopes. The mean woman who makes her life miserable bluntly tells her she is clinging to a fantasy. Even her friends say as much behind her back. Only we who view it all from a distance want her not to give up. Even before we see her father, we just know, as she does, that he has to be alive somewhere.

This delightful, warm story, which ends with the joyful reunion of father and daughter, would have turned into a tragedy, had the two characters never discovered each other.

In a similar vein, one of the greatest romantic tragedies ever written relies on the main character not knowing some important good news. I refer to *Romeo and Juliet*.

Shakespeare wrote a number of tragic plays. Usually the characters are seriously flawed and bring ruin on themselves or others. Not so with Romeo and Juliet. Their simple and wholehearted love fully endears them to us. But tragedy befalls them. Romeo hears that Juliet has died. Unaware that this is a ruse, part of Juliet's desperate plan to feign death in order to escape and be with him, Romeo determines to drink poison and die at her side. He reaches her resting place, and as he puts the poison to his lips, we want to cry out, "No! No!" It is all so needless. If only he knew that his beloved Juliet is about to awake . . . *If he knew!*

Drama in Real Life

The dramatic scenarios just described are symbolic of the real-life drama being played out in millions of lives today. Indeed, you may well be the little princess, clinging to a dream that someday all will be right with your life, even though now things look pretty dismal. Or, tragedy of tragedies, you may become Romeo. You may give up hope and die in grief, not knowing something wonderful that could have made all the difference in your life.

That something wonderful is this: *The fulfilling life you want most is near to you. It can be yours.* The frightening thing is that you may never know it.

This must not be! Just as I wanted the little princess to continue her search for her father, I want you to know that your dream of a better life can be fulfilled. It is not a fantasy.

From Illusion to Disillusion

Most people spend a big part of their lives chasing illusions. They believe their life will be wonderful when . . . you name it.

Children think they will be happy when they are old enough to get away from the control of their parents or the torment of their brothers and sisters.

Young adults imagine they will find fulfillment when they marry some beautiful person who will think them simply wonderful and love them forever.

Students think that finding the right job or career will do it for them. Those already in careers imagine life will be truly good when they reach whatever career goal they have set.

Married people often think that if they could just get rid of a bad partner and find a good one, life would be great.

The people we have been describing may or may not realize that they see fulfillment in these terms. However, the thing a person devotes himself to pursuing is the thing he sees as "what I need to make life good," whether he consciously thinks of it in those terms or not.

When people are disappointed in their search for fulfillment, they tend to do one of two things. First, they may substitute a new illusion for the old and keep chasing rainbows, looking for a pot of gold that isn't there. Second, they may become totally disillusioned old people (whatever their age), without any dreams.

God's Alternative: The Overflowing Life

The message of this book is that you don't have to live a life of illusion or disillusionment. You can have real fulfillment. You can experience what I have chosen to call the overflowing life.

The overflowing life is similar to the abundant life many Christians speak of, only better. The abundant life, as it is often understood and taught, can be quite self-centered: "I am to have abundance." By definition, the overflowing life reaches out; it overflows to others in addition to meeting my own personal needs.

The concept of overflowing life comes from the teachings of Jesus Christ. He said, "If a man is thirsty, let him come to me and drink. Whoever believes in me, as the Scripture has said, streams of living water will flow from within him" (John 7:37, 38).

Note the two elements here. First, there is water for you to drink. That is the abundant life. You need not go unsatisfied and unfulfilled. Second, beyond your being able to drink, a stream of living water will flow from within you. This is not a cistern or a reservoir of water stored up for your own use. The water "will flow from" you, not just be in you. God wants you to have an abundant life that also overflows to refresh a parched and thirsty world.

Replacing My Own Illusions

Like other people, I have had my share of illusions. I spent many years wanting to be "great." I was never quite as driven as some are—John Claypool confesses that he wanted to be president of the world—I just wanted to be widely known and recognized for the superior skills I believed I possessed.

There are two ways I could have become disillusioned. I could have realized I was never going to achieve the goals I thought would bring me happiness. (This is said to be an important element in the typical mid-life crisis.) Or I could have reached my goal, only to discover it was not nearly as fulfilling as I had anticipated.

In my own case, I achieved my goal. In 1970 I was summoned from a pastorate to the editor's desk of *Power* papers at Scripture Press. I had been an avid reader of *Power* from my teens. Even to write for *Power* was a great honor and achievement, in my mind. To become editor was close to the ultimate for me.

Still, who pays any attention to editors? Few readers of any publication can tell you who the editor is. It's a behind-the-scenes job. So, as much as I considered being the editor of *Power* an achievement, it did not satisfy my desire for wide recognition.

However, the *Power* position soon led to even better things. Scripture Press was beginning its book-publishing division at that time, and I was tapped to become the first editor of Victor Books. This led in turn to my writing some of their early books—and to the recognition I had always wanted.

My new stature was epitomized when our marketing division put me on "Mt. Rushmore." What I called Mt. Rushmore was a brochure that Victor produced to promote its books and authors. The way the pictures of the authors were displayed was suggestive (unintentionally, I think) of the famous South Dakota mountain where the faces of four American presidents are carved in stone.

There I was, on evangelicalism's Mt. Rushmore, along with such notables as Warren Wiersbe, Joyce Landorf, and Howard Hendricks. That was exhilarating. I had it made.

Over the next couple of years, however, it became apparent to me that recognition wasn't going to do all that much for me in terms of personal fulfillment. Yes, it was nice to have, but what good did it really do me? Even if millions of people came to know my name, I would never see them, never hear from them, certainly never know them, and really not know if they were blessed and helped by my writing. I realized that fame was a totally intangible thing that had little to do with the quality of my life.

Did you get that? Fame gives one no more inner resources than he has without it. One is not enriched by it, as a person.

There's your first important insight into the nature of the overflowing life: It is not dependent on externals such as fame, career success, wealth, privilege, popularity, and power. In the last analysis, you will either have an *inner* spring of water that satisfies your deepest thirst and overflows to water others, or you will go unfulfilled.

Why People Lose Out

The great news is that you can have this inner spring. The great concern is that you can be so close and yet miss it, as people all around us are doing.

I am convinced that a major reason people miss out on the overflowing life is that they have little idea what it is. They settle for "better than nothing" when they could have better than they dare to dream.

Recently, I met with a group of friends. We get together once a month to help one another with our various writing and speaking projects. Lodece read a draft of a speech she had prepared for the National Cancer Society. In her speech, Lodece cited frightening statistics about the relationship of cancer to smoking. For example, on an average, each cigarette smoked takes six minutes off the life expectancy of the smoker.

Maria commented that this kind of bad news is not very effective in stopping people from smoking. "Such statistics arouse fear," said Maria, "but as one who smoked for many years, I can tell you that fear would just make me reach for another cigarette."

Today people are well aware of the detrimental effect of smoking on one's health. Yet millions continue to smoke, unable or unwilling to give it up. The reasons for this are complex and may vary with the individual. But in most cases, it's not that people don't know smoking is bad, because they do. What they don't know is a good way to stop.

Later in the evening, Roberta read her story, "He Needs Me, He Needs Me Not." It concerned a young woman trapped in a relationship with a manipulative man. If she ever left him, he said, he would kill himself. Meanwhile, he was possessive and domineering.

It was clear to the young woman that the relationship was sick. That much she knew. What she didn't know was how to get out of it. What might he do to himself, or even to her?

The common thread in these two very different examples is that knowing something is wrong or bad is not enough. We need to know that there is a better alternative, and we need to know what that alternative is.

This principle applies throughout our troubled society. Ben is a drug addict. He knows very well that his drug abuse is bad for him. It damages his health, alienates him from his family and from straight society, and drains his money and energy from worthwhile pursuits. Ben has no doubts about these facts.

But drugs also make Ben feel good. He remembers his life before drugs. It was not all that good, and he doesn't want to go back to it. Ben knows all the bad news; what he needs to know is the good news. There is a way to live that is not only far superior to drug addiction but also far superior to that old life that left him so vulnerable to drugs in the first place.

Doreen is a fourteen-year-old girl. She definitely does not want to become pregnant and have a child. Actually, she doesn't even want to have sex with her boyfriend. But she also doesn't want to be "out of it." She doesn't want to be dropped by her boyfriend. She already knows about the negatives associated with sexual intercourse at her age, but she is on the verge of letting it happen. She doesn't know any good alternative.

If You Knew the Gift of God

Sometimes we can be scared or driven away from wrong, evil, and destructive practices. God knows the dangers are real enough, and we ought to be scared. But what we want, and too often don't have, is a better alternative.

Jesus once came face-to-face with a woman like that. She had lived with at least six different men; it's hard to imagine she didn't know how bad that was. Jesus did not try to inform this woman of the negatives associated with her chosen life-style.

Among the things that Jesus did *not* say are the following:

> *"If you knew what a fool you are . . ."*
> *"If you knew men are only using you . . ."*
> *"If you knew you will likely grow old all alone . . ."*
> *"If you knew you will never hold your grandchildren . . ."*
> *"If you knew what decent people think of you . . ."*
> *"If you knew the health risks you are taking . . ."*

My guess is that she knew all these things only too well. She also knew the emptiness of her life when there was no man in it, and figured what she had was better than nothing. She didn't realize she could have so much more.

Contrast the things that Jesus did not say with the words He did speak: *"If you knew the gift of God* and who it is that asks you for a drink, you would have asked him and he would have given you living water"* (John 4:10).

Jesus did not want this woman to live and die not knowing there is a gift of God that quenches one's deepest thirsts. And He doesn't want us to be ignorant of the gift of God, either.

No Piddling Gift

The gift of God is something truly wonderful: It is a life of personal fulfillment, overflowing with God's blessing.

Our expectations of God are often too small. We settle for meager lives and then drift into destructive substitutes for fulfillment because we don't grasp how abundant life can be.

Don't make the mistake Jehoash, king of Israel, made when Elisha the prophet told him God wanted to give Jehoash a wonderful victory over his nation's enemies, the Syrians. Elisha told Jehoash to beat the ground with his arrows as a symbol of his coming victory. Jehoash struck the ground three times and stopped. Elisha was angry. He told Jehoash that he should have struck the ground at least five or six times; then his victory would have been complete (see 2 Kings 13:18, 19).

I am angry, too, when I see people forfeiting the gift of God. They struggle and stumble along in life, hurting themselves and others, and it is all so unnecessary.

But if I am angry, the Lord Jesus Christ is grieved. It was out of sadness for her loss (as well as hope for her future) that Jesus said to the woman who had lived with six men, "If you knew the gift of God. ..."

It was out of sadness that Jesus more than once grieved over the holy city. "O Jerusalem, Jerusalem ... how often I have longed to gather your children together, as a hen gathers her chicks under her wings, but you were not willing. Look, your house is left to you desolate" (Matthew 23:37, 38).

Desolation lay in store for Jerusalem for the same reason the woman at the well was missing out. Neither of them knew the better thing that God had for them. Hear that plaintive note in the lament Jesus made over Jerusalem just before His crucifixion:

> As he approached Jerusalem and saw the city, he wept over it and said, "If you, even you, had only known on this day what would bring you peace—but now it is hidden from your eyes. The days will come upon you when your enemies will build an embankment against you and encircle you and hem you in on every side. They will dash you to the ground, you and the children within your walls. They will not leave one stone on another, because you did not recognize the time of God's coming to you."
>
> Luke 19:41–44

I believe Jesus weeps yet today over those who do not know what will bring them peace. He weeps over those who do not realize when He comes to speak to them.

At the last hour of His life, when Jesus was led away to be crucified and some of the women were wailing for Him, He turned and said, "Do not weep for me; weep for yourselves and for your children" (Luke 23:28).

Weep for yourselves! Yours is the consummate tragedy, when you do not know the gift of God.

In those moments when Jesus wept over the deprived of His day, we see a microcosm of human history. He wept for Jerusalem, yes, but He also wept for the little princess and for Romeo and for drug addicts and for people in abusive relationships and for all who do not know the gift of God.

Our Choice

For us who are still alive today, it is not yet too late. For us, Jesus not only weeps but, just as He reached out to the woman who had lived with six men, He also reaches out to us. He offers us a gift of God which, once we know and receive it, makes everything different. This gift of God provides us an alternative to all the half-measures and better-than-nothing compromises that have been eating us alive.

I know there is such a gift.

I also understand why you might be a bit skeptical about it. We live in a society of oversell, and anyone who is not at least somewhat skeptical about grand claims is quite likely to be victimized.

Even among Christians, overstatement and oversell exist on all sides. Some sell a Christian life so "spiritual" that God is their "all in all," and you begin to wonder if they even have to attend to their own bodily functions. At the other extreme are those who sell such an earthly, success-oriented Christianity that they might better symbolize their faith with a Cadillac or BMW insignia than with a cross.

Our own resident family humorist, our number-two daughter, Krystal, heard that I was writing a book entitled *The Overflowing Life: It Can Be Yours.* "Oh, I didn't know you wrote fiction!" she quipped. Humor often has a semiserious basis, and hers definitely did.

So then, just how seriously is one to take this overflowing life stuff?

Over quite legitimate skepticism, I would simply point out that we must face the claims of Jesus Christ. He is the one who said He came that we might have life to the fullest. He is the one who said that rivers of living water can flow from within us. I believe Him.

But if you don't believe it—if you can't accept the gift of God that can make your life right—then Juliet really is dead, and you may as well be, too.

—PART—
II

The Source
of the
Overflowing Life

—TWO—

God's Best Gift
—The End of
Your Search

Don't you know that you yourselves are God's temple and that God's Spirit lives in you?

1 Corinthians 3:16

God "is not far from each one of us" (Acts 17:27).

The Apostle Paul spoke those words to pagan philosophers of ancient Athens. If God was not far from them, I believe He is also not far from you now, as you read this book and ponder these thoughts.

The Bible teaches that this God, who is not far from each one of us, wants to be a great deal closer than we may realize—actually *within us*.

Until He dwells within us, we can never know the overflowing life. Remember, when Jesus said we could have streams of living water flowing from within, He was talking about the indwelling Holy Spirit (see John 7:37–39).

25

God's desire is to unite Himself with us, to join His Spirit so closely to ours that we can describe it as God-in-us.

This plan of God's is so radical that even longtime Christians may be slow to grasp it. Therefore, we need to build a solid biblical base for the God-in-you concept, and will devote the rest of this chapter to doing so.

The Mystery

Millions of people have received Christ as Lord and Savior without realizing fully, if at all, that *received Christ* is not a figure of speech for something else. It is not equivalent to "believed in Christ" or "trusted Christ." Believing and trusting are involved, to be sure, but *receive* means Christ comes to dwell within us.

The Apostle Paul said that this truth was not understood, indeed had not been revealed, before his day. He wrote about "the mystery that has been kept hidden for ages and generations, but is now disclosed . . . *which is Christ in you,* the hope of glory" (Colossians 1:26, 27, italics mine).

In biblical terms, a mystery is not a "whodunit." It is, as the above passage states, a truth previously hidden but now revealed. All through Old Testament times, devout people knew that God was for them up in heaven. People of faith also knew they could have God with them. In fact, "God was with him" is almost like a refrain throughout the history of the patriarchs of Israel. Scripture emphasizes it as the secret of success for Moses and Joseph.

God's people clearly knew He could be with them, says Paul, but they never understood or realized that He could be *in* them. Paul's ministry was to help make known that truth.

Paul lived and ministered almost 2,000 years ago. Ironically, though the truth of Christ-in-us was revealed so long ago, it is still essentially unknown and unrealized by masses of sincerely devout people.

Alexander Maclaren, a famous preacher at Union Chapel in Manchester, England, during the last half of the nineteenth century, had this to say about it:

> To begin with, let me say in the plainest, simplest, strongest way that I can, that that dwelling of Christ in

26

the believing heart is to be regarded as being a plain literal fact. . . . It is not to be weakened down into any notion of participation in his likeness, sympathy with his character, submission to his influence, following his example, listening to his instruction, or the like . . . but it is the presence of his own self.

I think that Christian people as a rule do far too little turn their attention to this aspect of the gospel. . . . Very largely the glad thought of an indwelling Christ who actually abides and works in our hearts . . . has faded away from the consciousness of the Christian church.[1]

So, what about you? Have you realized yet that if you have received Christ, He actually dwells within you? Do you have any idea how significant that is? If God is literally in you, isn't that by far the most significant fact of your life?

The Witness of Other Scriptures

As we have said, the concept is radical. Yet, this great truth that God can be in us is clearly taught in various places in the New Testament. In the following quotations, the key phrases are italicized for emphasis.

> Don't you know that you yourselves are God's temple and that *God's Spirit lives in you?*
>
> 1 Corinthians 3:16

> Examine yourselves to see whether you are in the faith; test yourselves. Do you not realize that *Christ Jesus is in you*—unless, of course, you fail the test?
>
> 2 Corinthians 13:5

> No one has ever seen God; but if we love one another, *God lives in us* and his love is made complete in us. We know that we live in him *and he in us,* because he has given us of his Spirit. . . . If anyone acknowledges that Jesus is the Son of God, *God lives in him* and he in God. . . .

God is love. Whoever lives in love lives in God, and *God in him.*

1 John 4:12, 13, 15, 16

Notice that these Scriptures speak of each Person of the Trinity being in the believer. The Spirit is in us; Christ is in us; God is in us.

The Witness of Jesus

Though Paul emphasized the mystery aspect of Christ in us, Jesus Himself also taught that we can be indwelt by God. We earlier quoted, as basic to the theme of this book, these words of Jesus: " 'Whoever believes in me . . . streams of living water will flow from within him.' By this he meant the Spirit" (John 7:38, 39).

In another place, Jesus spoke to His disciples about the Holy Spirit as follows: " 'You know him, for he lives with you and will be in you' " (John 14:17). " 'On that day you will realize that I am in my Father, and you are in me, and I am in you' " (v. 20). Jesus went on to say that if anyone loves Him, both He and the Father " 'will come to him and make our home with him' " (v. 23).

As the other writers did, Jesus also tells us that all three Persons of the Trinity can be in us: The Holy Spirit, Christ, and the Father. These will make their home with those who love Jesus. Did you get that? They are not merely visitors. They are residents, settling down to dwell in our hearts.

So often we think only in terms of someday making our home with God in heaven. It is true that we will someday go to be with Him. But it is also true that God makes His home with us, right now, here on earth.

That does not make earth heaven, but it certainly does bring gladness to our hearts. In fact, it brings us the overflowing life.

God Incognito

If God is actually in people, as we have been saying, one might well wonder why it's not a little more apparent. Where are these people in whom God dwells? Shouldn't His presence be unmistakable?

Actually, no. The Bible teaches that Jesus Christ was God in the flesh. We read, "For in Christ all the fullness of the Deity lives in bodily form" (Colossians 2:9). Yet, Jesus Christ was not so outstandingly different from everyone else of His day. In some ways He was, but not in anything apparent to His contemporaries.

Jesus' own family, those who lived with Him and knew Him best, did not believe in Him until after His resurrection (see John 7:1–5). That seems incredible. They lived with a sinless being, with Almighty God in the flesh, and they thought He was an ordinary person!

Not only was Jesus' family unable to see God in Him, but neither could the Jews. "They said, 'Is this not Jesus, the son of Joseph, whose father and mother we know? How can he now say, "I came down from heaven"?' " (John 6:42.)

Therefore, to say that God lives unobserved in His people today is not so farfetched. Scripture indicates that our relationship to God is incognito. "The creation waits in eager expectation for the sons of God to be revealed" (Romans 8:19). Something that is awaited obviously hasn't happened yet. Our sonship has not yet been revealed.

When Jesus Christ walked down the streets of Nazareth, nobody pointed to Him and said, "Look! There goes the Son of God!" Nobody says God is in us, either, because that has not yet been revealed. When it is, the whole creation will know it. We will then receive a glorious body like Christ's resurrection body, immortal and without flaw (see Philippians 3:20, 21). Until then, "we have this treasure in jars of clay," as Paul put it (2 Corinthians 4:7). The treasure is God in us; the jars of clay are the common, unimpressive bodies and personalities we presently have.

From Seed to Full Kernel

We have said, first, that this world cannot recognize God in anyone, even when that one is the perfect Lord Jesus Christ. We have said, second, that we have not yet been glorified, not yet revealed as God's sons.

There is another reason that God-in-us may be hard to observe, not only for outsiders, but even for us in whom God dwells. This third reason is that the life of God-in-us is not (for lack of a better way to say it) fully developed. That seems a clumsy explanation, because God is God and needs no developing. Nevertheless, Scripture describes the divine life in us as a seed (*see* 1 John 3:9). Jesus pointed out that seeds grow into fully mature plants through a process little understood.

> "This is what the kingdom of God is like. A man scatters seed on the ground. Night and day, whether he sleeps or gets up, the seed sprouts and grows, though he does not know how. All by itself the soil produces grain—first the stalk, then the head, then the full kernel in the head. As soon as the grain is ripe, he puts the sickle to it, because the harvest has come."
>
> Mark 4:26–29

It seems to me that this parable of Jesus, whatever else it may be intended to convey, describes a process by which God-in-us becomes fully realized. The development of life, whether of a human being in the womb or a seed in the ground, is gradual, mysterious, and difficult to analyze. So it is with the development of the life of God in us. Though it is initiated with the decisive implantation of a seed, spiritual growth is essentially a quiet work of God, and even the hindsight of many years may not be adequate to pinpoint its advance from stage to stage.

> How silently, how silently,
> The wondrous gift is giv'n!
> So God imparts to human hearts
> The blessings of his heav'n.
> No ear may hear his coming,
> But in this world of sin,
> Where meek souls will receive him still,
> The dear Christ enters in.
>
> Phillips Brooks
> "O Little Town
> of Bethlehem"

The Apostle Paul acknowledged the impossibility of detecting the life of God in people, especially in its early stages. He wrote, "My dear children, for whom I am again in the pains of childbirth until Christ is formed in you, how I wish I could be with you now and change my tone, because I am perplexed about you!" (Galatians 4:19, 20.)

He had thought they already had Christ in them, but certain things he learned about them caused him to doubt it. They certainly had no "full kernel in the ear," and Paul had to scrutinize the ground closely for the first appearance of a green stalk peeping through.

Understanding What It Is and Is Not

To say that God is in us is quite different from saying that God *is* us. Anyone who identifies himself as God is either crazy or a pantheist or something else other than a biblical Christian.

The Bible never confuses the creature with the Creator, as pantheism does.

Alexander Maclaren put it this way:

> We have got to keep very clear and distinct before our minds the broad, firm line of demarcation between the creature and the Creator, or else we get into a pantheistic region where both creature and Creator expire. But there is a Christian as well as an atheistic pantheism, and as long as we retain clearly in our minds the consciousness of the distinction between God and his child, so as that the child can turn around and say "I love thee," and God can look down and say, "I bless thee"; then all identification and mutual indwelling and impartation from him of himself are possible, and are held forth as the aim and end of Christian life.[2]

That we can be indwelt by God, that He can impart Himself to us, Maclaren says, is both possible and the aim of Christian life. He goes on to say:

> Instead of puzzling ourselves with metaphysical difficulties which are mere shadows, and the work of the understanding or the spawn of words, let us listen to the

31

Christ when he says, "We will come into him and make our abode with him," and believe that it was no impossibility which fired the Apostle's hope when he prayed, and in praying prophesied, that we might be filled with all the fulness of God.[3]

God's Kingdom Within You

Much of the rest of this book will deal with how God-in-you imparts an overflowing life. Let us take time now for one brief example.

In the year 1667 in France, Jeanne Marie Guyon was a young wife and mother only nineteen years old. She became troubled because she could not seem to pray the way she wanted to and felt she should. Being very devout and faithful, she never missed her twice-daily times of prayer. In those times, she says, "I endeavored to meditate, and to think on God without intermission."

It caused her "great anxiety," she continues, "to find I could not meditate, nor exert my imagination in order to pray."

At last, because of her father's concern and at his insistence, she went to see a spiritual adviser known for his devotion to God. She described her difficulties with prayer, and he replied:

"It is madame, because you seek without what you have within. Accustom yourself to seek God in your heart, and you will find him there."

Having said these words, he left me. They were to me like the stroke of a dart, which penetrated through my heart. I felt a very deep wound, a wound so delightful that I desired not to be cured. These words brought into my heart what I had been seeking so many years. Rather they discovered to me what was there, and which I had not enjoyed for want of knowing it.

O my Lord, thou wast in my heart, and demanded only a simple turning of my mind inward, to make me perceive thy presence. Oh, infinite Goodness! how was I running hither and thither to seek thee, my life was a burden to me, although my happiness was within myself.

I was poor in riches, and ready to perish with hunger near a table plentifully spread and a continual feast.

O Beauty, ancient and new; why have I known thee so late? Alas! I sought thee where thou wert not, and did not seek thee where thou wert. It was for want of understanding these words of thy gospel, "The kingdom of God cometh not with observation ... The kingdom of God is within you."

This I now experienced. Thou becamest my King, and my heart thy kingdom, wherein thou didst reign supreme and performed all thy sacred will.

I told this man that I did not know what he had done to me, that my heart was quite changed, that God was there. . . . I was suddenly so altered that I was hardly to be known either by myself or others.[4]

God was there. God's presence within changed Madame Guyon drastically. When God is there in your innermost being and you know it, you, too, will have found the fountain of living water.

God-in-you makes a difference that is beyond our words to describe. However, we can describe some aspects of it. That will be our pursuit in the pages that follow.

——— THREE ———

Why Life Gets So Messed Up, and What to Do About It

"For I know the plans I have for you," declares the Lord, "plans to prosper you and not to harm you, plans to give you hope and a future."

Jeremiah 29:11

The first thing the overflowing life does is reconcile Almighty God to us. Although He has been set against us because of our sin, He is now for us.

One can hardly exaggerate how important this difference is. As the Apostle Paul wrote, "If God is for us, who can be against us?" (Romans 8:31.) As someone else has said, "One plus God makes a majority."

Perhaps the best way to realize how great it is to have God for us is to think about the reverse—having God against us. Some would call it being jinxed! Even if we deny being jinxed, even if we deny one can be jinxed, when we aren't sure God is for us, we are likely to feel a general uneasiness and be prone to expect misfortune.

"I might have known!"

"Nothing goes right for me."

"I should live so long."

Even Murphy's Law, "If anything can go wrong, it will," suggests a conspiracy of nature against us.

Fact or Superstition?

We must face the evidence that God can, indeed, be against us. From ancient times, people have sensed intuitively that God sets Himself against certain individuals. God puts a curse on those who have especially displeased Him.

This notion is found in both biblical and pagan cultures. Fiji, for example, is a pleasant place to visit today, but was once a very bad place to be shipwrecked. Not that there is any *good* place to be shipwrecked, but Fijians once believed that those shipwrecked on their shores must have displeased the gods. Therefore, they were to be killed and eaten.

In Bible times, the inhabitants of the Mediterranean island of Malta had a similar view of catastrophe, although they were hospitable people and not cannibals. The Apostle Paul was shipwrecked on Malta. The friendly natives built a fire to warm the survivors, because the weather was cold and rainy. Wanting to help, Paul gathered sticks for the fire. As he arranged the sticks on the flames, a deadly snake came out of the bundle and set its fangs in Paul's hand. The natives said, "This man must be a murderer; for though he escaped from the sea, Justice has not allowed him to live" (Acts 28:4). When Paul showed no ill effects of the bite, however, they reversed their opinions and decided he was a god.

The pagan view that you can tell how wicked a man is by the misfortunes that come upon him is false. However, the idea that God sets Himself in opposition to those guilty of certain practices is true. Scripture specifically cites several behaviors that bring upon people a curse from God.

Persecuting God's People

One thing that stirs God's anger against people is persecution of His children. Notice that God's promises to Abraham included, "I will bless those who bless you, and whoever curses you I will curse" (Genesis 12:3).

History records a number of times when this curse has been imposed with devastating effect. One of the strongest examples is from modern times. Adolph Hitler tried to destroy the Jewish people, and God not only sent utter and complete destruction upon Hitler, but everlasting shame on his name.

An earlier example was Haman, who tried to destroy the Jews in the days of the Persian emperor Xerxes. He ended up being hanged on the very gallows he had prepared for his Jewish archenemy, Mordecai. In the middle of this story, Haman's wife and his advisers spoke these significant words to him: "Since Mordecai, before whom your downfall has started, is of Jewish origin, you cannot stand against him—you will surely come to ruin" (Esther 6:13).

Now, you can call it superstition if you want to, but there's no way I am going to raise my hand or voice against God's people, the Jews. I want to bless them, not curse them, because I want God to bless, not curse, me. I feel the same way about persecution of Christians, for they are also the children of Abraham by faith. (For that matter, I don't want to persecute anybody. All people, no matter how godless they are, belong to God by right of creation and are made in His image.)

Disobeying God's Law

A second thing that brings God's curse upon people is disobedience of His laws and precepts. In a remarkable portion of Scripture, Deuteronomy 28, we read, in verses 1-14, of all the blessings God promised to bestow on those who obey His law. The passage sums up these blessings by saying, "You will always be at the top, never at the bottom" (v. 13).

Next follows a description of God's curses upon those who disobey the law. Then we read, "All these curses will come upon you. They will pursue you and overtake you until you are destroyed, because you did not obey the Lord your God and observe the commands and decrees he gave you" (v. 45).

God's curse has a quality of inevitability about it. "These curses will come upon you ... pursue you ... overtake you." God's curse works like a heat-seeking guided missile. Homing in on the heat created by the target airplane's exhaust, the missile is deadly accurate, inescapable. The target literally draws the destroying missile to itself. That is what we do when we cast off God's holy law.

To decribe the same inevitability in natural terms, "It will be as though a man fled from a lion only to meet a bear, as though he entered his house and rested his hand on the wall only to have a snake bite him" (Amos 5:19).

If you feel you are "snakebit," maybe there's a reason. God is no respecter of persons, and He hasn't arbitrarily picked you out to be jinxed. But He does set Himself against those who scorn Him and His law. The Bible describes such people as having "only a fearful expectation of judgment" (Hebrews 10:27). Their guilty hearts tell them they deserve nothing good from God, so the best they can do is try to avoid Him.

Ahab, king of Israel, was a man who lived under the curse of God. Ahab resisted and disobeyed God all his life, and he had the uneasy conscience that went with it. God's guided missile caught up with Ahab when he planned a joint military expedition with Jehoshaphat, king of Judah. The story is told in 1 Kings 22.

Ahab had surrounded himself with false prophets who would tell him what he wanted to hear. They all predicted that the contemplated venture would be a great success. Ahab was apparently a strong believer in positive thinking, so he used these fellows to boost his confidence. "I can do it if I believe I can," was his motto.

Ahab's ally, Jehoshaphat, wanted a good word, too, but being a follower of the Lord, he knew more was involved than positive thinking. If *God* gave the good word, he could go forth to battle with confidence, but if not.... Well, Jehoshaphat had no desire whatever to fight against both God and the enemy forces. "Is there not a prophet of the Lord here whom we can inquire of?" he said to Ahab (1 Kings 22:7).

Ahab reluctantly admitted that there was one such prophet, a man name Micaiah. "But I hate him," said Ahab. "He always prophesies evil for me and not good" (see v. 8).

At Jehoshaphat's insistence, Ahab summoned Micaiah. Ahab tried his best to intimidate Micaiah, even while he was enroute to deliver his prophecy. Ahab's messenger told the prophet, "Look, as one man the other prophets are predicting success for the king. Let your word agree with theirs, and speak favorably" (v. 13). He might as well have said, "Don't rock the boat; it could go hard for you if you make trouble."

When Micaiah arrived, he told a surprised Ahab just what the other prophets had said and just what the king wanted to hear. "Attack and be victorious, for the Lord will give it into the king's hand" (v. 15).

Ahab was as shaken as he would have been if Micaiah had foretold his doom. He knew in his heart there was no way God was going to bless him. What was this crafty Micaiah trying to pull, anyway? Was he being sarcastic?

"Tell me the truth!" Ahab demanded.

Then Micaiah uttered his chilling prophecy. "I saw all Israel scattered on the hills like sheep without a shepherd, and the Lord said, 'These people have no master. Let each one go home in peace' " (v. 17).

Since Ahab was their master, he immediately recognized these words as a prophecy of his own downfall in the battle. Micaiah proceeded, however, to make it absolutely clear that Ahab would be going to his death (v. 20). He concluded with, "The Lord has decreed disaster for you" (v. 23).

Ahab's habit of rejecting the word of God and trying to sneak past God's judgment was strong, as it is with many people today. So, despite the clear warnings, Ahab proceeded with his battle plans. He did take extra precautions, however: He went into battle disguised as an ordinary soldier, so nobody could single him out for an arrow. Meanwhile, he persuaded his "friend" and ally, Jehoshaphat, to go into the battle dressed as a king.

Jehoshaphat was almost killed because the enemy soldiers were especially targeting the king of Israel, and they at first mistook Jehoshaphat for Ahab. Though they discovered their mistake and spared Jehoshaphat, they were never able to identify Ahab. His shrewd trick of wearing a disguise "worked."

Ahab's cleverness could not save him, however, from the guided missile of God's judgment. We read, "But someone drew his bow at random and hit the king of Israel between the sections of his armor" (v. 34). This was a double coincidence. First, the random shot just happened to strike Ahab. Second, the arrow just happened to strike in the small crack between his plates of armor, where the arrow could penetrate. So Ahab died.

Make no mistake: If God sets Himself against you, no amount of clever planning will save you. And God does set Himself against those who persist in persecuting His people or disobeying His law.

Returning Evil for Good

A third kind of behavior that provokes the wrath of God is doing evil to those who have done good to us. "If a man pays back evil for good, evil will never leave his house" (Proverbs 17:13).

To do evil is bad enough anytime, but to misuse someone who has been kind and good to you is especially foul in the eyes of God—so foul that He is not going to stand for it. Unless you repent and receive forgiveness, you are going to pay for that for the rest of your life. God Himself will see to it. He has set Himself against you.

There are a lot of young people against whom God has set His face, and they will never know any peace. They have returned evil for good to parents who loved them and tried to raise them right.

There are husbands and wives who have abused the love and kindness and forbearance of their spouses. They will never know joy.

There are employees who, though paid well and treated kindly, have stolen their employers blind. Some have betrayed their company to a competitor. God is the judge of all such.

There are employers who have exploited their workers and in some cases fired them after years of faithful service, just to avoid paying them the retirement benefits they need and deserve. Their sin cries out for judgment.

Worst of all, there are people who receive boundless good directly from the hands of God and repay Him with the evil of ingratitude and disobedience. God gives them breath, and they repay Him by using it to profane His holy name. God gives them health, and they repay Him by using their energies to pursue things He hates. God gives them money, and they squander it on their own pleasures, never seeking to glorify Him with it. God gives them time, and they use it for anything but to serve and worship Him.

Do you want to know why the world is in such a mess today? Why your own life is a mess? A curse from God is upon all who return evil for good. Evil never leaves their houses.

The greatest and most costly good that God did for you was to send Jesus Christ, His Son, to die on the cross for your sake. There Christ took upon Himself the curse you deserve. "Christ redeemed us from the curse of the law by becoming a curse for us . . . He redeemed us . . . so that by faith we might receive the promise of the Spirit" (Galatians 3:13, 14).

There we are, back to the best gift of all—God's gift of His Spirit, to dwell within us as an overflowing river of life. It is a gift made possible only by the redeeming love that sent Christ to die in our place.

To repay such love with indifference or scorn is the ultimate in returning evil for good. No wonder we read, "Whoever believes in the Son has eternal life, but whoever rejects the Son will not see life, for God's wrath remains on him" (John 3:36).

"God's wrath remains on him."

"Evil will never leave his house."

What an absolutely dreadful state in which to be!

Removing Every Curse

We have seen that God has pronounced a curse on those who persecute His people, disobey His law, or return evil for good. With God against them, such people must spend their lives in fearful expectation of judgment.

What a miserable way to live! Always under a cloud. Always sensing the frown of God. When things go well, you know it cannot last. When things go badly, you fear that the judgment you tried not to think about may now be falling.

When I was a boy living in Bend, Oregon, my older brother, Ron, and I used to go swimming at Curtis Pool in the summer. It cost a dime to get in, and that was money hard to come by. One day my brother showed me a way to get in without paying.

The bathhouse had an upper deck that was divided right down the middle by a wall. On one side, swimmers could lie in the sun. On the other side, visitors could watch their children or friends in the pool. It didn't cost anything to go up on the observation deck. Ron showed me how he could go to the observation deck, walk to the back of the dividing wall, reach around for a handhold on the other side, and transfer himself to the sunbathing section. From there it was simple to descend the stairs and enter the pool.

There was one rather formidable problem, as far as I was concerned. The back of the bathhouse was built right above the rocky riverbank, and that dividing wall reached clear to the edge of the building. To transfer from one side to the other meant swinging out in space over what looked—to this little boy—like at least a hundred-foot drop to that rocky riverbank. I can see it clearly in my mind's eye to this day.

Ron went ahead, got around the end wall with no difficulty, descended the stairs, and was soon swimming and splashing in the pool. As much as I wanted to join him, I was not about to risk that fall. But I also didn't have a dime.

The pool was very busy that day, and I decided I would rather chance being observed than falling to a certain death. When the attendants were especially busy with a group of kids who came all at once, I simply walked past them and slipped into the pool. I didn't enjoy my swim as much as usual, though, because I kept wondering if they would discover me.

I left earlier than I would have normally and went home. All evening I wondered if there would be a knock at the door and the swimming pool attendants would be there (maybe the police, too), to apprehend me.

The next day, some kids told me, "Hey, after you left yesterday, the attendants were asking us your name. They said you sneaked in without paying."

I was terrified. For several days, I stayed away from home as much as I could so that, if they came, I wouldn't be there. Of course I couldn't go swimming again, even with a dime, because they might recognize me as the boy they wanted. I lived in torment.

When the Bible talks about living with a fearful expectation of judgment, I know what it means. Believe me, it's no fun. I decided that I would never again try to sneak into Curtis Pool. It just wasn't worth the suffering.

To any who suffer from a fearful expectation of judgment, the good news is that the overflowing life brings a radical change in that situation. Christ has redeemed us from the curse, paying our dime plus penalties for us, as it were. Because we have trusted in Christ, God is reconciled to us. He isn't laying for us. He is no longer against us, but on our side.

When the weight of our sins presses upon our minds and guilt assails us, the greatest thing in the world is to know that Almighty God is for us. He is the one we most had to fear. He is the one against whom our worst offenses were committed. But now He drops all charges. Our judge has become our defender, and no one remains to press charges against us. As the Apostle Paul wrote, "Who will bring any charge against those whom God has chosen? It is God who justifies" (Romans 8:33).

The very God who once stood against us because we deserved it now clears us of all charges because of Christ's intervention on our behalf and because we have received the gift of forgiveness. Isn't that glorious?

It is what Moses had in mind centuries ago, when he penned Psalm 90. Reflecting on how short life is, like a single day (vv. 5, 6), Moses cried to God, "Satisfy us in the morning with your unfailing love, that we may sing for joy and be glad all our days" (v. 14).

Your time on earth is too short to live under the frown of a God who is against you. While it is still morning—or at least before any more of life's short day passes—the joy and gladness of God's unfailing love can enrich your life. There is no such thing as an overflowing life when God is against you.

Tell God you want Him to be for you and not against you, and whatever it takes to make it that way, you are willing.

You are, aren't you?

43

——FOUR——

What Makes Life Work as It Should

But life isn't just success and survival. Life is also a journey, and God is a wonderful traveling companion.

To talk about God being for us or against us, as we did in the previous chapter, assumes more than some people will accept. It assumes there is a personal God who relates to us individually.

Some imagine that if there is a God, He must be unknown and unknowable, a "first cause" or "ground of being." They look at a universe so vast and complex that our world is an insignificant speck of dust by comparison. On this speck called Earth, the human race has appeared for one brief hour of time as geologic ages go. Each of us is only one of millions of human beings who have come and gone. Surely we live out our few moments in obscurity, as far as the eternal Creator is concerned. We are but passing specks on a speck.

The idea that God involves Himself intimately and personally with us is mind-boggling.

The Bible does not ignore this problem but addresses it directly: "When I consider your heavens, the work of your fingers, the moon and the stars, which you have set in place, what is man that you are mindful of him, the son of man that you care for him?" (Psalm 8:3, 4.)

Nevertheless, the Bible consistently teaches that in this case, the marvelous is also true. God is mindful of us, and He does care about us.

God at a Distance

The overflowing life is predicated on the possibility that we can come into such a relationship with God that He will not only be aware of us and for us, but will actually be with us and in us. The overflowing life does not come from a distant God who is up in the stands of heaven, cheering for us. Admittedly, that's a whole lot better than having Him up there planning judgments against us. However, the overflowing life comes only from a close-at-hand God, one who is present to enrich our lives.

How close is God to you?

I'm afraid too many of us are like my friend Malcolm MacGregor once was. In his popular book *Your Money Matters*, Malcolm writes:

> I had an intellectual understanding of the "process" by which people became Christians. It all made sense to me, too, because some people were pretty wicked and they needed this. Personally, I already had it all together; I didn't need anything. I had a real good relationship with God: I didn't bother him and he didn't bother me.[1]

Another friend said, concerning her relationship with God, "He and I are just sort of tolerating each other."

This God-at-a-distance arrangement is not the overflowing life. It

45

is a life needlessly impoverished. We need God with us, and we need God in us for several very specific reasons. Let's look at a few of these reasons.

God in Us for True Success

I must tell you about one of the Angelo boys, Michel.

Michel Angelo was a noted artist and sculptor of the sixteenth century. He is famous for his great statues of Moses and David, as well as for his paintings on the ceiling and walls of the Sistine Chapel in Rome. (I was kidding about his name; it was really Michelangelo Buonarotti.)

There can be no doubt that Michelangelo was both immensely talented and highly dedicated to his art. The remarkable thing is that his success required more than both of those traits combined.

Michelangelo was just another sculptor living in Florence, Italy, in his early years. No one took his work seriously. The art critics of his day raved about ancient works of art dug out of old ruins, but they would hardly look at anything he did. He just could not get a fair shake from them.

Then one day there showed up, in the possession of Cardinal Raffaelo Riario in Rome, a sculpture of the *Sleeping Cupid*. The cardinal had purchased it for a large sum of money as an authentic ancient art treasure. It turned out to be a counterfeit, produced by an unknown twenty-one-year-old from Florence named—you guessed it—Michelangelo.

There are differing versions of just how all this came about. What we know for sure is that the cardinal was so impressed with the sculpture, though he had been taken on it, that he summoned Michelangelo to Rome. In the next five years Michelangelo produced a *Bacchus* and the *Pietà* and achieved great fame.

The rest is history.

It takes more than talent to succeed in life. Even a person so extraordinarily gifted as Michelangelo needed something more. He needed a stroke of luck (assuming he did not engineer the *Sleeping Cupid* affair himself) or quite a bit of resourcefulness (if, as I suspect, he did).

I do not know that Michelangelo's "something extra" had a spiritual base, though he certainly was a man of faith in God. What I do know is that having God with us and in us is the something extra that is most crucial to our success. We either have an inner resource from God that enables us to function the way He designed us, or we do not.

Something Lacking

Thousands of years ago, a keen observer of the human condition wrote:

> The race is not to the swift
>   or the battle to the strong,
> nor does food come to the wise
>   or wealth to the brilliant
>   or favor to the learned;
> but time and chance happen to them all.

Ecclesiastes 9:11

We see it so often.

So many who are fleet of foot stumble and fail to finish the race, much less win it.

So many strong people, beaten in the battle, are left crippled and defeated.

So many able people are reduced to trudging through life with little purpose and even less joy.

So many gifted people allow their gifts to fall into disuse.

Yet others, less swift, less strong, less able, less gifted, live full, productive, happy lives. As the passage suggests, time and chance may have a lot to do with the outcome, and we will deal with that shortly. However, the gifted often fail even when no misfortune strikes. When this happens, it seems clear that something is lacking inside those who are unable to capitalize on their advantages.

If you are unfulfilled, look inside. I say *unfulfilled* because my definition of success is not a worldly one, based on how our lives may appear to other people. Rather, success has to do with how we use our God-given talents and how well we balance all of life. An

47

inner deficit that keeps us from using our talents and from balancing our lives will leave us unfulfilled.

God can give you the something extra you presently lack for success, whether that something extra is inner release, confidence, discipline, motivation, or guidance—whatever it may be.

Perhaps you are blocked somehow and need release. The Bible says, "Where the Spirit of the Lord is, there is freedom" (2 Corinthians 3:17). You can become sufficiently filled with God's Spirit to be free inside.

Perhaps you are not so much blocked as blind. You may not be able to see your own gifts clearly. Michelangelo was not blind to his gifts; he saw them when others did not. He believed enough in his gifts and himself to take the initiative.

The world is full of people who are waiting for someone else to take the initiative on their behalf. "If someone else believes in me, opens doors for me, makes things happen for me, then I will use my gift." That is their attitude, and it is extremely unrealistic. Others will help us along the way, but we must take the initiative ourselves. Why should someone else believe in you, if you don't? Why should someone else make things happen for you, if you won't?

Jesus said that He came in the interests of "recovery of sight for the blind" (see Luke 4:18). When He dwells in our hearts by His Spirit, He provides that something extra we need to see our gifts and see how we can exercise them.

Perhaps you are discouraged because your poor talents are few and unimpressive. No need. The something extra you will have when God fills your life is a greater asset than any talent. Lacking many gifts, you will have God's best gift, and since fulfillment constitutes true success, you will never be unsuccessful but will experience a life enriched from within.

I have mentioned a few specific examples of how the operation of God in our lives can provide the something extra that makes the difference between true success and failure. Such examples could be multiplied by as many people as there are in the world. Whoever you are and whatever constitutes real success for you, God's power within you is the key.

God in Us for Strength

In the passage quoted earlier about "the race is not to the swift," the concluding observation was ". . . but time and chance happen to them all" (Ecclesiastes 9:11). The passage continues, "Moreover, no man knows when his hour will come."

Sooner or later, you and I are going to run into time or chance: We are going to face devastating circumstances. When we do, we will need God with us and in us.

In an earlier book, I dealt at length with many of the vicissitudes of time and chance. I described how real people have coped with awesome and overwhelming situations, including those in which the providence of God seemed conspicuously absent and there was no happy ending.

The story of one of those people, Captain Allan Gardiner, bears repeating here. We take up the story on December 17, 1850.

> It was on that date . . . that Gardiner and six intrepid companions landed at Patagonia on the southern tip of South America. Their task was to take the gospel to a people so primitive that the evolutionist Charles Darwin had said they existed "in a lower state . . . than in any other part of the world."
>
> Gardiner, a seasoned captain of the British navy, had made careful preparations for their mission. He had twice before visited the area, once staying for three months. He knew the natives to be treacherous cannibals and the land and weather to be severe.
>
> He took with him two double-deck launches, the *Pioneer* and the *Speedwell*, and six-months' supply of provisions. His team included a medical doctor and a ship's carpenter. In England he had a group of supporters who were to send him a second six-months' supply of goods.
>
> On December 18 Gardiner said goodbye to the *Ocean Queen*, the ship that had carried his party from England. "Nothing can exceed the cheerful endurance and unanimity of the whole party," he wrote. "I feel that the Lord is with us, and cannot doubt that he will own and bless the work which he has permitted us to begin."

The very next month Gardiner's supporters in England began seeking a ship to carry the next six-months' provisions to Patagonia. No one would risk it. Can you imagine the thoughts of the missionaries as day after day they searched the horizon for a ship that never came? Could the tempter have passed up such an opportunity to question the love and faithfulness of Almighty God?

Fighting scurvy, cold, and hunger, plus the hostility of those they had come to win, the little band must have known some dark days of discouragement.

In October of 1851, when a relief ship finally reached Patagonia, the horrified crew found the missionaries dead of starvation. Gardiner's body, clad in three suits and with wool stockings over his arms to ward off the numbing cold, was found lying beside a boat. In his journal was a record of the ordeal. At one point Gardiner wrote: "Poor and weak as we are, our boat is very Bethel to our souls, for we feel and know that God is here. Asleep or awake, I am, beyond the power of expression, happy."

God did not supply his physical needs. He and his companions had sought first the kingdom of God, but the material things had not been added unto them. Still, while he could not say God's provision was there, he could and did say, "God is here."[2]

I might point out that later the missionary agency founded by Gardiner succeeded in Patagonia. Charles Darwin wrote, "The success of the mission is most wonderful and charms me, as I always prophesied utter failure. I shall feel proud if your committee think fit to elect me an honorary member of your society."[3]

But none of that was known to Gardiner. He had to either find his solace in God or die with a soul as desolate as the land where he fell. Gardiner found his solace in God.

By contrast, even a warm, sterile hospital bed can be a desolate place for a person dying without God.

Certainly at death, and probably at many other points along the way, we will need the strengthening presence of God in our lives.

50

The good news is that we will have that presence with us when we need it. God indwells us.

Help Matched to Your Need

We die only once, but we have to live every day. Crushing experiences can and do invade our lives, seemingly from out of nowhere. Some of them last only a short time and, with God's help, we put them behind us. Others stay with us for years, and we need a strength that is not only immediate but lasting.

Can you imagine anything better, when time and chance combine against you, than to hear within your soul these words from the Lord?

> So do not fear, for I am with you;
>   do not be dismayed, for I am your
>   God.
> I will strengthen you and help you;
>   I will uphold you with my
>   righteous right hand.
>
> Isaiah 41:10

One thing I particularly appreciate about the Lord is His sensitivity when He helps me. I mean, have you ever had anybody try to help you when you didn't want help? They make a nuisance of themselves. You end up under obligation to them for giving help you neither needed nor wanted.

By contrast, God tailors His help to our situation. Notice the progression of thought in the Scripture just quoted. God will *strengthen*, or *help*, or *uphold* us, according to our need.

Every day I need strength, and God is always there to supply it. Sometimes, though, I need more than strength. I may be up against something I can't handle alone, no matter how strong I am. I need help. And beyond that, there are times when the Lord just about has to do it all; circumstances are too much for me, and I can only look to Him to uphold me.

One can trace these degrees of assistance in the lives of certain Bible characters. Moses, for example, agreed to lead Israel out of

Egypt after God said, "I will be with you" (Exodus 3:12). God being with him *strengthened* Moses to confront the Pharaoh with a demand for their release.

Moses was also *helped* by the signs God provided: the staff that became a snake, the healthy hand that became leprous and then healthy again, the water that turned to blood when Moses poured it on the ground.

Later, when the people and the leaders of Israel turned against Moses and spoke of stoning him to death, God *upheld* Moses. There was really nothing Moses could do about the situation, but God was with him and dealt with the problem (*see* Numbers 12, 14, 16).

How far do you suppose Moses would have gotten without God's help?

Dr. Adrian Rogers, a prominent Southern Baptist pastor, tells of a man who cut off the tail of a huge lion with only a pocket knife. As it turned out, the man did have help: Someone else had already cut off the lion's head.

I suspect most of my exploits are like that. I have had more than a little help. And thank God for that; I wouldn't care to take on the lions of time and chance without Him.

God in Us for Fellowship

We've said that we need God in us first for true success, and second, to receive strength according to our need. But life isn't just success and survival. Certainly, life overflowing is more than "grit your teeth and with God's help you will make it." Life is also a journey, and God is a wonderful traveling companion.

Recently my wife, Marge, and I visited Fiji and Australia for the first time. Do you know what the best part of the trip was? The people.

In Fiji we stayed with Don and Helen Stormer, missionaries from New Zealand. We not only got a lot of help but also a lot of enjoyable company from the Stormers. Helen knew how and where to shop, away from the tourist traps. Don took me to speaking engagements. Both of them answered our many questions about the culture, the people, the state of God's work there. Helen even persuaded two policemen, wearing their white skirts with deep vee hems, to pose for photos with us on the city streets of Suva, the capital.

One day I wrote picture postcards to friends and family back home. When Helen and Marge and I were next in town, I stopped in the post office for airmail stamps and then dropped the cards in the mail slot. Outside I noticed a trash can that could almost have been mistaken for a mailbox. When Helen asked me if I had mailed my cards, I couldn't resist. "Yes," I said, pointing to the trash can, "I dropped them in that mailbox."

Well, Helen is a woman of action. "Oh, no," she said as she headed for the can. "We must get them out of there!"

Of course, I couldn't actually let her dig into the trash can, so I laughed, and confessed my ruse. Marge confirmed that I really do have a warped sense of humor. Fortunately, Helen thought it was pretty funny, too.

In Australia, we enjoyed similar good fellowship with Jim and Ruth Meharg. True, his was an unusual last name, Jim told us almost as soon as we met. He had researched its origin and discovered the family name was originally Grahem. One of his forebears, wanted for murder, had reversed the spelling of his name to help him escape the law. Since we knew Australia was settled as a British penal colony, the story had a degree of credibility.

What good times we had, talking and laughing about the strange expressions and customs of our respective lands!

Several times on that trip, I thought about an acquaintance of mine who traveled around the world in about one week, all by himself. What a waste! You know, wherever you go in this world, a major airport is a major airport, a big city is a big city, and a motel room is a motel room. They are virtually interchangeable, from one country to another. My friend might as well have spent his week sitting in O'Hare International Airport in Chicago, where he started. He certainly did not see much of the world that he circled.

New acquaintances, friends, people—they make places colorful and interesting. I wouldn't care to go at all, if I had to go alone, stay alone, see the sights alone.

In a similar way, God with us and in us enriches our life's journey by His presence. He is good company. He laughs with us—even when we really do drop our mail into the trash can—and He enjoys what we enjoy.

Yes, God with us and in us truly is God's best gift. In all the ways we have suggested here, and many more, He is the source of over-flowing life.

—PART—
III

Characteristics
of the
Overflowing Life

———— FIVE ————

You Can Be Fundamentally Right, Not Wrong

"I will give you a new heart and put a new spirit in you; I will remove from you your heart of stone and give you a heart of flesh. And I will put my Spirit in you and move you to follow my decrees and be careful to keep my laws."

Ezekiel 36:26, 27

We all have elements of good and bad in our lives. In fact, most of our basic characteristics have both a good and a bad side, according to how they are expressed. For example, traits that are generally good can turn bad:

- Are you *congenial*?

To be friendly and responsive to people's requests is good; to be played for a sucker because you are unable to tell anyone no is bad.

- Are you *mellow*?

To be relaxed and easygoing is good; to be so laid back that you never accomplish anything with your life is bad.

57

• Are you *ambitious?*

To aspire to and pursue a meaningful life is good; to want to "reach the top" so much that you scramble over people or burn yourself out in the process is bad.

Just as good traits have bad aspects, so bad traits can have good aspects:

• Are you *angry?*

To lose your temper and destroy things, injure people, or use foul language is bad; to be angry over injustice or your own folly and to harness that anger to correct the situation is good.

• Are you *quiet?*

To be so introverted or withdrawn that you become isolated from others or bottle up things that need to be talked out is bad; avoiding senseless chatter and quietly listening to others is good.

• Are you *lazy?*

To let things go, to neglect your duties, to waste your potential just because it takes work to develop it, is bad; to be able to relax or play without feeling guilty, even when there's work to be done, is good. There is *always* work to be done, if you have a mind to do it.

Your life, then, is not 100 percent good or 100 percent bad, and most of its bad could become something good, if redirected and controlled. As long as you live, you will need to continue to fine-tune your character, seeking good and constructive expressions of your natural inclinations.

Building on a Solid Base

The critical thing is to have a solid base from which you may successfully build your own uniquely balanced life. That base is your identity as a person who is fundamentally right, rather than fundamentally wrong.

Let me illustrate. A certain young man was frequently in trouble of one sort or another. One day his mother sensed he might be in trouble again, and she asked him, "Is something wrong?"

He replied, "Something has *always* been wrong."

This fundamental sense of something being wrong is devastating, for it undermines all a person's good intentions. It is like Lawrence of Arabia's complaint when his life went bad. Though he had done great exploits and became world famous early in life, he lived in un-happy obscurity in the years before his death at age forty-six. In describing himself then, Lawrence said, "There is something broken in the works . . . my will, I think."

Whether one feels that he has "always been wrong" or that he now has "something broken in the works," the results can be posi-tively terrifying. Such a person might well say: "This is *me* we are talking about. I am not some disposable dime-store trinket, a cheap ornament that hardly matters, whether it works or not. I am all I've got, and if I am intrinsically defective, then I am doomed to a life of dismal struggle, at best."

Many who never talk that way, even to themselves, nevertheless do have feelings that all is not as it should be. These feelings are so threatening that they are usually buried or denied.

Any person who consciously or unconsciously feels fundamen-tally wrong desperately needs to replace that feeling with the assur-ance that, as the old hymn says:

> Whatever my lot, Thou hast taught me to say,
> It is well, it is well, with my soul.

This assurance that all is well, that you are fundamentally right, is a great treasure. Without it, you will always suffer pangs. You will see the continual small and great calamities that invade your life as evidence of the unhappy truth you have always known and never wanted to face: You are a loser. Count on it: Things will al-ways be going wrong in this world. You have no hope of being well in your soul until you can look yourself in the eye in the mirror and say with conviction, "However wrong my world goes, and no mat-ter how much my own blunders have contributed to my problems, I myself have been made right. I am not a loser, but a chosen and be-loved child of God."

A Job for the Creator

Be clear about this: We are not saying you need to convince your-self you are okay. We are saying you actually need to *become* okay.

This is a job for the Creator. You cannot make yourself funda-

59

mentally okay. Scripture says, "Can the Ethiopian change his skin or the leopard its spots? Neither can you do good who are accustomed to doing evil" (Jeremiah 13:23).

But God can change you fundamentally, and the good news is that He is willing to do that. It's all a part of the gift of God, of which we have been speaking all along.

You should pray and ask God for the gift of a fundamentally right heart, as others have done before you. David prayed, "Create in me a pure heart, O God, and renew a steadfast spirit within me" (Psalm 51:10).

The prophet Ezekiel described the change as follows:

> "I will give you a new heart and put a new spirit in you; I will remove from you your heart of stone and give you a heart of flesh. And I will put my Spirit in you and move you to follow my decrees and be careful to keep my laws. You will live in the land I gave your forefathers; you will be my people, and I will be your God."
>
> Ezekiel 36:26–28

The Apostle Paul said, "Therefore, if anyone is in Christ, he is a new creation; the old has gone, the new has come!" (2 Corinthians 5:17.)

Being made fundamentally right by God does not mean you become perfect. You still exhibit a mixture of good and bad elements. But there is a great deal of difference between being a fundamentally flawed person with some good traits and being a fundamentally right person with some bad traits. It is the difference between being a Hitler (who gassed millions of Jews but showed kindness to a pet) and being a Paul (who blessed millions of people with the Gospel but was sometimes covetous or contentious).

One could argue against my distinction here. For example, someone might say, "Being right with wrong mixed in is no different from being wrong with right mixed in. It's two ways of saying the same thing. A zebra could as well be called black with white stripes as white with black stripes."

I'll grant that's the way things may appear on the surface. However, a zebra is not six of one and half a dozen of the other. A zebra is definitely white with black stripes, as one can tell by looking at the unstriped areas of the body, such as the stomach.

So it is with those who receive the gift of God. The Bible teaches that we become fundamentally right. The gift of God is, in fact, an impartation of something of the very nature of God to us (see 2 Peter 1:4). That nature is not only right but incorruptible; it will *always* be right. How's that for good news?

An Influence for Right in a Gone-Wrong World

People who are fundamentally right overflow into the world as an influence for right. It is not so much that they are crusaders. Sometimes a crusader is a person trying desperately to compensate for being fundamentally wrong inside. Such people are basically hypocrites. They are the rigid, unloving, driven, self-righteous, critical, shove-it-down-their-throats type of crusaders.

Fundamentally right people become a force for right in the world not so much because of what they *do*—the causes they support, the positions of power they hold—but because of what they *are*.

We had a county commissioner whose stand on social issues gained him the outspoken support of many conservative Christian leaders. He was against all the things they were against—in his public pronouncements. Later, evidence came out that he personally did the very things he publicly denounced. He was driven from office in disgrace.

Contrast this political leader with the Apostle Paul when he was imprisoned in Caesarea. Paul languishes in jail for months while legal proceedings grind on interminably and his whole future remains in doubt. Jewish leaders are pressing serious charges against him. Many of the Roman authorities, who hold his fate in their hands, are corrupt. One wants a bribe from him; another is intent on doing political favors for Paul's enemies. Color his world gray. His conditions are miserable. His outlook is bleak.

Paul is a man who is fundamentally right in his soul. He is experiencing the overflowing life, despite his circumstances. When he has a chance to present his case to King Agrippa, he is so enthused about Jesus that Agrippa remarks, "Do you think that in such a short time you can persuade me to be a Christian?" (Acts 26:28.)

Paul responds, "Short time or long—I pray God that not only you but all who are listening to me today may become what I am, except for these chains" (Acts 26:29).

There it is! "I pray God all may become what I am."

That is how fulfilling Paul's life was. The chains were no fun, and he said so, but his life was of such quality he would not have exchanged places with anyone who did not know God. He only wished that they might also know the kind of life he had found.

Can you say that? If you can, I'd say it's a pretty good indication that you know something of the overflowing life.

SIX

You Can Live
With Confidence,
Not in Fear

"So do not fear, for I am with you; do not be dismayed, for I
am your God. I will strengthen you and help you; I will uphold
you with my righteous right hand."

Isaiah 41:10

Everybody seems to be living life on the ragged edge. On
one of our regular walks recently, my wife, Marge, and I were talking about that. We noted how it is true of those closest to us—our
married children. They are all solid citizens, and their lives seem serene enough to outsiders, but every one of them must deal with
threatening or disturbing situations.

Our oldest daughter, Kathy, seems like a totally "together" person. She is a mother of three children still at home and a capable
part-time secretary in the insurance office of her husband, Mort. But
for years Kathy has been fighting periods of depression, PMS, and

63

headaches. Sometimes the kids almost drive her batty. In addition, she and Mort recently went through the trauma of leaving their church when their personal convictions became irreconcilable with church policies.

Our daughter Krys and her husband, Bill, are on the edge financially. Bill makes a good income working for the postal service, and Krystal augments that with a small part-time wage from the school district. They are good money managers. Still, they often feel hard-pressed. They have three children and are determined not to deprive them of a good start. For example, all three presently take piano lessons, at a combined cost of one hundred dollars a month.

Bill and Krys can't afford many extras. Unforeseen expenses can pose a serious problem. Last year the water line to their house broke. Before they discovered it, a huge water bill had accrued. To help pay that bill and to dig up and replace the line, their church came to their rescue.

Our son Steve is a lawyer. He worked long and hard to put himself through school. Now he is associated with a prestigious law firm, enjoys his work, and has bright prospects for the future. I'm sure he is the envy of many people, as well as a model for younger members of the family.

But Steve also has problems. His work situation makes it hard for him to spend much time with his wife, Bev, and their new baby. He is finding himself financially pressed, too; he has so many more expenses now than he faced during his simpler student days.

Our daughter Karen and her husband, Dave, while far from rich, are getting by okay financially, right now. It's a good thing, because they recently decided they had to get their oldest son, Joshua, out of public school and into a private school.

Marge and I talked about how the lives of all these loved ones of ours appear perfectly serene to outsiders. We know other people well enough to glimpse below the surface, too, and we know they fight some desperate private battles while seeming at peace. This makes us suspect that the rest of the human race is not much different.

"Nobody really has life under control, except us," I said to Marge jokingly. "And we are kept on the ragged edge with our concerns over everybody else."

Accidents, illnesses, children in trouble, dashed dreams, personal conflicts, financial reverses, lawsuits—these and many other disasters can strike any of us. The overflowing life does not exempt us from such experiences, but it does enable us to live confidently, in spite of them.

The Failure of Groundless Optimism

The overflowing life must not be confused with the baseless optimism so often a part of the so-called "American dream." That optimism, with its marriage to materialistic values and worldly concepts of success, is something else entirely. The American dream can destroy those who pursue it all their lives and then end up feeling betrayed by it.

Willy Loman, the leading character in Arthur Miller's *Death of a Salesman*, is a prime example. Willy spent his life believing that if he persistently worked hard and was well liked, he would make it big in sales. To be well liked was important. Some people were liked but not well liked. He himself was well liked by his customers in New England.

Biff, his son, was well liked, too. He was a high-school football hero. True, he had only drifted since high school and had even gotten into a few scrapes with the law, but when he settled down, Biff would make it big.

Ultimately this house of cards collapsed around Willy's head. Less and less effective on his job but too old and stubborn to give up his delusions and settle for other work, he was finally fired. Meanwhile, at age thirty-four, his son Biff still hadn't settled down.

Willy committed suicide, betrayed by his dreams but still pursuing them. (Surely Biff would be magnificent with the insurance money Willy left him.) But Biff had no such dreams and bitterly declared of his father, "He never knew who he was!"

Now, I am fully aware that people often pursue dreams and fulfill them. Doing so usually turns out to be less wonderful than they had imagined, but that's another matter. Some people do, indeed, gain great material and vocational success. They constitute visible evidence that it can be done.

Their high visibility is part of the problem. The people for whom life does not turn out all roses are not so visible. They have no inspiring story to tell, and nobody wants to listen to a "crybaby," so they quietly fade away.

But believe me, they are out there in great numbers. You need only pause long enough to look. Some, now unemployed after twenty or thirty years on the job, face in their declining years a life that is nothing like they expected. With no good work prospects, few assets, small if any vested retirement benefits, perhaps without even health insurance as they approach the years when they will need it most, their lives are bleak. These weren't all play-it-safe people, either. Some grabbed for the gold, made investments that proved bad, and now face their declining years in poverty.

Such people don't all end up suicides like Willy Loman. Some just become bitter, disillusioned, and thoroughly defeated in spirit.

Looking Reality in the Eye

The confidence that comes with the overflowing life is not based on a stubborn, wish-fulfilling, ultimately destructive optimism like Willy Loman's. The overflowing life enables one to look reality straight in the eye, with all its dangers, difficulties, and disappointments, and still be confident.

You see, there are basically three ways we can react to life's threatening situations. We can:

1. Live in paralyzing, tormenting fear.
2. Maintain a false confidence based on a "Willy Loman" type of optimism.
3. Be at peace because we have been infused with confidence from God Himself.

An incident from the life of Jesus may help us appreciate the differences among these three responses. The disciples and Jesus were in a boat on the Sea of Galilee. "Without warning, a furious storm came up on the lake, so that the waves swept over the boat. But Jesus was sleeping. The disciples went and woke him, saying, 'Lord, save us! We're going to drown!' " (Matthew 8:24, 25).

That's how we feel, when we are on the ragged edge. We are alarmed and afraid we may drown.

Now, several of the disciples who were in the boat with Jesus that day were fishermen. The sea was their home. They had looked to the sea for their livelihood, perhaps for prosperity, but now the very system they had tried to make serve them threatened to destroy them. How like Willy Loman!

There were also several landlubbers in the boat with Jesus. Matthew, the tax collector, for example—what did he know about the sea? He was in an unfamiliar environment, facing a storm that had even the veteran seamen frightened. He was like us when a doctor tells us we face some dread disease we have never even heard of, or when we discover our child is homosexual or addicted to drugs. We are completely out of our element, overwhelmed.

Jesus told the disciples—both seamen and landlubbers—" 'You of little faith, why are you so afraid?' " (v. 26).

These words of Jesus have often been misunderstood. They have been taken to imply that the disciples should have known they were safe from drowning as long as Jesus was with them in the boat. One hymn based on this account says:

No water can swallow the ship where lies
The Master of ocean, and earth, and skies.

Now, personally, I am convinced that this is nonsense. Water has swallowed many a ship occupied by disciples of Jesus, with whom Jesus says He is always present. Do you suppose there were no Christians on the *Titanic*? Certainly there were.

Christians are not exempt from drowning. Dawson Trotman, founder of a worldwide discipling organization called The Navigators, drowned. Not only was he a devoted Christian, but he was trying to save someone else's life at the time.

When Jesus said, "You of little faith, why are you so afraid?" He was not saying that there was no danger of drowning. He was saying that even if they did drown, they really did not need to be afraid. They were in the hands of a loving heavenly Father. To sink in the stormy sea would have been to rise to their Father.

This kind of indomitable spirit marked the early followers of Jesus. One counselor to the Roman emperor described the difficulty in persecuting them something like this: "If we kill them, they say they are going to be with Christ which is far better. If we spoil their goods, they rejoice that they are counted worthy to suffer for Christ's sake. Nothing we can do seems to hurt them."

Those disciples did not live in fear. Neither did they rest in the false confidence that nothing bad could happen to them, that life would surely treat them royally if they only pushed the right buttons. Their confidence came from God Himself. It was the confidence of an overflowing life, and we can have it, too.

──── SEVEN ────

You Can Be Powerful, Not Pathetic

"Everything is permissible for me"—but I will not be mastered by anything.

1 Corinthians 6:12

God intends you to become a person of great power. Someday He intends you to judge the angels. Did you know that? It's true, according to Scripture. "Do you not know that we will judge angels? How much more the things of this life!" (1 Corinthians 6:3.)

If you and I are to judge angels someday, we had better shape up and start judging, or managing, the things of this life now. God wants to prepare us here on earth for even greater things hereafter. He is not planning to wave a magic wand over those of us who have been pathetic here and suddenly make us powerful there. Instead,

He wants to build into our lives and characters now the traits that will qualify us to judge angels—and exercise authority in many other ways—hereafter.

The Plan

God's plan, from the time of your creation, was to make you a person of power. In fact, when the Bible says that man was made in the image of God, that refers primarily to our delegated power. Notice how the two concepts are joined in the Bible's first reference to man. "Then God said, 'Let us make man in our image, in our likeness, and let them rule . . . over all the earth' " (Genesis 1:26).

The human race was intended to rule the earth, and each of us is to govern our personal world. Jesus taught that if we govern our personal world well, God will expand the area of our authority. He will say, as the parable of the talents puts it: " 'Well done, good and faithful servant! You have been faithful with a few things; I will put you in charge of many things' " (Matthew 25:21).

The Pathos

Unfortunately, many people cannot govern their few things well. They do not rule their own affairs; their lives are out of control. Sometimes they are captives unaware. Pathetically, they brag of freedom while in almost total bondage.

Perhaps a parable will illustrate the point.

There was once a young prince, whose father turned the kingdom over to him before going away to a far country. The prince at first thought it wonderfully exciting to be in charge of the kingdom, and he was full of ideas about what he would do.

However, an enemy soon attacked the young prince, sending a powerful army against him. Capturing both the prince and the castle, the enemy confined the young prince to the castle dungeon.

After a long time, the king returned and discovered the sad state of his kingdom. Immediately he laid siege to the castle, drove out the enemy, and threw open the dungeon door. "My son," he cried. "Rise! Come forth! I have come to set you free."

The prince did not move. "Set me free?" he said dully. "I am al-

ready free." He held up his hands. "See, I am bound by no chain."
He swept his hand around the tiny cell. "No one is here to tell me
what I must do. Now you come and want me to do whatever you
say. I am sorry, but I just cannot give up my freedom."

Like this prince, many who were called to rule have been so long
and so utterly confined that they no longer even know what freedom is. They imagine that not having to obey God is freedom, so
they turn away from the One who made them to rule.

Progressive Deterioration

Powerless people are pathetic when they are unaware of their
captivity. They are also pathetic because of the progressively worse
state into which they are moving. Sin sometimes does not seem destructive in its early stages. "Sin, when it is full-grown, gives birth to
death" (James 1:15).

No one provides a more dramatic example of progressive deterio-
ration than the addict. A chemical substance, whether alcohol, marijuana, tobacco, cocaine, or some other drug, has taken control. In
the early stages of addiction, the slavery and degradation may not
be apparent. Nevertheless, the process has begun. Unless there is a
change of course, the end is certain to be tragic.

Ward B. Phipps describes the degradation into which alcohol can
cast a person:

> When I was a boy, I would pick up three whisky bot-
> tles and sell them to the saloon keeper on the corner for a
> nickel. My mother did not like for me to do it. She told
> me the saloon was an evil place.
>
> I thought the saloon was a pretty place. I thought
> Mother was prejudiced against that nice, clean place.
> One day the keeper told me to set the bottles in a back
> room. When I did so, I saw something that I did not know
> about the place before. Back of the room where I set the
> bottles was another room that I learned they called the
> "bull pen."
>
> In that room were five drunk men, lying in disarranged
> piles on the floor. They were bruised, dirty, covered in
> their own and each other's vomit. Flies were all over

71

them. In their half-delirious condition, they were cursing and groaning.

I got out as quickly as I could and never again did I want to go back to any saloon. There I began to learn that while the front door of a place of sin may be pretty and clean, the back door is terrible. At the front there may be music and song and laughter and lights. But at the back door there are moans and groans and darkness.

Young people go in the front door looking for and expecting a glorious time. They may have a hilarious time. But little by little, the devil through his subtlety winds his web of delusion around them, and then they come out the back door broken and ruined, but often still deceived.

When people writhe in pain, out of their minds and covered with vomit, it is plain to see their condition is pitiful. What we don't see, and they don't, either, is how pathetic their condition really was for a long time before it ended in degradation.

These are people for whom God intended a progressive expansion of dominion. Instead, they have progressively become more enslaved. They are like cashmere sweaters used as car rags. They are like fine engravings used as dust pans. After a while, they bear little resemblance to what they were originally intended to be.

Caught in a Web

Addiction is by no means the only kind of progressive enslavement. Jesus said, " 'I tell you the truth, everyone who sins is a slave to sin' " (John 8:34). Drug addiction spins physical and psychological webs around a person, but sin of any kind entangles us spiritually and decimates our power to resist.

I once saw a spider kill a mouse. I could hardly believe my eyes. I suppose that mouse was several hundred times larger than the spider. For a while, the mouse seemed to ignore the spider, and as the spider spun its web around the mouse's legs, I marveled at its audacity. Clearly the mouse could break those fragile strands anytime it chose.

Patiently the spider worked as the mouse continued nosing around in some crumbs and dust on the floor. At length, the mouse's movements began to be hindered by the spider's web. It began to kick, and I expected it to break free easily.

Just at that moment, with unbelievable quickness, the spider darted at the mouse and injected it with poison. The mouse began to kick frantically but only succeeded in suspending itself in midair, where it was securely held by the flexible but unbreaking web of the spider. In moments, it was all over; the mouse was dead.

Our problem is that we have all been entangled in sin's web at some point or another. We'd like some hope that our entanglement won't prove fatal. We need timely intervention. We need someone who will break the web before the spider injects his fatal poison. Christ is the one who can do exactly that.

One-Eyed Warriors

Powerless people are pathetic when they are captives and don't know it. Powerless people are pathetic when they become progressively more degraded by their sinful habits. Powerless people are also pathetic when their powerlessness leads to their being irreversibly maimed or crippled.

An incident from the Old Testament illustrates both the danger of being maimed and the way to prevent such a tragedy.

The account is found in 1 Samuel 11 and concerns the city of Jabesh in the land of Gilead, a part of ancient Israel. An overwhelming enemy army from Ammon besieged the city of Jabesh, and it seemed to the citizens that their best way out was to negotiate a surrender. They knew they would be subservient to Ammon after that, but at least they could survive the immediate crisis. Later, perhaps they could manage to overthrow their oppressors.

The Ammonite leader said he would accept their surrender on only one condition. Every man of Jabesh would have his right eye thrust out. This horrible action was not proposed simply as a way to inflict painful punishment on an enemy. No, Ammon had a clever plan that would leave the men of Jabesh able to serve but unable to resist their foreign masters.

In the hand-to-hand combat of that day, a man held a shield in his left hand and a sword in his right hand. The shield primarily protected the warrior against assault from his left. Meanwhile, he watched and did battle toward his right side. With no right eyes, the men of Jabesh would be severely handicapped as warriors. Meanwhile, they would hardly be hindered at all in working, as they would if the Ammonites cut off their right hands, for example.

Therefore, for Jabesh to surrender to the Ammonites meant much more than losing one particular battle. It meant they would be less able to resist their enemy in the future.

When we surrender to sin, much the same thing happens. Our ability to resist is drastically affected. As Jesus said, we become slaves to sin.

Jabesh is representative of us in another respect, also. They were told that Ammon would "gouge out the right eye of every one of you and so bring disgrace on all Israel" (1 Samuel 11:2). Beyond the personal tragedy these men would experience, they would be a reproach to their nation.

Israel was a people famed for their valor. God had appointed them to drive pagan worship out of the land and establish a kingdom of righteousness and peace. No pagan nation had been able to stand against them. For a troop of God's men to become squinting wood choppers and water carriers for a godless alien power would have been a tragedy for the whole nation.

Like Israel, you were created to glorify God, not to grovel under the heel of the devil. You were designed to be powerful, not pathetic. It is a reproach on God and on all the people of God when you are degraded. Let this travesty stop!

Let it stop *now*. A critical time element may be involved here. Once a person's eye is gone, it's gone. Submitting to the power of sin could maim you permanently.

When the citizens of Jabesh realized their dilemma, they decided to surrender only "if there is no man to save us." They sought help, and their appeal came to the ears of Saul, who, although he was king, had never before been recognized or followed by them. Angry at the indignity Ammon intended to inflict on Jabesh and all Israel,

Saul gathered a force of 330,000 men. He marched on the Ammonite army and so thoroughly defeated and scattered them that no two of them were left together.

Do you know that Jesus Christ, your King—perhaps too little recognized and followed by you in the past—has overwhelming forces available for your rescue? He can scatter your enemies and restore your freedom and dignity. You don't have to be maimed.

I'm not saying there will be no battle. To the contrary, the struggle may be long and fierce. The outcome, however, is not in doubt. The overflowing life will make you powerful, not pathetic.

A Spirit of Power

The overflowing life confers upon us a new inner power, both to rule our own lives and to rule that portion of God's creation that He entrusts to us. We have said that God indwells His people. Well, one of God's attributes is omnipotence. If He is in us, we ought to be people of power.

Yet people in churches everywhere acknowledge that they lack power. Much of the depression, worry, fear, discouragement, frustration, and even anger, that we see in people's lives traces back to a sense of powerlessness.

When you are worried, for instance, it is not simply because you have a problem. It is because you have a problem that you fear you do not have power to handle well.

When you are depressed, it is not simply that things are not as you might wish. Rather you feel powerless to make them right or to cope well with the "wrongness."

The feeling or attitude of powerlessness has no place in the life of one called to rule. As Paul wrote, "For God did not give us a spirit of timidity, but a spirit of power, of love and of self-discipline" (2 Timothy 1:7).

Part of our problem is that we don't really believe God's power is available to us; we think we are weak. We try to be "good strong Christians," but since we know we are weak, we inevitably fail.

This is no small problem. How can we believe we are strong when we know—and have proved repeatedly—that we are weak?

Hope for the Struggling

I know how frustrating it is to try to claim God's power in one's daily life and to fail. I know what it is like to try in vain to resist temptation. I know about the doubt, the self-loathing, the near despair.

If that describes your state now, let me encourage you. As hard as it may be to believe, you are closer to the overflowing life than those who don't experience the kind of struggle you do.

If you feel weak and powerless and ashamed, you are at least one giant step ahead of the complacent captives of sin.

Providing You With Power

I think every Christian has to learn for himself how to have God's power for his daily life. Prayer, fasting, support groups, deeper spiritual experiences, Scripture memory and meditation, counseling— all these have been helpful to many.

Whatever it takes, seek and find the help you need. *It will all boil down to laying hold on God's power within.* How to do that is the question.

For me, Scripture memory and meditation helped a lot. In all honesty, it also contributed to my frustration for a while. For example, I knew by heart such verses as Psalm 119:11: "I have hidden your word in my heart that I might not sin against you." But I still seemed powerless to resist temptation.

I memorized 1 Corinthians 10:13: "No temptation has seized you except what is common to man. And God is faithful; he will not let you be tempted beyond what you can bear. But when you are tempted, he will also provide a way out so that you can stand up under it."

The passage was helpful in giving me hope, but it was also frustrating, because I could not find the way out that the verse assured me existed.

Two other passages of Scripture eventually did bring some practical help, a way out for me. The first was 1 John 5:4: "For everyone born of God overcomes the world. This is the victory that has overcome the world, even our faith." God told me through this verse that

I needed to have more faith and I needed to exercise my faith in a different way than I had before, when I failed. I had often prayed to God for forgiveness and for help, and I used all the faith I could muster when I did so. But the next day, or whenever the hour of temptation came, I fell again. I finally realized that if I had faith in God *at the moment of temptation,* then faith really did ovecome the world. I could say no to temptation at that moment.

The second passage that helped me was Romans 12:21: "Do not be overcome by evil, but overcome evil with good." This proved to be a dynamite practical principle for me.

When I was tempted and lacked strength to resist, I now had a one-two punch I could use against Satan.

1. The punch of faith: I could pray quickly to God for strength and believe He was giving it.

2. The punch of action: I could immediately involve myself in doing something I knew was pleasing to God; that way I couldn't do the evil.

I don't say these two principles solved all my problems. I don't know how well they will work for you. But they certainly did help me.

What I can say with certainty is that there is a way out for you. You can be a person with power to do the will of God. Seek, and keep on seeking, and you will find!

There was once a man who felt weak, as you perhaps do now. He could neither do the good things he wanted to do nor resist the evil things he didn't want to do. Sin was his master, and he cried, "What a wretched man I am! Who will rescue me from this body of death?" (Romans 7:24).

That same man, the Apostle Paul, was later able to say, " 'Everything is permissible for me'—but I will not be mastered by anything" (1 Corinthians 6:12). *I will not be mastered.* Paul was no longer expressing a wish or a longing when he spoke those words. He was asserting power. He was staking out a territory. It was a territory God had assigned him long before: to rule his own life first, and then increasingly to rule over the creation.

This is your calling, too. "I will not be mastered," can become your watchword, as it was Paul's. It is all a part of the overflowing life.

An Arsenal of Faith

I know the principles of God's word can make you a person of power. Therefore, I want to offer you the following passages to commit to memory.

Before you say or think that it's just too hard and you can't memorize these Scriptures, consider two facts:

1. You are being prepared to exercise power, not only for here and now, but also for hereafter. You are not learning the principles of God's word as some quick fix to a temporary situation. You are becoming a person qualified to judge angels. It makes sense to work a little to qualify yourself.

2. The idea that learning these verses of Scripture is difficult has little basis in fact. Granted, learning long passages that have no importance or meaning to you would be difficult. But these are practical principles for daily living.

Furthermore, each verse is only ten words long. Ten words! That's hardly any longer than your full name and address, so don't say you can't learn it.

Take one verse a week for ten weeks, and it will be a snap. Write one verse out on a card you can carry with you this week. Study it when you have spare moments. In each succeeding week, add a new verse, reviewing the old ones, too. In the tenth week, you will be learning the tenth verse and reviewing the other nine.

Get a friend or mate to learn the verses along with you, and both of you will profit.

Most of the Scriptures are quoted from the New International Version. Some are adapted slightly, to keep them to ten words. Here are the dynamite ten:

"I can do everything through him who gives me strength."

Philippians 4:13

"Be not overcome by evil, but overcome evil with good."

See Romans 12:21

"God gives a spirit of power, love, self-discipline, not fear."

See 2 Timothy 1:7

"The Lord is my helper; I will not be afraid."

Hebrews 13:6

"There is now no condemnation for those in Christ Jesus."

See Romans 8:1

" 'Everything's permissible'—but I will not be mastered by anything."

See 1 Corinthians 6:12

"God cannot be mocked. A person reaps what he sows."

See Galatians 6:7

"One who sows to the sinful nature will reap destruction."

See Galatians 6:8

"One who sows to the Spirit will reap eternal life."

See Galatians 6:8

"We will reap a harvest if we don't give up."

See Galatians 6:9

You have probably heard of various self-improvement plans. "Six weeks to a new, slim you." "Three months to prosperity beyond your wildest dreams." "Twenty minutes a day to physical fitness." Here's something far better than any of those. These ten power principles can be an asset to you from this day on, for as long as you live. There's only one catch: You have to use them.

———EIGHT———
Your Life Can Have Purpose and Meaning

One generally assumes that a boomerang returns to the thrower; actually it returns only when the thrower has missed his target. Similarly, man returns to himself, to being concerned with his self, only after he has missed his mission, only after he has failed to find meaning in life.[1]

Viktor Frankl

Psychologists and other students of human nature have widely recognized that a sense of purpose is one of man's deepest emotional needs.

Dr. James D. Mallory, Jr., author of *The Kink and I,* puts it this way: "People need meaning and purpose in their work and in their lives, and . . . everything deteriorates without it."[2]

He quotes Friedrich Nietzsche, "He who has a *why* to live can bear almost any *how*," and George Bernard Shaw, "Every man is ill at ease until he has found his niche."[3]

If these observers are correct, it is clear that the overflowing life, in order to be such, must give a person a sense of meaning and purpose.

Why Not Just Live?

Certainly not everyone lies awake nights fretting about life's purpose. However, just because that may not be a top-priority concern doesn't mean it's unimportant to your life.

Without a satisfactory sense of meaning, people suffer emotionally, whether or not they realize what is at the root of their problem. Viktor Frankl says that humans can be symbolized by boomerangs.

> One generally assumes that a boomerang returns to the thrower; actually it returns only when the thrower has missed his target. Similarly, man returns to himself, to being concerned with his self, only after he has missed his mission, only after he has failed to find meaning in life.[4]

Ours has been called the "narcissistic generation." People are preoccupied with themselves. Frankl would argue that such preoccupation is a symptom of a generation lacking in meaning and purpose, whether people think in those terms or not.

If you have a disquieted spirit, if you tend to be focused on yourself, perhaps it is because you have failed to find adequate meaning in your life. Your energies have boomeranged.

A Basis for Purpose

Some years ago, newspapers carried the story of a Fairbanks, Alaska, man who had built a "nothing machine." As I recall, the machine had about 270 moving parts. It was an impressive assembly of whirring gears, shafts, and wheels. However, it didn't *do* anything.

The nothing machine was novel enough to rate space in the newspapers. That alone tells us something: We expect everything to have a purpose. If it doesn't, that's news.

Yet there are those—a few—who would tell us the entire universe is only a super-colossal nothing machine. This complex universe, from the orbiting particles inside one atom to the largest star system in space, just *are;* they don't mean anything.

By that reckoning, man is totally insignificant, since he is only a little scum (or a speck, as we said before) on one tiny planet in the huge system. Our lives really cannot have any meaning but are, in the words of Shakespeare, "a tale told by an idiot, full of sound and fury and signifying nothing."

Most people, however, see it quite differently. They believe, at the least, that some purpose is behind it all. Christians believe more specifically that everything was created by God. He has a plan for the whole creation and for every part, especially for man.

Christians With No Purpose

There is a huge gap between believing God has a purpose for everything and living with a sense of purpose. Some Christians are, in fact, more vacuous and trivial than many who don't even know the Lord. The Christian who dreams of creature comforts, ease, and pleasure is put to shame by the wealthy people of this world who aspire to something better.

Gordon Peter Getty, for example, was once asked if it pleased him to be considered one of the richest men in the United States. He replied:

> No, certainly not. I'd rather lapse back into obscurity. But if my music became well respected, I wouldn't mind becoming well-known for that. The best things in life require effort and study rather than money. You can't buy an education, and education is worth more than a billion dollars.

Society is full of good, solid citizens, including Christians, who are so lacking in purpose that their lives are just plain boring. Frankl writes, "Boredom is now causing, and certainly bringing to psychiatrists, more problems to solve than distress."[5]

J. I. Packer describes the situation this way:

> The world today is full of sufferers from the wasting disease which Albert Camus focused as Absurdism ("life is a bad joke"), and from the complaint which we may call Marie Antoinette's fever, since she found the phrase that describes it ("nothing tastes"). These disorders blight the whole of life: everything becomes at once a problem and a bore, because nothing seems worth while.[6]

Long before Marie Antoinette colorfully captioned the emptiness of a life without purpose, King Solomon wrote a book about it: Ecclesiastes. " 'Meaningless! Meaningless!' says the Teacher. 'Utterly meaningless! Everything is meaningless' " (1:2).

Continuing in the same vein, he said, "All things are wearisome, more than one can say" (v. 8). And again, "Yet when I surveyed all that my hands had done and what I had toiled to achieve, everything was meaningless, a chasing after the wind; nothing was gained under the sun" (2:11).

It's worth noting that Solomon was not bored from having nothing to do. He had not only involved himself in the world's various pleasures but had also "toiled to achieve" things that he undoubtedly thought were worth achieving at the time. Yet, he came up feeling empty afterward; even his achievements seemed meaningless. Clearly, then, finding purpose involves more than being busy, or even being busy with productive work.

The Christian's Struggle for Meaning

Sometimes I myself have wandered in a wilderness, unable to make my life as purposeful as I sense it ought to be. I observe the same frustration in others. We know we have "found it" in Christ, but somehow we can't put it all together and make it work as it should.

What Happened to the Wonderful Plan?

The Four Spiritual Laws, which originated with Campus Crusade for Christ, have been used to introduce great numbers of people to

Christ. The first of these laws states, "God loves you and has a wonderful plan for your life."

Now, I do not wish to argue with the truth of that statement, for I wholeheartedly believe it. However, the wonderful plan may be hidden deep in the counsels of God. What many Christians see in their own lives is decidedly unwonderful, and if there is any plan, it is extremely hard to decipher.

Most Christians live rather ordinary lives. The wonderful plan, as they have understood that phrase, has been overbooked. Just as the airlines sometimes sell more tickets than there are seats on the flight, so the soul winners have recruited more believers than there are extraordinary roles to fill.

Let's face it: In any church, the vast majority of the people are ordinary members, a few are prominent leaders, and only one is the senior pastor.

The same scarcity of extraordinary roles pervades our society. Famous Christian musicians give concerts before crowds numbering in the thousands. The musicians experience God's wonderful plan for them, but the thousands mostly just live from day to day. The high point of their week (or year!) in an otherwise dull existence was to hear these wonderful musicians.

A best-selling author can live out the wonderful plan only because the multitudes are, at least so far as the author/reader relationship goes, only anonymous readers.

If high achievement or privileged position is the object, then God has a wonderful plan for a few people, but the pyramid is very small at the top.

Either we have been sold a bill of goods and there is no wonderful plan for most of our lives, or else the wonderful plan must be found in the ordinary give-and-take of daily life.

Finding Meaning in Your Work

One problem is that we too often seek purpose and meaning in a single dimension of life. Christians tend to seek all their meaning in religious or spiritual activities. Secular people seek all their meaning apart from the spiritual. But God's plan is not one-dimensional. One can have purpose in life in various ways. But we are talking about the overflowing life. We are talking about fulfillment, not just escape from a sense of utter futility and boredom. The overflowing life lends meaning and purpose to everything we do.

One place to find meaning and purpose is in your work. Now, it is possible to make an idol of one's work, and many people do. But while our work can be an idol, it can also be service to God and a great source of fulfillment. Far from feeling guilty about our work, we ought to throw ourselves into it enthusiastically.

The first thing God ever said to man was, "Be fruitful and increase in number; fill the earth and subdue it" (Genesis 1:28). To subdue the earth, to rule it and use it wisely and well, is what work is all about.

God also gave Adam work to do in paradise, before sin entered the picture. "The Lord God took the man and put him in the Garden of Eden to work it and take care of it" (Genesis 2:15).

So then, we were made to work. Therefore, we get a sense of satisfaction, we experience fulfillment in a desirable career or work setting because we are functioning as God made us to function. We are fulfilling our purpose.

Retired people who no longer work often waste away and die because they have no purpose for living. In fact, people of any age are more susceptible to illness when they have nothing compelling to do. Many times I have felt a cold or flu coming on but shook it off because I simply didn't have time to be sick; I had important work to do. Maybe you find that hard to believe, but I ask you, have you ever known a bride to get sick on her wedding day? I don't say that it can't happen. I don't say I could always shake off any illness if I were busy enough. I simply say that having a purpose makes a big difference.

In his book *Anatomy of an Illness,* Norman Cousins says, "A highly developed purpose and the will to live are among the prime raw materials of human existence." He continues, "I became convinced that these materials may well represent the most potent force within human reach."[7]

Cousins went on to describe the remarkable effect of purpose in the life of famous Spanish cellist, conductor, and composer Pablo Casals. Playing his music seemed to transform the man. "Twice in one day I had seen the miracle. A man almost ninety, beset with the infirmities of old age, was able to cast off his afflictions, at least temporarily, because he knew he had something of overriding importance to do. There was no mystery about the way it worked, for it happened every day."[8]

Cousins described a similar phenomenon in Albert Schweitzer at an advanced age. "Albert Schweitzer always believed that the best medicine for any illness he might have was the knowledge that he had a job to do, plus a good sense of humor."[9]

God has given us all some work to do, and we can find much purpose and meaning in life by doing it wholeheartedly.

With this in mind, one can understand why people get involved in their work and get so much satisfaction out of it. They are supposed to! Even people who do not know God can therefore have some sense of purpose in life. Their work can give them the definite feeling that "This is for what I was made!"

Finding Meaning in Fellowship

As we have said, our problem is that we too often seek a one-dimensional answer to the question of meaning and purpose. So, while our work can give meaning to our lives, we need to ask what other elements are also important.

The *Westminster Catechism* suggests another answer to the question of our purpose for being. "The chief end of man is to glorify God and to enjoy him forever." The "glorify God" aspect of that statement no doubt includes our work, but the "enjoy him" part speaks more of relationship and fellowship.

Immediately, much that we have read in the Bible springs to the support of the view that our purpose is to company with God. Jesus said, " 'Now this is eternal life: that they may know you, the only true God, and Jesus Christ, whom you have sent' " (John 17:3).

The story of Mary and Martha also applies. Martha was busy serving Jesus; Mary was sitting at His feet, fellowshiping with Him. Jesus said that Mary chose the better part.

Our purpose is to be found not only in what we do for God—in our work—but in God Himself. What a wonderful release! We don't have to perform all the time. We can relax and enjoy God's creation, giving Him praise for it, and thus fulfill at least a part of our purpose.

Even if we are incapacitated for most work, we can fellowship with God, which is one thing God had in mind when He created man in the first place.

We must not embrace fellowship *instead* of the work ethic, however. We must add it. The opening chapters of Genesis suggest this balance. God came to meet with Adam and Eve in the garden in the cool of the day, but He also told them to tend the garden and keep it. They didn't concentrate all their time and energy on one of these purposes, but pursued both. There is a performance element and a fellowship element in God's purpose for each of us.

A Third Purpose

There is yet a third purpose that should absorb us and lend meaning to our lives. It is serving others, and particularly serving the cause of their redemption.

This is not mentioned in the opening chapters of Genesis, as are fellowship with God and tending the garden, because man had not yet fallen. In our time, however, this third element of purpose is critical. Serving the cause of redemption may well give us a sense that we are living for a purpose—more than anything else we can do.

Jesus said, " 'Whoever wants to become great among you must be your servant, and whoever wants to be first must be slave of all. For even the Son of Man did not come to be served, but to serve, and to give his life as a ransom for many' " (Mark 10:43–45).

Any kind of service we render can contribute to our sense of meaning and purpose. Some services, however, are more significant than others. Saving someone's life is worth more than washing someone's windshield.

Imagine, then, what a service it would be to contribute to someone's eternal salvation. Scripture says, "Those who lead many to righteousness [will shine] like the stars for ever and ever" (Daniel 12:3).

Some time ago in the city of Chicago, two small children perished in a fire that destroyed the seedy apartment where they lived. Police arrested the father on a charge of negligent homicide. It seems he was so drunk that he accidentally caused the fire, stumbled out of the place in a daze, and didn't even tell firemen that his children were still inside. News accounts described the father as devastated with guilt and grief, as one might imagine.

Suppose that before the fatal day you had been with this man. Suppose you had been able to "lead him to righteousness" so he quit his destructive drinking habit. You would have saved the lives of those children and spared the man immeasurable suffering. Can you think of any greater service you or anyone else could possibly have rendered that man?

All over our world, children and adults are suffering greatly because of sin. What a service it is when somebody turns an unrepentant sinner to righteousness! No wonder those who turn many to righteousness will shine as the stars forever!

A Price to Pay

Here, then, is a glorious purpose for which to live. But it can also be costly. Our redemption cost Jesus His life on the cross. Fulfilling our purpose by serving the redemption of others also involves a crosslike cost.

For a fuller treatment of this theme, read my book *When Death Means Life: Choosing the Way of the Cross*. Here is an example from that book of how the principle of the cross operates in the life most full of meaning and purpose.

> Consider now, as perhaps the premier exhibit, the life of the woman blessed above all others—Mary the mother of Jesus.
>
> When the angel Gabriel first announced to Mary that she would bear a child, he said, "Greetings, you who are highly favored! The Lord is with you" (Luke 1:28).
>
> Later, Mary's cousin Elizabeth said to her, "Blessed are you among women, and blessed is the child you will bear" (v. 42).

Mary responded, "My soul praises the Lord, and my spirit rejoices in God my Savior, for he has been mindful of the humble state of his servant. From now on all generations will call me blessed, for the Mighty One has done great things for me" (vv. 46–49).

What could be better?

"Highly favored."

"Blessed . . . among women."

Blessed for all time "from now on."

God doing "great things" for her.

We need to ask exactly what it entailed for Mary to be blessed so markedly.

First, it meant she was suspected by her fiancé of being immoral. Joseph thought she had been with another man. Only the direct intervention of God deterred him from rejecting her completely.

We don't know what the other people of Nazareth thought and said and did about the apparent illegitimate pregnancy of Joseph's girlfriend. Knowing Joseph's initial reaction, we can guess. I doubt that the pair would even try to convince the neighbors that Mary was still a virgin and was with child by the Holy Spirit.

In any case, we know that Mary had to take a long arduous trip to Bethlehem when she was in the last stages of pregnancy. She had to take lodging in a stable and give birth to her first child far from home and loved ones.

This was the beginning of her sorrows. At the dedication of the Child, a devout man named Simeon prophesied of his destiny. Then he said to Mary, as if an afterthought, "A sword will pierce your own soul too" (Luke 2:35).

Thirty-three years later, when Mary stood at the foot of the cross and saw a Roman spear pierce the side of her crucified Son, we may be sure the sword pierced her soul.

Blessed of God?

Highly favored?

Great things?

Not if "blessed" means free from sorrow and difficulty. Not if "favored" means knowing a life of ease and prosperity. Not if "great things" have to do with earthly power and prestige and success.

How, then, was Mary blessed? Ah, she knew the glory of living for a divine purpose, of having transcendent meaning in her life. She, an obscure maiden from the despised town of Nazareth, was the direct agent of Messiah's coming.

I believe everyone wants meaning in life. Still, we would just as soon have it without a sword in our soul. Without the cross.

Mary couldn't.

Jesus couldn't.

Neither can we.[10]

The God of Purpose

Remember, the overflowing life is God-in-us. God is a God of purpose. The people of God have always been people of purpose. Scripture says we are to run with perseverance the race marked out for us (see Hebrews 12:1). Too many people not only won't run but don't even cheer the runners on; they simply don't care about the great purposes of God. If you don't care anything about the race, if you are just hanging around the stadium for the peanuts, popcorn, and soft drinks, your life is going to be a pretty dismal event.

The choice is yours. You can loiter around the stands, or you can run your God-appointed race. You can have a life in which "nothing tastes," or a life that overflows with meaning.

I hope you will decide you want to get running. I believe that, with God in you, that's exactly what you will do, for God has three great purposes for you:

- To know God and fellowship with Him.
- To use your abilities and energy in pursuing a work on earth.
- To serve other people, especially to serve their redemption.

Say, that sounds like a pretty wonderful plan, at that!

──── NINE ────

You Can
Expand
Your World

You and I wouldn't even exist if God had a ghetto mentality. He created us because He is a God of new departures. He made man in His own image when there was not, and never had been, any such creature.

There once was a man who was carried every day to beg at the Beautiful Gate of the temple in Jerusalem. The man had never walked, being crippled from birth. His life was mostly a burden, not only to him, but to those who cared for him. Imagine the chore it was to carry a grown man to the temple gate each morning and back home each night!

This poor beggar's world was in every respect a narrow one. He was confined physically to the spot where he was placed by others. He was limited vocationally to begging for a living. He was deprived emotionally, with little to look forward to. Socially, he was an outcast. He did not even enjoy the satisfaction of being able to contribute something of value to others, on whom he continually had to impose.

This man's constricted little life revolved around how much he took in each day by begging. If someone dropped a larger than usual coin in his hand, it kind of made his day. He liked to fantasize that someday a wealthy worshiper, entering or leaving the temple, might feel especially blessed and give him some "real money."

One day, about the middle of the afternoon, two men entering the temple paused to speak to him. His pulse quickened. They didn't look rich, but one never knew. *How much?* he thought. *How much are they going to give me?*

"We don't have any money," the one man said, and the beggar's heart sank. "But what we do have, we give to you. In the name of Jesus, rise up and walk." At the same time, the man reached out to take him by the hand.

The lame man took the hand of the Apostle Peter, for that is who (with the Apostle John) had stopped to speak with him. Instantly his feet and anklebones were strengthened, and he came up with a leap (see Acts 3:1–10).

Everybody around was startled, for they had seen this lame beggar sitting there for years, and now he was walking.

The miracle, great as it was, was even greater for what it portended. This man received much more than the ability to walk. A door was flung open to him—a door to an incredible world he never could have entered before. His new world, in contrast to the old, was characterized by almost limitless possibilities.

No longer did he need to be one of society's takers, a burden and a chore for his family and friends, a sad spectacle at the Beautiful Gate of the temple, a pitiful creature whose high moments occurred when he got a bigger than usual coin. No, now his options were practically unlimited. He could go anywhere, do anything, become whatever he chose.

The narrow, confining boundaries of his little world had disappeared.

God's gift of overflowing life is like that beggar's healing. The overflowing life is not just a larger coin in our beggar's basket. It is a personal inner healing that takes a once dependent, crippled, confined person and makes him or her whole and free. It's an inner adequacy that is better than any external gift—even a pile of gold—could ever be.

Understand that receiving the gift of God doesn't necessarily mean your physical handicaps will vanish. That's not the critical issue. It is lameness of spirit that cripples a person. Millions of people in our society today are quite well, physically, but seriously handicapped in their spirits. We see them on every side. By contrast, people such as Joni Eareckson in our day and the Apostle Paul, in his, have some physical affliction that they must live with, but they do so with grace and beauty and strength. They are whole persons, with an inner well of water continually flowing.

Little Followers of a Big God

Christians are frequently accused of being narrow-minded. Often the accusation is false, as when Christians are ridiculed for declining—out of conviction—to participate in popular but destructive practices.

In sticking by our convictions, and in many other ways, we need to be narrow. We need to be narrow about what we allow to take first place in our lives. Only God can properly have that priority.

We need a certain narrow-mindedness in pursuing our work. It is called concentration. I can complete this book in timely fashion only by focusing my attention on the task.

We need to be narrow about vicious and hateful attitudes that have no place among Christians.

So then, narrow is not necessarily bad.

Unfortunately, we sometimes become narrow-minded in ways we ought not to be. We become strange little followers of a very big God. This is contradictory to the basic truth on which the overflowing life depends. That truth is God-in-us. We cannot at the same time be indwelt effectively by a big God and remain small in our minds and souls.

The God of Incredible Diversity

Marge and I enjoy watching nature shows on TV. Sometimes we see bizarre creatures that live in deserts or frozen wastelands far from human habitation. Other times we watch microscopic life forms or observe denizens of the deep not normally exposed to human scrutiny.

"Why did God make so many weird creatures that people rarely even see?" Marge asks.

I, with my usual wisdom, reply, "I don't know. I guess He wanted to."

Christians ordinarily think that God made the earth and everything in it for us to use and enjoy. Marge's question seems to assume that is the fact. If we humans don't use it, why does it exist?

I believe that mankind truly is God's first concern; we alone are made in God's image. It was as man, and to redeem man, that God came to earth in the Person of Jesus Christ. Nevertheless, God made everything else, too. Apparently, He has an incredibly broad interest in zoology.

Furthermore, the wide and weird world of animals that we know about does not begin to exhaust the diversity of God. According to the *Encyclopedia Britannica,* "More than 1,000,000 species of animals and more than 300,000 species of plants had been named by mid-20th century; probably at least twice this number will ultimately be recognized when the knowledge of the world faunas and floras approaches completion."

Think of it! Nearly three million different species of animals and plants! And that's just on this little speck in the universe called Earth. We have no idea what creatures may inhabit the far reaches of space.

In addition to the incredible biological diversity created by God, there are other complex systems. Everything man studies under the headings of geology, physics, chemistry, and astronomy was God's idea first, to say nothing of art, music, literature, and philosophy.

Everywhere we look, there is complexity and variety. Our telescopes cannot see to the end of the universe's bigness, and our microscopes can't see to the end of its smallness. And the Lord God made it all.

Therefore, my proposition to you is this: *The overflowing life, which in essence is God within, will not narrow the scope of your life but will incredibly expand it.*

You see, the overflowing life is not the study of God or a search for God. That could be pretty narrow. The overflowing life is the life of God-in-us, and that has to be broadening, to say the least.

What Makes Life Small?

Since God-in-us expands or even explodes the dimensions of our lives, what makes life small? The obvious answer is the absence of God-in-us in a dynamic way. We need Jesus Christ to come into our daily experience in as effective a way as He came into the life of the beggar at the Beautiful Gate of the temple. We need Him to come and quicken us, so that we experience life not as a dreary, unchanging existence but as an incredible profusion of options and opportunities.

Rather than explaining our constricted lives simply as the absence of God-in-us, however, we need to see the role we play in shrinking our own world. We shrink our world in several ways, one of the most common being by allowing idolatry in our lives. Idolatry, which we can define as worshiping anything other than the true and living God, inevitably makes one's life smaller than it would otherwise be.

Idolatry focuses your life on whatever it is you worship, and that thing is always too small.

Drug addiction is a graphic example. Talk about the lame beggar having a constricted life! No person lives in a smaller world than the drug addict. His world shrinks and shrinks, until nothing matters to him except his drugs. He inhabits a world full of wonders and sees none of them. Family, friends, job, hobbies, material things—all become less and less important.

A similar constricting of life may be observed in those obsessed with sex or with eating or with money or with career or with anything else. Some people are simply obsessed with themselves. In every case, the false god diminishes and constricts the life of the worshiper. Yet people continue in their idolatries because they think their particular idol offers so much! What blindness!

Mark it well: Idolatry will increasingly take away your options, until you have no good choices left. Life will become a wearisome burden.

By contrast, God does just the opposite. He will expand and increase your options, until you wish you had several lives to spend in pursuit of all the wonderful, exciting, and worthwhile things that beckon you.

I am a writer and a speaker, and I love my life. I would also like to be a lawyer, a legislator, a broadcaster, an educator, a scientist, an astronaut, a doctor, a theologian, an operator of heavy equipment, a builder, an artisan in western red cedar, and ... well, you get the idea.

Other Life Shrinkers

Idolatry, devoting one's life to false gods, is not the only thing that can constrict one's world. Captivity to our attitudes, habits, and culture can do the same thing.

Some years ago I wrote a story about the early years of Haddon Robinson, now the distinguished president of Denver Seminary. Haddon Robinson once lived a very constricted life, though he grew up in one of the world's largest cities, New York.

I called the story, "He Escaped Mousetown," because the Mousetown section of Harlem, where Haddon lived, was literally a psychological prison, not only to him, but to hundreds of others. Scores of Mousetown people never got as far as Times Square, let alone to the rest of the city, state, nation, and world. Haddon was an avid fan of the New York Giants baseball team but only got to Ebbets Field once to see them play.

Only two miles from the garbage-littered streets of Mousetown was the "Acropolis of the Modern World" where Columbia University, Union Seminary, and other fine institutions stood. The former general and future president Dwight Eisenhower lived there when he was president of Columbia. As for being remote to Mousetowners, that area might as well have been the Acropolis of Athens. Yet, nothing kept the people of Mousetown confined, except the invisible boundaries of their own attitudes, habits, and culture.

Haddon's narrow world began to expand when, at age fifteen, he was fortunate enough to visit a cousin in Pennsylvania. When he returned to Mousetown, the garbage in the streets, unnoticed before, stunk. The elevated train that had thundered past for years, a hundred yards from his window, now seemed almost to run right through his room.

Haddon began attending Sunday school at a Presbyterian church near Mousetown. This further expanded his world and led ultimately to his attending university, then graduate school, and on and on. He had escaped the ghetto.

Mousetowns of Our Own Making

You don't need to live in a big-city ghetto to have a ghetto mentality. If you never . . .

- *go anywhere new*
- *read anything different*
- *get to know anyone outside your small circle*
- *learn new skills*
- *explore new interests*
- *think new thoughts*

. . . you are effectively locked in your own too-small world.

This is not overflowing life. It is not what God-in-you would produce. I say that because it is unlike God. We have already described something of His diversity.

You and I wouldn't even exist if God had a ghetto mentality. He created us because He is a God of new departures. He made man in His own image when there was not, and never had been, any such creature. Later, God Himself came where He had never been—into human form and substance—to pursue His grand adventure.

Expanded World, Expanded You

When you begin to move into an expanded world, your world isn't the only thing that changes; you change.

Today Haddon Robinson is a far different person from the rough-edged teen who sometimes had the Presbyterian youth leader, Mrs. Barnes, in tears.

Likewise, the used-to-be beggar at the Beautiful Gate of the temple must have experienced continuing change when he began walking. Instead of having an "every day's the dreary same" attitude, he could view every day as a new adventure. And every succeeding new experience left its mark on him and worked its change.

No question—an expanded world leads to an expanded you.

A Caution Sign Is Not a Stop Sign

It would not do to leave the impression that an expanded world brings only joy and satisfaction. It hasn't worked that way for God. The man He made in His own image fell into sin and plunged the world into darkness and grief, from which it is still in the process of being recovered. The humanity that God took upon Himself when He came into our world as the Christ knew rejection, sorrow, and scorn.

For us, as for God, an expanded world can be painful. To leave our secure little safety zones is frightening. Who knows what may happen to us out there?

Certainly, the paths an able-bodied man will walk are not as safe as just lying at the Beautiful Gate of the temple would be. If one climbs the mountain, he might fall from its heights. If one wades the stream, he might slip and get a drenching. If one so much as walks the streets, he risks being hit by a passing vehicle.

Can we take the chance?

God did. And because He did, we will, too, if we are animated by His Spirit dwelling within us.

Doing what we can to minimize our risk as we walk through this sometimes treacherous world makes sense. But sitting out life to avoid the dangers inherent in living life fully does not make sense.

God Is Not Passive

The idea of sitting out life brings us to the third element that can shrink a person's world. We have identified the basic problem as a practical absence of God-in-you. We have said that two elements of this are idolatry and captivity to one's attitudes, habits, and culture.

The third element, which we come to now, is passivity. God is not passive. He doesn't sit around waiting for things to happen; He makes things happen.

At the same time, God does not use force to impose His will on anyone. He is active but not coercive. He also is not impulsive. What He does is well conceived and patiently pursued.

Patience and planning are appropriate for us, then, but passivity is not. We need to act, to initiate, to participate in life. When we do so, our world will begin to expand, however small it may be in the beginning. As our world expands, our options will increase.

Who Gets the Shiny Spoon?

When our children were growing up, they had their share of family chores. One was to take turns setting the dinner table. Our silverware then consisted of odds and ends we had picked up where we could. Most of it was dull and tarnished, but there was one shiny spoon.

One day a fuss erupted just before dinner. Krystal had set the table and put the shiny spoon at her own place. Kathy had come along and switched the shiny spoon to her place. Krystal was calling foul.

I settled the dispute by establishing a new household rule: The person who sets the table decides who gets the shiny spoon.

I think God has a similar rule for His household: Those who are passive will have to settle for what they get.

In the real world, what passive people get is likely to be not much. As the Scripture says, "A little sleep, a little slumber, a little folding of the hands to rest—and poverty will come on you like a bandit and scarcity like an armed man" (Proverbs 24:33, 34).

The passage does not teach that one can never rest, but it does teach that one cannot be passive when he ought to be active, without incurring great loss. The principle applies both to material and personal well-being. To be passive is to confine yourself to a small world of poverty and scarcity.

So, do something. Even if your opportunities seem severely limited right now, start to involve yourself actively in life. Take authority over setting the table and deciding where the shiny spoon goes.

Jesus devoted an extended parable to warning against being lazy and passive. If you don't already know the parable about the servants who received five talents, two talents, and one talent respectively, read it in Matthew 25:14–30. Ask God to open your eyes to its meaning. And don't miss the main point: The servant who did badly was the one who was passive, who hid his talent and did nothing with it.

Be passive and you will lose out with God and with life, too.

A Checklist

If your world is small, narrow, constricted, and confined, look to the three world shrinkers we've described as possible causes:

- *Idolatry*
- *Captivity to your attitudes, habits, and culture*
- *Passivity*

All of these things make for a small world. But God-in-you expands your world infinitely.

The lame beggar of whom we wrote at the beginning of this chapter was healed by the power of Jesus Christ when he reached out in faith and took Peter's hand. He jumped to his feet and "went with them into the temple courts, walking and jumping, and praising God" (Acts 3:8).

I pray that these words might be as a hand of God reaching out to you. I pray that as you respond, a flow of energy will surge inside of you. If you have been sitting, lame and inactive, may you now walk and jump. Praising God, may you go out into a new and much wider world.

—PART— IV

Counterfeits of the Overflowing Life

TEN

Romantic Love and Other Broken Cisterns

Romantic love is a vision of a possibility far greater than itself, a vision of the overflowing life.

I love homemade chocolate-chip cookies. My wife, Marge, makes such good ones! My favorites are the chocolate chip, filbert, and coconut cookies I can get her to make only occasionally. It seems quite a process is involved in making them. She has to mix the dough with her hands and refrigerate it overnight before baking.

In any case, a good way to ruin what would otherwise be a batch of delectable cookies is to substitute margarine for the shortening called for in the recipe. Don't ask me why. Both products are made of vegetable oil, and by itself, margarine certainly tastes better than shortening, but the cookies made with margarine spread out flat and sort of crispy on the cookie sheet, while those made with shortening have a crumbly, toothsome texture.

(You didn't know you were going to get a baking lesson in this book, did you? Well, if you've had problems with your cookies and you have been using margarine, just try shortening next time.)

Cookies and the overflowing life may seem unrelated, though if you ate one of my wife's chocolate chip, filbert, and coconut cookies, I think you might see the similarity. However, it is the ruinous effect of substituting margarine for shortening that illustrates an important truth: *We lose out on what could be an overflowing life by ruinous substitutions we make.*

Scripture puts it this way in Jeremiah 2:13: " 'My people have committed two sins: They have forsaken me, the spring of living water, and have dug their own cisterns, broken cisterns that cannot hold water.' "

God Himself is the spring of living water. He is the gift that becomes in us a spring of water, both quenching our thirst and flowing out to a parched world.

But let's face it: God is a gift not altogether to everyone's liking. The water we want, yes. The overflowing life, certainly. But God Himself? We are not so sure. God is so, so . . . well, what *is* God like? We are not sure about that, either.

Because we don't know what God is like or aren't too pleased with what we think we know about Him, we would just as soon (maybe rather) find overflowing life our own way. With our own cisterns full of water, we would not have to rely on a spring. We could be independent. True, we are substituting margarine for shortening, but margarine tastes better, anyhow.

The trouble is that substitutes may not work very well. "Your cisterns leak," says God. They won't hold water.

Man, the Cistern Maker

Let's be clear: There is nothing wrong with cisterns, in their places (or with margarine). If you live in the middle of a desert and can neither drill a well nor run a pipeline, a cistern is probably your best choice, preferably a cistern that doesn't leak. But to rely on a leaky cistern when there's a fresh-flowing fountain nearby is crazy.

Unfortunately, man is an inveterate cistern maker, even when he doesn't need to be. He substitutes other things for God, and he also substitutes his own inventions for God's provision. Often he doesn't realize his cistern leaks, or that it has other problems, until he faces a water crisis. Sometimes he wakes up to reality only when he comes to the cistern desperately thirsty one day and finds it empty. Or he discovers a dead rat floating in it. Then he wonders how long the rat has been there, and what the consequences may be to his health, to say nothing of his sensibilities.

Though all of the data is not yet in, I suspect that some of man's leaky cisterns of recent years may include:

- *nuclear power plants*
- *artificial sweeteners*
- *tranquilizers such as Thalidomide and Valium*
- *deficient baby formulas*
- *fluorocarbon aerosol sprays*
- *sexual anarchy*

All of these man-contrived substitutes for something else have created problems potentially more serious than those they were intended to solve. In some cases, the new problems virtually threaten the survival of the human race. The dead rats in the above-mentioned cisterns can cause cancer, deformities, and AIDS.

Even when our broken cisterns are not evil in themselves, they can be damaging, because it is unwise substitution we are talking about. We must understand that even things good in their place can be disastrously poor substitutes for other things. Nothing, however good or even glorious it may be, can substitute for God in your life.

Subtle Substitution

Most people do not consciously substitute other things for God. They don't think in those terms. They substitute without even realizing it and may heatedly deny they are doing so.

Recently I participated in a local television forum discussing "The Powers of Darkness." Ex-Satanists and victims told hair-raising tales of human sacrifice and sexual abuse. They claimed to speak from firsthand experience, seemed credible, and made Satan worship come out looking horrible, to say the least.

No one came to the defense of the horrors, but quite a few participants did want everyone to know that there was a distinction between Satan worship and witchcraft. Several said they were witches who followed the "old religion," paganism. They spoke of the forces of nature, which they identified with a "female deity," the goddess. This old religion, they said, existed long before Christ. And they used it only for good.

Then it was my turn to speak. I agreed that there was a distinction between Satan worship and witchcraft. "But these witches just serve Satan under another form," I said.

The witches were incensed and interrupted me with their protests.

However, I was still on the microphone and camera, so I continued, ". . . *because* the first commandment is to worship God with all your heart and to have no other gods. These people tell us they worship nature, or a nature goddess. That means, at best, they serve and worship the creature rather than the Creator. Any worship that does not glorify the one true and living God serves Satan."

You see, while Satan worship is blatantly evil, Satan's chief work is nothing so sensational or obvious. His chief work is to tempt people and get them to turn away from the true and living God. What they turn to matters little. One broken cistern is as good as another in diverting people from the spring of living water.

In the remainder of this chapter, we will look at one of the subtlest of all the substitutes for God—romantic love. Talk about margarine tasting better than shortening! Romantic love seems more exciting than God to most people any day of the week, including Sunday.

I happen to think that romantic love is not a bad thing. It comes about as close to being glorious as anything on earth can. The problem is that, in spite of its glories, it can't substitute for God. It is a broken cistern as far as being a source of the overflowing life.

While few people would seriously argue that romantic love can substitute satisfactorily for God, not a few people *live* as if it could.

And it is our lives, not what we say, that demonstrate what we really believe.

Let's look, then, at a biblical case in point. I will tell the story at length and take the liberty of filling in details so we may better glimpse how romantic love subtly substitutes for God.

The Man at the Well

She paid little attention at first to the man who was the only other person at the roadside rest area. However, she did recognize at once that He was a Jew and not one of her own people. Beyond that, He seemed of little interest. She assumed the feeling of indifference was mutual. He was hardly likely to take much notice of her.

Ah, but there was a time when He'd have taken notice, she thought. That was one thing she had always had going for her: She was attractive to men. Even now, this one seemed to be watching her. *More likely critical than attracted,* she thought.

Men!

How far she was now from that starry-eyed girl she had been when she first wrapped all her hopes and dreams in a handsome young man who said he would love her forever.

She had been bitter when their marriage failed. She had tried so hard to make it work, hoping he would change, forgiving him, starting over fresh again and again, praying to God to intervene and do something. In the end she had been just too weary, too defeated, too hopeless to go on.

Love starved, insecure, lonely, she embarked on marriage number two much too soon. The guy was eligible, he was fun, and he represented a second chance at happiness. It was a combination she couldn't afford to pass up. How many chances could a girl expect?

Unfortunately, the man was basically immature. What had seemed to be a fun-loving attitude in a suitor turned out to be irresponsibility in a husband. This man didn't need a wife; he needed a mother, and preferably a well-to-do one at that, since it was clear he would never provide for a family.

So marriage number two turned sour quickly, and she bailed out. No way did she want to go through another slow, painful death, like she had endured the first time. This so-called marriage of theirs wasn't going to work, and the best thing to do was to end it as quickly and painlessly as possible. Under their law, she couldn't initiate the proceedings, but she could make sure life was so miserable that he would.

It worked. Single again, she realized one thing clearly: She hadn't gotten to know her second husband well enough before they married. Next time would be different. Mr. Dependable, that's who she wanted. She'd make sure he was somebody she could respect, first of all. She could learn to love him later.

The third marriage seemed much better, and for a long time she was sure they were going to make it. There was a lot to say for being the wife of Mr. Dependable. He provided for her very well. He was there when she needed him. He gave her security. He was considerate, respected in the community, and a good father to their children.

He was so good, in fact, that she felt terribly guilty for her underlying feeling of dissatisfaction, which grew as the years passed. She rebuked herself sternly for her ingratitude. True, there was little romance in their marriage, but she did love him . . . in a way.

But why did she tingle like a schoolgirl when the new neighbor smiled at her the first time they met? When he only stood near her, it made her heart beat faster. She could not look him in the eyes for fear he would see into her very soul.

Was it her imagination that he seemed to be attracted to her as she was to him? Whenever she ventured a glance his way, he was looking at her. And his smile—it nearly dissolved her.

He brushed her hand with his one day, innocently it seemed, but she was sure he cared. She could hardly sleep that night for the excitement. It was as though she had been only half-alive all the years of her marriage to Mr. Dependable.

When it finally happened—when she and her lover were ready to go away together—she was torn over leaving. She didn't want to hurt her husband. But in the end, she went. This had not been _life._ She knew that now. She had been only existing. As for her Mr. Dependable, maybe he could find a woman whose love would make him come alive, as she had. This new love of hers was so beautiful, so wonderful; it had to be of God.

They married; it was her fourth. She knew in less than a month that the magic was not going to last. But though the magic would not last, she would. She had paid too high a price for this man to give him up. She would stick with him forever. No more dreaming for her.

But it was not to be. He had changed his mind, he told her. He was sorry, he said. He hadn't meant to hurt her, but he thought—no, he knew—that they had made a mistake.

There were other words, but she didn't hear them. They didn't matter. Nothing mattered. Her life was over.

She would go on, of course. Like everyone else. Existing.

And from among the rest of the living dead, she would find a man. She still had some looks, and almost anyone would be better than being alone. So she married again. Number five. No, he wasn't the greatest, but she was no prize, either. They deserved each other.

Later, when number five left for good, she hardly noticed. He hadn't been around that much, anyhow. What a joke their "marriage" had been. Well, now she was through. *No more!* she decided. *No more!*

But dreams die hard. In her heart she still longed for someone who would love her, someone who would make her feel alive again. Someone who would see her as beautiful and desirable, and whose love would make her into that beautiful person she longed to be.

From time to time she met men who almost made her hope it could happen. But these were only memories of her dream, not the dream itself. The dream was dead. *She* was dead.

So she never married any of the men whose paths crossed hers, and after living with one or another of them for a while, she was always glad she hadn't.

But now the man at the well was speaking. To her? No one else was there; it had to be to her. What was He saying? Oh, He needed a drink. Humph! Most Jews would go thirsty before they would ask a Samaritan for anything.

She wasn't the clever, indirect type, so she blurted out her surprise. "How can you ask me for a drink?"

He answered strangely. "If you knew the gift of God and who it is that asks you for a drink, you would have asked him and he would have given you living water."

She had always hoped for too much from men and been disappointed. Now this stranger was saying He was somebody special, somebody who could enrich her life with a gift of God that He called living water. She eyed Him suspiciously and tried to size Him up. She had met big talkers before. Who was this man with big claims and no way even to draw a drink of water for Himself?

"Where can you get this living water?" she asked. "Are you greater than our father Jacob, who gave us the well?"

"Everyone who drinks this water will be thirsty again," the man said, "but whoever drinks the water I give him will never thirst. Indeed, the water I give him will become in him a spring of water welling up to eternal life."

It sounded good. Too good. She had reached for dreams before, many times, and she had always come up with nothing but smoke. Still, she could call His bluff. What did she have to lose? He hadn't asked her for anything, yet, except a drink of water. She'd give that much to a dog.

"Sir, give me this water," she said.

"Go call your husband," the man replied, "and come here."

Her mind worked fast. _Was this His way of finding out if she were available? Well, she was . . . maybe._ "I have no husband," she said.

"You are right," the man replied. "The fact is, you have had five husbands, and the man you now have is not your husband. What you have just said is quite true."

She was awestruck. Maybe her reputation was all over town, but it surely hadn't traveled so far as to reach the ears of this wayfaring stranger. "I can see that you are a prophet," she said.

Her mind juggled the fascinating possibilities. _A prophet! Exactly what was needed to settle the thorny controversy that long had separated their two peoples: Where was the proper place to worship God?_ Not only was that an issue of intense interest, but it was also much less threatening a subject than her marital status. She would ask His opinion.

Still, the remarkable thing was that this Jewish prophet should talk to her at all. He not only knew she was a Samaritan, but He also knew about her living arrangement. Why, the people in her own town thought they were too good to speak to her, yet this man had offered her living water as a gift of God. All this danced through her thoughts, even as she asked and He answered her questions.

"God is spirit," the man was saying now, "and the way he is worshiped is crucial, not the place."

"I know that Messiah is coming," the woman said. "When he comes, he will explain everything to us."

The man replied, "I who speak to you am He."

Her mind raced to put it all together. Here was one who somehow knew about her failed and sinful life. Yet He had not scorned her but had offered to give her "the gift of God" that would be a well of water springing up within her.

All her life she had looked for a man to make her life fulfilling and happy. Right up until this very day, she had clung to the notion that such a thing was possible, as if she had not proved otherwise again and again. But now, suddenly, it was crystal clear to her. No man had provided what she sought because none of them possibly could. She had been looking all this time, unwittingly, for the Messiah, for a Savior, for Christ. And now He had come!

Romantic Love and Christ's Love

Debbie Boone scored a hit a few years ago singing "You Light Up My Life." Though it was a love song, I heard that Debbie, a Christian, was thinking of Christ as the one who can light up our lives.

I heard a few people pooh-pooh the idea that such a song could be addressed to Christ, but to me that is believable. Sometimes when I turn on the radio, I have to listen quite intently for a while before I can be sure whether I am hearing a contemporary Christian song or a romantic song. Both the music and the lyrics can be quite similar.

Being a heterosexual male, I've never been too keen on songs about Jesus that have overtones of romance, but I've gotten used to them.

If some songs about Jesus are too romantic, however, even more songs about romance are too worshipful. They describe the lover in terms appropriate only for a Savior:

- *"Only You"*
- *"Some Day My Prince Will Come"*
- *"Heaven Is in Your Arms"*
- *"You Are My Sunshine"*
- *"There Goes My Everything"*
- *"You're the First, the Last, My Everything"*
- *"You Are My Destiny"*
- *"I'm Yours"*
- *"I Was Made for Lovin' You"*

Many other songs that do not reveal it in the title say in the lyrics either that "life means nothing to me without you" or "life is great, solely because of you."

Now, I know this is poetic license, overstatement, and all that. I also think it means something. Romantic love has certain striking similarities to the overflowing life that Christ offers us. Romantic love is the only exciting, fulfilling thing—or the most exciting, fulfilling thing—many people have ever experienced. By considering the similarities and differences of romantic love and the overflowing life, perhaps we can learn more about both.

To compare romantic love with the overflowing life is not as radical a departure as it may seem. Marriage has long been compared to the life in Christ. The Bible speaks of Christ as the bridegroom, of His church as the bride, and of our eventual gathering to Him as the "marriage supper of the Lamb." While marriage and romantic love are not the same thing, I believe both have spiritual implications.

Here are some things that romantic love and the overflowing life both involve, or seem to involve:

I Have Found My Ideal

Imagine a scene with me.

I am walking through a busy shopping mall when I see her. She has her back to me, she's wearing a raincoat, and she is beautiful.

I can't see her face. Her figure is shrouded in the raincoat, which could conceal almost any flaw short of a shape like a Sumo wrestler's. All I can really see is her beautiful hair, but my mind fills in the rest of the picture, and it is gorgeous.

I am intrigued enough to move closer to this vision of loveliness. I circle her to get a better view. When I do so, what a shock! The craggy face on this woman is nothing like the enchanting loveliness I had mentally created to go with the hair.

Why are there so few really good-looking women? I think.

Okay, end of scene. Now, what would an incident like this reveal? First, whether I was conscious of it or not, I had in my mind a concept of feminine beauty, a physical ideal, if you will. Except for her hair, this woman turned out not to fit my ideal.

The incident also reveals that when all I see of a person is one particularly attractive characteristic, I mentally manufacture the rest of the person to fit my ideal.

Often all it takes to disillusion me is a closer look. I see the craggy face or whatever, and am disappointed. But what if both the face and figure, and then the personality, match the hair? Zap! I'm in love!

The problem is that I still see little of the actual person. I am still filling in the unknowns with my ideals.

At this point I might be so enamored of this creature I think I have found (but actually have in part created) that I refuse to see her faults. I don't want to mar the ideal.

This is the classic love-is-blind situation. I think I am deeply in love, and maybe I am. But I am also infatuated, a word that literally means "made a fool." I have lost my head over this person.

She may or may not be very lovely. However lovely she is, though, one thing is sure: This flawless, totally appealing person I am falling in love with is an illusion. Nobody is like that, except Jesus Christ.

So while I may or may not have found a person I can love as long as I live, I definitely have not found someone without blemish or flaw, however much I may feel that way.

The overflowing life is like romantic love in that both make us feel we have found our ideal. Only the overflowing life actually involves an ideal person in our lives. In romantic love, our supposed ideal person is never 100 percent perfect and is usually nowhere near that.

If you elevate your lover to ideal status, you will surely get into trouble. When your lover is wrong, you will either fail to see it and go wrong, too, or see it and suffer crushing disillusionment. Women too often follow erring husbands right into disaster. Some have so idolized their husbands that they accept physical abuse without complaint.

My own wife used to think too highly of me. I basically could do no wrong in her eyes. She followed my lead in everything and viewed me as a tower of strength who certainly needed nothing from her spiritually.

When life eventually proved otherwise, she floundered for a while before she could accept my weaknesses without resenting me and see my strengths without exaggerating them into perfection.

Thank God, in Christ we have One we can fully trust. His wisdom is perfect. His character is without flaw. His love never fails. I can adjust my life at His direction and know I am not going astray. In all the world, there is no other such Person. I have found my ideal.

My Ideal Loves Me

One reason romantic love is so powerful and so wonderful is that, when it is reciprocated, it gives me a huge ego boost. To have anyone love or admire me is heady stuff, under any circumstances. The weaker my self-esteem is, the more gratifying it is to have someone else think I am great.

In a romantic love relationship, I am admired and loved—not by just anyone—but by the one person I perceive as the most wonderful, beautiful, and nearly perfect person in all the world. That is not just gratifying; it is wildly intoxicating.

This ego-boosting aspect of romantic love sometimes makes the temptation to have an affair almost irresistible. One man described his vulnerability to an affair like this: "She was the kind of girl I was nuts about in high school and who wouldn't give me a second look. When this one looked at me as if I was God's gift to womankind, I was sunk."[1]

When the closest-to-perfect person in my world loves me, in spite of my faults, and sees me as the wonderful person I long to be, I am immensely affirmed, warmed, and fed.

But now, you see, there is great danger that a romantic delusion will develop or deepen. Not only is my beloved actually far less perfect than I imagine her to be, but her love is not what I imagine it to be, either. She does not love me *in spite* of my faults. Instead, she is oblivious to my faults, which are only too real and will one day manifest themselves unmistakably. She also does not see me as the wonderful person I long to be. She sees me as the wonderful person she longs to have love her.

Once again, romantic love is like the overflowing life. Both give me the inexpressibly wonderful feeling that my ideal loves me. In the case of the overflowing life, Christ really does, in spite of my clearly seen faults. He sees beyond my faults, to the wonderful person I was intended to be. His love will help me become that person. What could be better?

My Ideal and I Belong Together

A third reason romantic love is so wonderful is that it joins me with my ideal person. Long before any marriage ceremony formally establishes the fact, there is a sense of pairing. No longer do we simply talk about "you" and "me." Now there is an "us."

When a woman (or a man) wants to make clear that a romantic attraction is one-sided and she doesn't share it, she refuses to talk about "us." She responds to any such suggestion by saying, "There is no 'us.'"

When romantic love blooms into full flower, our sense of pairing becomes so strong that we feel we have been only half-alive until now. Without the other person, we have only existed.

The overflowing life is like that, on both grounds. First, it truly unites us to Christ. Second, we were only half-alive before we became paired with Him.

The pairing produced by the overflowing life is deeper and longer lasting than that produced by romantic love. Romantic pairs come and go. Ultimately they are dissolved by death, if by nothing else. The one who is truly ideal and who truly loves us with all our faults, Jesus Christ, enters into a match with us that is eternal.

The Apostle Paul specifically described this parallel between human love and the overflowing life. Alluding to sexual union, he writes, "For it is said, 'The two will become one flesh.' But he who unites himself with the Lord is one with him in spirit" (1 Corinthians 6:16, 17).

Think of it! To be one with the Lord Jesus Christ!

Nothing compares to being united with the Lord. This is overflowing life, indeed!

Taking Romance Away From People

Our theme is the overflowing life. You don't produce that by taking from people the good things they have. Romantic love is wonderful. It brings a beautiful person into our lives. It makes us feel very special. It makes us feel fully alive. It makes our whole world sing.

Please do not imagine that I want you to substitute formal religion for romance. I don't. I am not even suggesting you renounce romance in favor of the reality of Christ in your life, because there is no reason you cannot have both.

What I am urging is that you don't seek in romance what you can never find there. Those deepest desires of your soul, which must be met if you are to experience the overflowing life, can only be found in a relationship with Jesus Christ.

Remember when Christ met the woman who had lived with six men? He told her that He had living water for her. He said that if she drank the water from the well beside which they talked, she would thirst again, but the water He would give would be in her a well of water, springing up to eternal life.

Do you think Jesus had something against well water? Was He trying to take that away from her? Certainly not. And He has nothing against romantic love. Just don't let it be a substitute for the better, deeper realities that it dimly mirrors. Instead, let romantic love call you on, with all its beauty and tenderness and excitement, to the ideal one who truly loves you and wants to be united with you, both now and forever.

Nathaniel Branden writes that lovers are "moved by a passion they do not understand toward a fulfillment they seldom reach, they are haunted by the vision of a distant possibility that refuses to be extinguished."[2]

The vision of a distant possibility. That's what romantic love is, in a sense far more profound than Branden meant. Romantic love is a vision of a possibility far greater than itself, a vision of the over-flowing life.

Because that vision has refused to be extinguished, because you are still haunted by it, you are reading this book. You are still seeking. Take courage, then, for Jesus said, "Blessed are they who seek and keep on seeking for they shall find" (*see* Matthew 5:6; 7:7).

——ELEVEN——

Man Doesn't Live by Bread Alone, But He Sure Gets Hungry Without It

The overflowing life comes from putting all of life's pieces in their proper places.

Recently, while in Sydney, Australia, I met a woman who told me a strange story. She had heard a Bible teacher in the community describe a recent fast in which "the Lord led" him to abstain not only from food for thirty days, but also from water. The wonderful thing was, he said, that he had neither experienced thirst nor suffered any ill effects.

The woman who told me about this "miracle fast" hardly knew what to think. I told her I was more than a little skeptical about the story, and about any person who would make such a claim. I pointed out that there is biblical precedent for going without food for up to forty days, but none for going without water.

To totally deprive oneself of water for thirty days would be fatal. A standard reference work states the situation as follows:

> One may live for weeks without food but only for a few days without water. One can lose all reserve carbohydrate (glycogen) and fat, and about half the body protein without real danger, but a loss of ten percent of total body water is serious, while a loss of 20 to 22 percent is fatal.[1]

To deprive oneself of water deliberately "at God's leading" would be like jumping from the top of a skyscraper with the same kind of prompting. Jesus taught us by example how we should respond to any suggestion such as that.

> Then the devil took him to the holy city and had him stand on the highest point of the temple. "If you are the Son of God," he said, "throw yourself down. For it is written: 'He will command his angels concerning you, and they will lift you up in their hands, so that you will not strike your foot against a stone.' " Jesus answered him, "It is also written: 'Do not put the Lord your God to the test.' "
>
> Matthew 4:5–7

Jesus rejected such irrational behavior, even when Scripture was cited that seemed to support it. How much less should one do such a thing on the basis of an *inward* impression!

The Secular Mind and the Fanatical Mind

In the previous chapter we described the error of trying to substitute other things for God. This is a common mistake of the secular mind. It makes the overflowing life impossible because it excludes from one's life the true and living God, whose place cannot be filled by another.

We need to realize that there is an opposite error: *substituting God for other things*. This is a common mistake of the fanatical mind. It makes the overflowing life impossible because it fails to use the means provided by God for normal fulfillment.

A superspiritual attitude combined with fuzzy thinking leads to the unwise substitution of the spiritual for the natural. Unfortunately, the person with a genuine hunger for God may be particularly susceptible to this error.

Earlier we cited Madame Guyon as one whose life was transformed by the realization that God could be and was within her. She made the mistake, however, of wanting God to be everything to her. She writes, "I now quitted all company, bade farewell forever to all plays and diversions, dancing, unprofitable walks and parties of pleasure."[2]

She lamented that her beauty tempted her to be vain, and she began to "pray to God incessantly, that he would remove from me that obstacle, and make me ugly. I could even have wished to be deaf, blind and dumb, that nothing might divert me from my love of God."[3]

In her life story, Madame Guyon speaks often of how unkind her husband was to her and how he tried to make her pray less. I don't wonder. She admits that she was "so deeply engaged within" that she forgot things without. She was to report to him about the condition of the garden one day, and here is her account of what happened:

> I went thither on purpose to notice everything, in order to tell him and yet when there did not think of looking. I went ten times one day, to see and bring him an account and yet forgot it.[4]

No wonder they say it is hard to live with a saint. One more passage will suffice to show how far into fanaticism one can go:

> Meanwhile the possession which the Lord had of my soul became every day stronger, insomuch that I passed whole days without being able to pronounce one word. The Lord was pleased to make me pass wholly into him by an entire internal transformation. He became more

and more the absolute master of my heart, to such a degree as not to leave me a movement of my own. This
state did not hinder me from condescending to my sister,
and the others in the house. Nevertheless, the useless
things with which they were taken up could not interest
me.[5]

All of this fanaticism, as I judge it to be, is still bearing bad fruit to
this day. The very account of it frightens some away from God,
while others are cast down by it, thinking they could never attain
such "holiness."

Madame Guyon's example, like going on a fast of both food and
water, represents an unusual and extreme manifestation of the
error of trying to substitute the spiritual for the natural. Other less
radical forms of it, however, are rather common.

God Is No Substitute for a Lover

To begin where we left off in the previous chapter, let's take romantic love as an example. While romantic love will fail us as a
substitute for God, the reverse is also true. God is no substitute for
romantic love.

I can't tell you how many times I have known people to err here.
A woman—let's say she's a young widow—divulges that she feels
so alone and hungers for a man to love her. At that point, the
preacher (or whoever may be counseling her) smacks her with
Isaiah 54:5: "For your Maker is your husband—the Lord Almighty is
his name."

Never mind that the woman addressed in Isaiah is the nation of
Israel and that the prophecy pictures God as having abandoned Israel temporarily (vv. 6–8). Ignoring this context, the counselor suggests that the lonely woman should find in God the answer to her
sexual romantic needs.

The Scripture, however, teaches exactly the opposite, in plain
language and without the use of analogy.

Consider 1 Timothy 5:9–15:

> No widow may be put on the list of widows unless she
> is over sixty. . . . As for younger widows, do not put them

> on such a list. For when their sensual desires overcome their dedication to Christ, they want to marry. Thus they bring judgment on themselves, because they have broken their first pledge. Besides, they get into the habit of being idle and going about from house to house. And not only do they become idlers, but also gossips and busybodies, saying things they ought not to. So I counsel younger widows to marry, to have children, to manage their homes and to give the enemy no opportunity for slander. Some have in fact already turned away to follow Satan.

Notice this statement: "When their sensual desires overcome their dedication to Christ, they want to marry." Clearly, dedication to Christ is not a satisfactory substitute for sensual desires. If it were, the sensual desires would not rise up and overcome the dedication.

In the New Testament, then, when a widow's sensual desires overcame her dedication, it was because a situation had been encouraged that should not have been allowed in the first place. An attempt had been made to substitute dedication to Christ for sensual desires. The two desires then became unnecessarily and unwisely pitted against each other.

When you have a situation like this, the result is going to be frustration rather than fulfillment. Sooner or later, the frustration is likely to produce:

1. Compensatory behavior: "not only do they become idlers, but also gossips and busybodies" (v. 13).

2. Breakdown. Eventually the frustration of dealing with unrealistic demands may well lead the woman to chuck the whole thing. "Some have in fact already turned away to follow Satan" (v. 15).

Paul states the remedy for all this unhappy business: "So I counsel younger widows to marry" (v. 14). Let romantic love fulfill the need for romantic love, and let God fulfill the need for God.

Obviously not every widow can remarry, since there are not enough eligible men to go around. Furthermore, the single woman ought not to rush into an unwise marriage just to satisfy her needs. It may be that a woman will find herself unable to remarry. Certainly, in such a case, God will be her refuge and strength. God's grace is sufficient for us in any extremity. By means of the strength Christ gives, the single woman can cope with being single, as with any other adversity. But that's quite different from saying that her singleness is no adversity because God will be her "husband."

By the same token, those who would help the widow ought to assist her in finding a suitable mate, if they are able to do so. Short of that, they should at least show kindness and concern. What they ought not to do is mislead her with impractical spiritual talk. As James writes, it does no good to tell a hungry and ill-clad person to be fed and clothed (*see* James 2:15, 16). It likewise does no good—and can do harm—to tell a lonely single person to be satisfied with God.

Not on Bread Alone

The error of unwise substitution in both directions between the natural and the spiritual is addressed beautifully in Scripture. " 'Man does not live on bread [or food] alone, but on every word that comes from the mouth of God' " (Matthew 4:4; *see also* Deuteronomy 8:3).

When I first proposed entitling this chapter "Man Doesn't Live by Bread Alone, But He Sure Gets Hungry Without It," one of my critics said it sounded flippant, irreverent. Was I mocking the Scripture?

Well, I do hope the title is catchy, but I am far from mocking the Scripture. To the contrary, I am bringing out what the Scripture teaches.

It says not on bread *alone,* signifying that we need God and His word in our lives, too. But it doesn't say not on bread at all, because we need bread. Not only will a person get awfully hungry without it, he will die.

Other Scriptures similarly maintain this commonsense balance of spiritual and natural needs. For example, Jesus said that He is the bread of life; we need Him for spiritual sustenance (*see* John 6:35). But Jesus also taught us to pray, "Give us today our daily bread." We need food for our bodies, too. It is not a question of choosing one or the other, but of having both to supply our different needs.

Note the balance in Psalm 23. "The Lord is my shepherd." There it is: We need God first of all. "I shall not be in want." Not "I need nothing else," but "I shall not be in want," because God provides. "He makes me lie down in green pastures, he leads me beside quiet waters." The way God provides is by natural means. He does not meet my needs for sustenance miraculously, apart from food and water, but He leads me to where I can eat and drink. ·

Worldly Pleasures

The attempt to make God serve in place of other things is, I fear, almost as widespread as it is damaging. The following example comes readily to mind.

Young people are often taught that they should not seek "worldly pleasure." Such pleasures are fleeting, they are told, and then they may be given a Scripture verse. One favorite is Psalm 16:11: "In thy presence is fullness of joy; at thy right hand there are pleasures for evermore" (KJV). The implication is that real pleasures are to be found only in God.

This teaching misses the mark. Certainly some pleasures are to be avoided; not, however, because we should be finding all our pleasure in God. If a pleasure is sinful or destructive, it should be avoided for that reason. If it is vulgar, we may want to encourage more elevated tastes. On the other hand, there is no reason to forbid a legitimate pleasure.

When I was converted to Christ and joined the church at age twelve, my Sunday school teacher taught that we shouldn't go to see movies. When I asked why, he quoted 1 John 2:15: "Do not love the world or anything in the world. If anyone loves the world, the love of the Father is not in him."

Though I didn't understand how or why that verse applied to movies but not to other things (such as radio, newspapers, and magazines), I eventually accepted what I took to be the prevailing wisdom. From age sixteen on, I never went to movies.

When my wife and I raised our own family, movies were off-limits to our children. We were Christians, and movies were "worldly pleasures." This worked out fine, as long as the children were small. When Kathy, our oldest, got into her middle teens, everything began to be challenged.

Kathy sneaked off and went to a few movies without our knowledge. Then one day we were debating some other "heavy moral issue," like whether or not she could shave her legs. I was against it.

"Why should I accept your judgment of right and wrong?" Kathy demanded. "You made me think movies are all scandalous, rotten, and immoral, too. Well, I found out they are not!"

Kathy thought the movies she had seen were decent, and she felt almost betrayed by me. If I had misled her so badly about movies, how could she trust me on other issues?

I was stymied. I realized I had no valid basis for prohibiting decent movies. So it was that G-rated movies became acceptable at our house. By enlisting the support of Ann Landers, Kathy even won the argument about shaving her legs.

With the hindsight of years, I can tell you (and Kathy would tell you) that her life has not been marred by the movies. We can't say the same about my overstrict demands. The damage done to my credibility as a dependable guide in spiritual and moral matters contributed to a pretty rocky transition from Kathy's teen to adult years.

"Oh, but you were more right than wrong," someone says. "Worldly pleasure can never satisfy the deep needs of the human heart."

Of course not; God does that. But while pleasure cannot satisfy our heart's deepest needs, it can satisfy our need for pleasure, a desire we should not expect God to satisfy spiritually, any more than we expect Him to sustain us without our eating and drinking.

From 1 Timothy 5:15 we learned that some widows "turn away to follow Satan" after they are unwisely led to substitute dedication to Christ for sensual desires. A similar frustration and collapse is likely to strike young people when they are told to substitute fellowship with God for pleasure. Thank God, that didn't happen with our children, but it certainly has with some.

What About Money?

One of the worst snares and traps we can encounter in the Christian life is money, or material things. Jesus said, " 'Be on your guard against all kinds of greed; a man's life does not consist in the abundance of his possessions' " (Luke 12:15). We also read that the love of money is a root of all evil, that it drowns men in perdition, that money is filthy lucre, and that materialism is like thorns crowding out the good seed of God's word.

So we shouldn't desire money and material things, right?

Wrong. We shouldn't put them first. That would be to substitute them for God. But money and possessions have an important and legitimate place in our lives, and we should not try to fill that place with God.

Bishop Desmond Tutu of South Africa was quoted in the newspapers as repeating an old tale. The gist of it is that years ago, when the missionaries first came to his country, the natives had the land and the missionaries had the Bible. The people listened to the missionaries, with the result that now the natives have the Bible and the missionaries have the land.

That is not a satisfactory swap. Certainly the eternal welfare of one's soul is more important than holding title to a parcel of land, but why should we see it as an either/or matter? People need God, but they also need things.

Possessions give one a needed sense of dignity. Look at a small child with a new pair of shoes. How happy the child is! How excited! How important he or she feels! What adult has not bought new clothes and experienced a lift of the spirits? Some people are even known to combat depression by going on shopping sprees.

The desire for possessions is not evil. It is a natural trait of human beings, placed in us by God. Otherwise, God would not appeal to this desire. God doesn't tempt us to sin. Yet God said to Abraham, " 'Lift up your eyes from where you are and look north and south, east and west. All the land that you see I will give to you and your offspring forever" (Genesis 13:14, 15).

Even at the very time He is telling us to put God first, Jesus also addresses our concerns about having the material things we need. " 'But seek first his kingdom and his righteousness, and all these things will be given to you as well" (Matthew 6:33). Note that Jesus says to seek the things of God *first*, not *only*. It is clear from this passage that we aren't to make the acquisition of things a priority, but it is also clear that God views material things as needs that He intends to supply.

Other Examples

If we thought about it for a while, we could probably cite many other examples of unwise substitution of God for other things. Some people have a strong tendency to renounce medical treatment in favor of faith. Happily, most Christians realize they can and should avail themselves of both medicine and God.

Some preachers try to substitute God for study and thought. One said that, for inspiration, he kept his Bible under his pillow as he slept. Both his preaching and his life would have benefited a lot more if he had kept the Scriptures on his mind while he was awake.

Assessing the Damage

All error tends to cause harm, and trying to substitute God for other things is no exception. At least two very serious consequences may follow.

The first consequence is that some people will actually try to replace food, romance, pleasure, or whatever with God. These are the earnest souls who intend to live their faith and not just talk it. Since a superspiritual approach to life doesn't work very well, the situation tends to be self-corrective and usually doesn't continue indefinitely. However, as already pointed out, it can lead to great frustration, to destructive compensatory behavior, and to a major breakdown in one's spiritual life. Those are no small dangers.

A second consequence is experienced by people who do not actually live out this superspiritual life-style but do buy into the concept, or into some elements of it. Multitudes of Christians think this is how they *ought* to live. If they were truly spiritual, God would be everything to them, and this world would be nothing. Thus they are brought into condemnation and guilt. A heavy yoke is placed upon their necks—one that neither we nor our forefathers were able to bear, as the Apostle Peter put it (see Acts 15:10).

My father-in-law was a victim of this misguided God-should-be-everything mentality. In my book *How to Build Your Christian Character,* I tell of a conversation I had with him a short time before his death.

127

Recently I asked him, "If you had it all to do over again, what would you do differently?"

He didn't have to think about it. "I'd be a missionary," he answered at once.

Now, mind you, Dad did not neglect a missionary call early in life. He didn't even become a Christian until he was in his forties, with a wife and seven children.

But almost from the time of his conversion, Dad bought into the notion that if he were really to do the will of God it would mean selling out everything and becoming a missionary. Since that wasn't feasible, he didn't see how he could truly be the Christian he should be. And with that attitude, he wasn't. Oh, he lived as good a life as the next church member—probably better than most—but he didn't live as close to God as he would have if it hadn't been for the guilt and the feeling, "Well, I'm not really what I ought to be anyhow, so what's the difference?"[6]

The Well-Ordered Life

When a person falls into the error of trying to make God everything, the overflowing life of the indwelling Spirit of God is actually stifled. This does not need to be. There is a happy ground of truth that lies between secularism and fanaticism. You can find that ground. Give God His rightful first place in your heart. Guard that first place diligently. Then fill up the hollow recesses of your life with those things specifically designed by God to go in there.

When our children were small, they received a "shape sorter," a plastic polyhedron and plastic pieces of various shapes. The idea was to place the plastic pieces inside the polyhedron through the holes sized and shaped just right to receive them. At first the children often tried to force the pieces into holes where they would not fit, but they soon learned that when they got things right, the pieces fit easily.

The overflowing life comes from putting all of life's pieces in their proper places. And God? He is not one of the pieces; He is the polyhedron.

—PART—
V

Making the
Overflowing Life
Truly Yours

──TWELVE──

To Have
and
to Use

**"The word is near you; it is in your mouth and in your heart,"
that is, the word of faith we are proclaiming.**

Romans 10:8

The overflowing Life is a gift. Its effect is far-reaching. Its implications are incalculable. We will be a lifetime learning all that it means. But it doesn't take a lot of instruction to receive it.

However, it does take some.

Remember what Jesus said to the woman at the well: "If you knew the gift of God and who it is that asks you for a drink, you would have asked him and he would have given you living water" (John 4:10).

You see, it is really quite simple: "You would have asked . . . he would have given." The basic how-to for receiving the gift of God is to ask for it.

Jesus did indicate that the woman needed to know a couple of things: *What the gift is* and *who He is.* Obviously, if one has no idea what something is, one can't intelligently ask for it. And if one does not know who has it to give, one won't know whom to ask.

We have dealt at length with what the gift is. Essentially, we have said the gift is God Himself, taking up residence in our lives. We have not said much about who Jesus is, that He should be the one we ask for this gift.

Jesus Is Not a Promoter

The world is full of pretenders, people who offer us the moon but are really out to take advantage of us. Almost every week, it seems, I get the good news in the mail that I have been selected and will definitely receive one of several wonderful free gifts.

I hardly consider these offers anymore. Just to confirm my skepticism, I do check the fine print for my odds of winning, which the promoters reveal because the government requires it. My chances of winning the new car are usually about 1 in 99,999. The same is true of the other valuable prizes. By contrast, the odds are 99,995 to 1 that a cheapy telephone or stereo or camera would be my prize. To get it, I would have to drive three hundred miles and listen to a lengthy, high-pressure sales pitch for some fraudulent or overpriced real-estate development.

Jesus is not running a promotion. Jesus is not trying to sign us up with misleading promises in order to take advantage of us. Jesus is the Son of God, the one who gives us the Holy Spirit to be a river of living water in us. But how can we know that?

How to Know Jesus Is the Son of God

I once faced the very dilemma the woman at the well faced and you may be facing now. How could I know that Jesus is who He claims to be?

I was at the opposite end of life from the woman at the well. She had been through the mill; I was just starting out. I was twelve years old.

My mother suggested it was time I be baptized and join the

church. I told her quite honestly that I was not interested, because I didn't believe any of that God stuff. It sounded like Superman to me.

My older brother, Ron, got me aside later and straightened me out. "You hurt her feelings," he said. "It wouldn't hurt you a bit to be baptized. I don't believe any of that stuff, either, but I'm going to be baptized."

Seeing what a thoughtless and inconsiderate son I had been, I told my mother I had decided to be baptized after all. She wanted to know why I had changed my mind, so I told her exactly what had happened.

"No," she said, "you can't do that. I don't want you to be baptized if you don't believe."

This experience served to do one thing: It focused my attention on some heavy questions: Is there a God, or not? Should I believe the Bible? Are the claims of Jesus true?

I knew my mother would answer each of these questions in the affirmative. I also felt sure my father would answer each one in the negative. So what should I believe? How could I decide? I needed my own independent source of information.

I decided to conduct a test. I would find out about God for myself; I would pray and see whether God would answer. But what should I pray for?

At that time, I had a very serious personal problem that caused me much embarrassment and shame. My mother would literally rail at me because of this particular weakness, this failure of mine. I felt terrible about it, but I seemed powerless to help myself. I wet the bed.

So I prayed. I said, "God—if there is a God—if You will help me not to wet the bed tonight, I'll believe in You."

The next morning I awoke a dry convert.

I can't say I was dry every morning thereafter, clear into eternity. But I have been a believer ever since.

Two Kinds of Evidence

I am fully aware that my evidence for God is hardly conclusive. No atheist is likely to rush to the nearest church and ask for baptism on the basis of what I have just written. On the other hand, the experience was quite convincing for the guileless twelve-year-old atheist who had the experience.

If you want harder evidence, there is plenty of it. This is not a book on Christian evidences, but you can get one—or several—at your nearest Christian bookstore or through your public library.

Furthermore, Jesus is quite willing to give you personal evidence. It won't be the kind that would stand up in court, but it will be the kind that is convincing to you.

Do not assume that the personal evidence of which I speak is just silly subjectivism or wishful thinking. It is far more than that. Perhaps I can illustrate.

I was awaiting a flight out of Chicago one evening, when my attention was drawn to a happy reunion taking place before my eyes. From an arriving plane came a dark-haired little charmer I guessed to be about eight or nine years old. She was met by a beaming elderly couple. "Look who's here!" the man said, and the little girl flew into his arms.

The woman's turn was next. She embraced the girl, whose dark eyes glowed as she exclaimed, "Grandma! Grandma!"

What happened next seemed utterly ridiculous. A woman employee of the airline had escorted the girl from the plane and now stood observing the happy scene. This woman said to the elderly couple, "May I see some identification?"

Identification? Everybody in the vicinity could have identified that couple as the little girl's beloved grandparents.

Of course, the airline employee was only doing her duty. It was appropriate to require formal identification before she turned the girl over to these people.

It is also appropriate for you to require formal identification from Jesus, if you wish. That is no problem to Him. True, a few religious types may tend to get bent out of shape if you question any of their dogma about Jesus, but He doesn't feel that way. When He was here, He freely cited various evidences of His identity. You may read about these for yourself throughout the Gospel of John. One place where several evidences are offered within the space of a few verses is John 5:31–47.

Jesus also offered one supreme sign, one irrefutable proof that He was the Son of God. He said that after they had crucified Him, in three days He would rise again from the dead (*see* John 2:19–22). That He did indeed rise is one of the best-attested facts in history, and if you don't see how that proves anything, you try doing it.

But while Jesus offers formal identification, that is not the only kind there is. The little girl had no need to see her grandparents' driver's licenses. She knew them personally.

Jesus said something like that is true of Him and His people. He said, " 'I am the good shepherd; I know my sheep and my sheep know me . . . I have other sheep that are not of this sheep pen. I must bring them also. They too will listen to my voice, and there shall be one flock and one shepherd' " (John 10:14, 16).

Later, Jesus alluded to both His formal and informal credentials when He said, " 'The miracles that I do in my Father's name speak for me, but you do not believe because you are not my sheep. My sheep listen to my voice; I know them, and they follow me' " (John 10:25–27).

So it was with the woman who had lived with six men. How did she come to know who Jesus was? It was not through some formal evidence that would stand up in court. It was through the personal interaction between them. She later told the townspeople, " 'Come, see a man who told me everything I ever did. Could this be the Christ?' " (John 4:29).

He hadn't actually told her everything she had done, but He had told her enough to convince her that He could.

Something Supernatural

The laws of evidence and logic are all well and good. Jesus Christ has nothing to fear from investigation on that level. But our relationship with Him involves something not only more personal, but also supernatural. The fact that Jesus knew about the woman's many husbands, though it helped convince her of His identity, was not sufficient in itself to change her life. He also offered—and gave her—the gift of God.

It was not only my dry bed that made me a believer; it was a supernatural inner witness. Jesus said, " 'If anyone chooses to do God's will, he will find out whether my teaching comes from God or whether I speak on my own' " (John 7:17).

"He will find out." With or without formal evidences, an inner conviction of truth can come from God Himself.

On one occasion, Jesus asked His disciples what people were saying about His identity. They reported on the current speculation. Some said Jesus was John the Baptist, recently executed but now returned to life with miracle-working power. Others said He was one or another of the Old Testament prophets, sent again by God to proclaim His message to the people.

After hearing their report, Jesus next asked the disciples, " 'But what about you? Who do you say I am?' "

Simon Peter answered, " 'You are the Christ, the Son of the living God.' "

Jesus replied, " 'Blessed are you, Simon son of Jonah, for this was not revealed to you by man, but by my Father in heaven" (see Matthew 16:13–17). With a similar revelation in our hearts of who Jesus is, we are prepared to ask Him for the gift of God.

If You Don't Know

It is crucial that you know who Jesus is.

Because the Jewish leaders did not know who He was, they rejected the one whom God sent to be their glorious King.

Because the Roman authorities did not know who Jesus was, they crucified as a criminal the one truly innocent man in the entire Roman empire.

Because the woman who had lived with six men did not at first know who Jesus was, she nearly passed by both Him and His great gift without paying heed.

Because I once did not know who He is, I lumped him along with Superman, as a far-fetched figment of man's fantasy.

If you don't know who Jesus is, you will never receive from Him that gift of God which would make your life one of fulfillment.

"Why Doesn't It Work for Me?"

I am certain there are some readers whose hearts will cry out that they do know Jesus, that they have "found" God, but that they still do not have overflowing life.

Why not? If it is truly a gift, why don't they seem to have it?

This can be quite a quandary, and I know what they are talking about. I cannot reply, "You are simply wrong. Jesus said it's a gift, so if you don't have it, you obviously have not received Him." That would be unkind, but worse than that, it would be untrue. I certainly have not experienced overflowing life ever since I first trusted in Christ, and neither have millions of other sincere Christians.

At this point one is tempted to start chipping away at the concept of the free gift. Do we have to do anything, or not? If we do, then the so-called gift is no longer free. If we do not, then why do so many Christians lack the overflowing life?

This problem is not as insolvable as it may appear.

Suppose I were to give you a new car as an outright gift. All you do is ask for it, and I turn it over to you—the keys, the title, and the car itself. It is all yours.

Suppose that this is a very nice new car. It is beautiful. It is luxurious. It is fun to drive. It is prestigious. It is even economical on fuel. Along with the new car comes full-coverage insurance and a lifetime service contract. Everything is a gift.

Suppose you accept this gift, take it to your home, drive it into your detached garage, shut the garage door, *and never again do anything with that car.*

Do you have the car, or don't you?

Technically, you have the car. Everything that car represents is potentially yours.

Actually, however, you may as well not own the car. It is doing you no good whatever. It doesn't transport you anywhere. It doesn't provide you with the pleasure of driving. The insurance and the service contract are both being wasted. The beautiful car does not even adorn your driveway, because it is hidden away in a garage that no one ever enters.

You could, of course, begin to use the car whenever you chose, though it might seem a bit strange when you first began doing so. Nevertheless, it is yours to use.

Notice this, however: The only way you can ever use that car is by giving yourself to it to some degree. You cannot even enjoy or admire its fine craftsmanship, its gleaming finish, or its soft uphol-stery without giving some attention to it.

If the car is to fulfill its original purpose of transporting you in style and comfort, you will have to commit yourself to it. That is, you will have to get in it, spend some time there, and operate the vehicle. The more you involve yourself with that car, the more you will "have" it, in a practical sense.

That's the way it is with the gift of God. The gift can only effec-tively be yours to the degree that you involve yourself with the gift.

Why don't you have the overflowing life despite the fact that you have received Christ? The reason could well be that you have not given yourself to Him sufficiently to make what is potentially yours actually yours.

A Sham Marriage

Another reason people lack the overflowing life is that they have not accepted the car at all, but only the brochure. Slick, glossy, and appealing as the brochure may be, it won't transport you anywhere.

In other words, Christ does not dwell within everybody. For Him to dwell within us, our very spirits must be joined to the Spirit of God. Remember that the Scripture says, "But he that is joined unto the Lord is one spirit" (1 Corinthians 6:17, KJV).

The context compares that union with God to the sexual union of a man and woman. In the eyes of the law, a marriage is not a mar-riage unless it has been consummated. The couple may have gone through all the formalities: license, ceremony, merging of assets, even adoption by the wife of the husband's surname. But unless they have merged their bodies in sexual union, they are not married.

God stands ready to merge His Spirit with your spirit, but this is not accomplished by formalities. It is accomplished only by direct and intimate interaction between you and God. This interaction in-volves faith and prayer.

Prayer and Faith

From the depths of our being, we talk to God. That is prayer. We ask God for His great gift, the one that means we won't suffer anymore from unslaked thirst. We ask for the well of water that will spring up within us until it flows out from us as a river of life to the world. We ask God for the gift of Himself.

We pray believing.

We don't get all tied in knots over how strong our faith is or is not. We remember that we are not *earning* the gift by our strong faith. It is a free gift, and all the faith we need is to reach out and take it.

"Anyone who comes to him must believe that he exists and that he rewards those who earnestly seek him" (Hebrews 11:6). That is all the faith you need, and that kind of faith is pretty much your choice. I mean, there is nothing to keep you from believing that God exists and that He rewards those who seek Him, is there? You can believe it, can't you?

If you can't, then you do have a problem. It's not an insurmountable problem because God is quite willing to provide you with evidences, as we detailed earlier. So settle that first. Then, once able to believe, you simply choose to do so. You then pray believing. You ask, and God gives Himself to you.

Let no one excuse unbelief with the argument that faith itself is a gift of God and it is therefore up to God whether or not one has it. Faith is indeed a gift of God, like everything else good, but He has already given it to you. Now you must choose how to use it. You may believe in God or against Him.

We are constantly making choices to believe or not to believe in our day-to-day lives. We hear various accounts from our friends and associates—accounts of everything from their success at fishing or on the golf course to the great deal they got or loss they suffered in buying a dinner, a car, or a house. As we hear all these accounts, we are inwardly believing or disputing them. We would almost stake our lives on the reports of some people because we trust them. We believe them even if there is considerable evidence to the contrary, or even if they give us a stranger-than-fiction story. Other people might tell us something quite believable in itself. Because we view them as unreliable, empty talkers, however, we doubt that they are telling us the truth.

139

Thus our belief or lack of it says something about the relationship that exists between us and the source of the information. That is why unbelief as it relates to God becomes a moral matter.[1]

Since Christianity is credible, you can believe it, if you want to. That is the bottom line. There may be steps to go through—investigation, evaluation of evidence, thought, prayer—but in the end you *decide*. To decide against God, when you could as easily have decided for Him, effectively excludes Him from your life. That is the life impoverished. Why choose that?

God is ready to help you with every aspect of a better choice. He will "strengthen you with power through his Spirit in your inner being, so that Christ may dwell in your hearts through faith" (Ephesians 3:16, 17).

False Faith and True Faith

It is important to understand the difference between faith and "trying to believe." Faith is not trying to believe; faith is believing. Trying to believe is unbelief attempting to become faith.

Trying to believe does not bring the overflowing life, because it is still unbelief.

The story is told of a public-school teacher who opposed the Christian faith. At the beginning of the year, the teacher announced that by the end of the year, none of his students would believe in God.

However, one boy let it be known that not only did he believe in God, but he knew God personally. That boy became a special target of the teacher's attacks.

The teacher didn't use lead-pipe tactics. He just went about subtly undermining faith when the opportunity presented itself. In a "nice" way, he kept putting the Christian student on the spot. All year long this continued.

On the last day of school, the teacher reminded the class of what he had said at the beginning. "But Christian, here, still believes. Is that right?" The boy nodded his head vigorously.

"Well, we are going to settle this God business right now," the teacher said. He took from his desk drawer an egg, walked around the desk to stand before the class, held the egg above the floor, and said, "I am about to drop this egg. But before I do, Christian, here, is going to pray that it won't break. We'll see whether or not there is a God!"

There was absolute silence in the room as the boy began to pray. "Dear Lord," he said, "when teacher drops that egg, I pray that it will shatter into a thousand pieces . . . and he'll drop dead!"

The students gasped. Had you been near the front of the room, you could have seen an almost imperceptible tightening of the teacher's grip on the egg. Slowly he walked back behind his desk, opened a drawer, and carefully deposited the egg inside. Then he announced, "Class dismissed."

I love to tell that story. Audiences love it, too. I don't know whether it's true or not, but it sure gives what-for to the opposition. Ha! That teacher's faith in his unbelief wasn't nearly as strong as he wanted everyone to think. In fact, his attempts to destroy the faith of others were mostly due to his need to shore up his own weak faith in atheism. He was trying to believe that there is no God.

I hardly ever tell that story, however, without pointing out that our faith in Christ can be as weak as that teacher's was in his unbelief. Even our efforts to witness can be an attempt to shore up our own weak faith.

God doesn't want our aggressive efforts to prove how strongly we believe. He doesn't want a "trying to believe" that really doesn't and that will betray itself when the chips are down. He doesn't want the kind of faith that Mark Twain cynically defined as believing what you know is not true.

I have chosen to believe that God exists. After all these years of knowing God, I could still doubt that, and once in a while I probably do. But I am absolutely and utterly convinced that unbelief requires at least as much faith on my part as belief does. Under those circumstances, I'd be a fool to choose against God.

Besides, unbelief doesn't offer an overflowing life.

—PART—
VI

The
Overflowing Life
in Action

—THIRTEEN—

Giving
and
Forgiving

We should give because the God of the cheerfully giving heart lives in us.

For some years now, I have been engaged in an ongoing debate with a good friend over the issue of whether God intends His people to prosper materially. My friend maintains that God does want to bless us materially, as well as in all other ways. He says Jesus died to redeem us from sin's curse, and that includes the curse of poverty.

I say that the full fruit of Christ's redemptive work is not yet ours. Just as the curse of physical death is still at work in us, causing our bodies to die, so dishonesty, laziness, exploitation, and other evils are also still at work in our fallen society, causing poverty. God's will is not yet done on earth, as it is in heaven. Rich and powerful people can and often do exploit the poor. Furthermore, Christ's kingdom is not of this world, and we are to seek His kingdom, not earthly prosperity. Scripture warns us that, "People who want to get rich fall into temptation and a trap" (1 Timothy 6:9).

It is in this area of prosperity that I see one of the most significant contrasts between the abundant life (as it is often understood and taught) and the overflowing life. The abundant life focuses on what we can get (prosperity). The overflowing life focuses on what we can give (service). Overflowing puts us in company with the Apostle Paul, who described himself as "poor, yet making many rich; having nothing, and yet possessing everything" (2 Corinthians 6:10).

Giving in Order to Get

The idea I find most objectionable in abundant-life teaching is that one should give in order to get. It is clear, however, that the Bible itself does link giving with getting. Consider a few passages:

> "And everyone who has left houses or brothers or sisters or father or mother or children or fields for my sake will receive a hundred times as much and will inherit eternal life."
>
> Matthew 19:29

> "Give, and it will be given to you. A good measure, pressed down, shaken together and running over, will be poured into your lap. For with the measure you use, it will be measured to you."
>
> Luke 6:38

> Remember this: Whoever sows sparingly will also reap sparingly, and whoever sows generously will also reap generously. Each man should give what he has decided in his heart to give, not reluctantly or under compulsion, for God loves a cheerful giver.
>
> 2 Corinthians 9:6, 7

In light of these and other Scriptures, there can be little doubt that God promises to reward those who give.

What a Deal!

But hold the phone just a minute. Something doesn't quite add up here. This promise of a hundredfold return on investment described in Matthew 19:29—that's quite a deal! That comes out to a 10,000

146

percent return on your investment. Any investment opportunity claiming to double your money in a year would be considered highly speculative and risky in financial circles. Yet Jesus promises not just double, but 100 times what you invest, though He didn't say how long it would take.

Understand, I am not doubting what Jesus said. I believe it: He gives 10,000 percent return on what we give up *for His sake.* Don't miss that aspect of motive. He didn't say He would give a hundred-fold return on anything we give up with the idea of making a killing but just on anything we give up for His sake.

One's motive is critical here.

You see, otherwise, Jesus and the disciples were missing out on a terrific recruitment tool. They could have been standing on every street corner in Jerusalem, saying something like this:

"Hey, buddy, you got ten dollars? How'd you like to turn it into one thousand dollars? I know this surefire investment, backed by the full faith and integrity of God Himself. However much you want to invest, we can guarantee you one hundred times as much back."

They didn't do that, and I think we can understand why.

Question: If I'm offered a hefty return on investing in the kingdom of God, how can I keep my motive pure? I am supposed to be giving for Jesus' sake, but that one-hundred-fold return I've been promised is a bit diverting, to say the least.

If no material gain was promised me, then it would be pretty clear I wasn't being motivated by greed. But now, who knows what my motives are? Can I even be sure of my own heart?

Some of us might well cry, "I wish you hadn't told me about the reward, Lord! You have robbed me of my unsullied gift of love."

Whose Idea Was This?

Without doubt, Jesus promised that those who give will get back much more. It is also clear that Jesus did not use that approach to recruit people. Much to the contrary, He told the crowds that if anyone did not hate "even his own life," he could not be a disciple (Luke 14:25, 26).

Jesus told one would-be follower, " 'Foxes have holes and birds of the air have nests, but the Son of Man has no place to lay his head' " (Luke 9:58). Clearly He wasn't trying to entice the man with promises of prosperity.

Even in the same chapter of Matthew where we read of the one-hundred-fold return, we also read that Jesus told a rich young man to "sell your possessions and give to the poor." The young man "went away sad, because he had great wealth." You see, Jesus omitted telling this young man he was going to get one-hundred-fold for anything he gave. Rather, He offered him a vague assurance of "treasure in heaven" (*see* Matthew 19:21, 22).

In fact, if you read on in the same chapter, you'll discover that the one-hundred-fold promise was not volunteered by Jesus at all. It was an elicited response to a very specific question from the Apostle Peter. " 'We have left everything to follow you! What then will there be for us?' " (Matthew 19:27).

Making a Deal With God

Jesus answered Peter's question with the promise of a one-hundred-fold return, but it's important to understand that His answer did not stop there.

One of the worst jobs anybody ever did of "helping" us to understand the Scriptures was performed by the unknown person who chopped up the Gospel of Matthew into chapters and verses centuries ago. One tends to assume that some sort of break exists between Matthew 19 and Matthew 20. This is definitely not the case.

In Matthew 19 we read Peter's question about what he could expect to get for having given up so much for Jesus. In the parable of Matthew 20:1–16, we find most of Jesus' reply to that question. Matthew tied the whole reply together, beginning and ending it with the words, "But many who are first will be last, and many who are last will be first" (*see* Matthew 19:30 and 20:16). The parable that lies between the two statements of that principle is intended to help us understand the principle. Unfortunately, what Jesus and Matthew joined together, some editor put asunder.

In this parable we can see why we should not operate on the basis of "What am I going to get out of this?" in our relationship with God.

The parable concerns a landowner who early one morning hires workers for his vineyard. He agrees with the workers to pay one denarius for a twelve-hour day. He goes to the marketplace again at nine, at noon, and at three. Those hired then have no specific wage promised. The landowner simply says, "I will pay you whatever is right."

At 5:00 P.M. the landowner hires yet more workers, making no mention at all of what pay they can expect.

At six o'clock quitting time, the landowner orders payments, with the last hired being the first paid. When the all-day workers see how much the one-hour workers get—a full day's wages—they figure this is one generous landowner and they are going to get paid handsomely. However, when they only get one denarius, they are steamed about it and begin to complain.

The parable was a warning to Peter and to everyone else who begins to develop a calculating spirit in serving the Lord. Do we want an agreement, a promise, a contract assuring us a fair return from God? Peter never raised such questions when he began following the Lord, but now a calculating spirit has crept in and he wants to know what he is going to get out of the deal.

Jesus' parable indicates that we would be a lot better off to leave the question of reward up to Him. Those who want to strike bargains not only fare less well, but they end up complaining against the Lord that they haven't been treated right. And though the parable doesn't say so specifically, they likely felt some animosity toward the other workers, too.

The Kind of Giver God Loves

Scripture says that God loves a cheerful giver (*see* 2 Corinthians 9:7). Once again we see an emphasis on the spirit in which one gives—not cold and calculating, but warm and happy.

I can readily understand why God feels that way, because I do, too. If I see a person giving in order to worm into someone's affections or to place him under obligation with a future favor in view, I am repulsed. On the other hand, cheerful giving that has no hidden agenda is a blessing to behold.

My grandson Jason is a likeable fellow, and his giving spirit is one reason for it. When Jason was about six, he could hardly wait for dark on Halloween, so he could go door to door trick-or-treating. Finally, his mother, Kathy, yielded to his pleas and said that even though it wasn't time yet, she supposed it would be all right if he went just to the people right next door on each side of their house.

Before she knew what was happening, Jason had grabbed the big bowl of candy she had ready for evening visitors and had gone next door. When the people answered his knock, Jason happily shouted, "Trick or treat," then thrust his bowl in their faces and told the surprised neighbors, "Here, take some!"

Why Does God Give?

If God loves a cheerful giver, I have to believe that God also *is* a cheerful giver. We should give, then, not in order to get, but because the God of the cheerfully giving heart lives in us. And I'm not talking only, or even primarily, about money. I'm talking about being a giving person, someone who wants to help others. Though we know we will be rewarded, our giving is not calculating. When we give, we don't think about how this giving might come back to benefit us.

Jesus said:

> "And if you lend to those from whom you expect repayment, what credit is that to you? Even 'sinners' lend to 'sinners,' expecting to be repaid in full. But love your enemies, do good to them, and lend to them without expecting to get anything back. Then your reward will be great, and you will be sons of the Most High, because he is kind to the ungrateful and wicked. Be merciful, just as your Father is merciful."

> Luke 6:34–36

Notice who is held up as our example for giving. We should give as God gives, for He is our Father, and indeed He dwells within us.

That is why the overflowing life cannot be selfish or self-contained. The overflowing life is God within, and God simply gives because He is a giver. This means that when you have the over-flowing life, it will be good news for those around you.

Not long ago I went fishing with Bill Brown at the mouth of the Columbia River. We got only one salmon, which Bill caught, but we also witnessed a highly entertaining display by the pelican popula-tion of the area. These huge, ungainly birds would fly a few feet above the river's surface, then suddenly plunge into the water as if crashing. Usually they seized one or more small fish, probably her-ring, which they then proceeded to gulp down.

I noticed that each pelican had two or three sea gulls hanging around it. The gulls flew with the pelicans and set down in the water everytime the pelicans crashed. Then I realized what was happening: The gulls were getting the overflow—the fish or pieces of fish that fell from the pelicans' bills.

Those who have overflowing life are pelicans, not gulls. They are not scavengers trying to snatch whatever morsels they can from the beaks of others. Instead, they are drawing on the abundant re-sources of God to such a degree that others are almost incidentally fed in the process.

This is the basic difference, let me remind you, between the over-flowing life and the abundant life as it has often been misunder-stood. The abundant life, in theory at least, can be selfish; the overflowing life cannot.

The concept of abundant life, like overflowing life, comes from the teachings of Jesus. He said, " 'The thief comes only to steal and kill and destroy; I have come that they may have life, and have it to the full' " (John 10:10). The King James Version renders it, "I am come that they might have life, and that they might have it more abundantly."

Unfortunately, when we take this passage alone and try to fash-ion our lives by it, we can think totally in terms of ourselves. We are to have abundance, period. Who cares about anybody else?

This is certainly not what Jesus intended. We aren't supposed to take one statement of His out of the context of everything else He ever said. The abundant life and the overflowing life are not contra-dictory concepts; they are complementary. The abundant life is the spring of water welling up within us, and the overflowing life is that same spring becoming a river and flowing out to the world. The abundant life and the overflowing life are two aspects of the same gift of God.

So, then, the abundant life is to be seen as a means to the overflowing life, not as an end in itself. A vessel does not ordinarily overflow until it is full, so we need the abundant life. Sadly, though, many have spoken and acted as if one's own personal abundance were the ultimate end, the highest good in life. Jesus clearly taught otherwise. He said, " 'It is more blessed to give than to receive' " (Acts 20:35). If the abundant life is a great blessing from God (and it is), then the overflowing life is yet a far greater blessing.

Looking Out for Number One

The overflowing life shows genuine, honest caring for and giving to others. What a treasure this is, in a world in which people's expressions of interest in others are often totally self-serving.

We have an automobile dealer in our area who regularly concludes his television commercials by saying, "If you don't come and see me this weekend, I can't save you any money."

Personally, I have a strong hunch that saving me money is not his primary interest. If it is, though, I have great news for him: I got a better deal somewhere else.

Paul found a self-seeking attitude common, even among Christians of his day. Timothy was an exception. Paul wrote, "I have no one else like him, who takes a genuine interest in your welfare. For everyone looks out for his own interests, not those of Jesus Christ" (Philippians 2:20, 21).

Please notice what Paul said here: Self-seeking crowds out *both* caring for others and seeking the things that are Christ's. The unfulfilled person has one supreme, crying concern, and that is himself or herself. There is little room left over to give much consideration to either God or others.

The fulfilled person, the one who has the overflowing life, gives continually, just because that is the kind of person God has made him by releasing His Spirit in him. He doesn't make a production out of giving; it isn't his career. It is simply part and parcel of his daily functioning.

Sir Bartle Frere, British governor of Bombay, was said to be such a person. His wife once sent a driver to meet Sir Bartle at the railway station. "But how shall I know him?" asked the driver, who had never seen Sir Bartle before.

"Oh," said Lady Frere, "just look for a tall gentleman helping somebody."

The description proved adequate. The driver went and found Sir Bartle helping an old man out of a railway car and knew him at once.

If you are totally occupied with looking out for your own interests, it's a pretty good bet that you don't enjoy a fulfilled and overflowing life. The fact that so many are preoccupied with themselves is testimony to how few have found—or been able to continue in— the overflowing life.

The Key to Forgiving

I don't need to say a great deal about forgiving that I have not already said about giving. Not that forgiving isn't important. It is absolutely critical to our health and wholeness. And not that unforgiveness isn't a common problem. It insinuates itself or comes barreling into our lives often.

But the reason I need not expound at length upon forgiving is that it flows from the same inner presence of God that prompts giving. God is both a giver and a forgiver, and God in us leads us to be both givers and forgivers.

Jerry Cook touched on the key to forgiveness when he defined it not simply as an act but as a *climate*. There is no question, when we do something wrong, as to whether or not we will be forgiven. Likewise, there should be no question about our granting forgiveness. Forgiveness should be assured—the climate in which we live and relate to one another.

We read that when we confess our sins to God, "He is faithful and just and will forgive us our sins" (1 John 1:9). God doesn't have to think about it for a while. He forgives. And since He indwells us, we forgive.

Now, I don't want to make it sound too easy. I'm describing an attitude we should make our own. We may need a lot of grace to do so. We also may need to apply to God for that grace again and again. C. S. Lewis responded to Jesus' statement that we should forgive others seventy times seven by suggesting we might have to do that for just one offense. Right now we forgive, but that doesn't guarantee that old feelings and resentments will not rise again. In that realm, it seems the devil has power to raise from the dead!

So I may need God's grace to forgive repeatedly. But the good news is that grace is always available. The God of grace is not far off in heaven, but right here in my heart.

A Model for All of Life

Giving and forgiving are good examples of the overflowing life in action. These two things alone can transform our dreary, choked, unhappy lives into vibrant ones. They also bless other people. Thus they serve as a model of how God intends the overflowing life to work.

We can trace the process as follows. You ask God in faith, and in the name of the Lord Jesus Christ, to fill your heart and life with His Holy Spirit. God hears your prayer and comes to dwell in your heart.

Next, you draw on His presence. As the opportunity arises, you give or forgive, needing no other reason than that He prompts you. You are saying yes to the indwelling Spirit of God.

Look! The promise has already been fulfilled. You came to Christ to drink, and streams of living water have begun to flow from within you, as Jesus said they would (see John 7:38, 39). Your own inner joy increases, and you feel good about the evidence of the overflowing life within you. Meanwhile, someone else has received the benefit of your giving or forgiving—your overflow.

By contrast to the overflowing life, all other motivations for giving and forgiving wear thin. Do so in order to gain something, and when the return seems small, you are likely to be discouraged. Do so out of a sense of obligation, and you are likely to grow weary and resentful. Give to gain favor or power, and . . . well, let's face it, that is really not giving at all; it's a trade.

However, give and forgive because God prompts you from within, and your motivation will continue, regardless of any "results" you see or don't see.

That's how the overflowing life works; it springs from within you.

—FOURTEEN—

God's Light and Wisdom in You

If you have a problem of any kind and you are having trouble resolving it, the first thing to do is get more light on it.

In the last chapter, I expounded at length on how giving should flow from the influence of the Spirit of God within us. I did so because the process is a model for other aspects of life. The Apostle John, in his first epistle, cites one thing after another that is true of God and therefore has implications for us in whom God dwells. Let's notice these in the order John cites them.

God's Light and Our Sin Problem

John writes:

This is the message we have heard from him and declare to you: God is light; in him there is no darkness at

155

all. If we claim to have fellowship with him yet walk in the darkness, we lie and do not live by the truth. But if we walk in the light, as he is in the light, we have fellowship with one another, and the blood of Jesus, his Son, purifies us from all sin.

1 John 1:5–7

What does it mean to be indwelt by the God who is pristine light?

We might be inclined to say that we also should be full of light, with no darkness of sin in us at all. Yet the Apostle John immediately affirms in strong terms that we do have sin in us. "If we claim to be without sin, we deceive ourselves and the truth is not in us" (1 John 1:8).

At this point, an important distinction we made earlier comes into play. We must always distinguish between the idea that God is *in* us and the idea that God *is* us. God has no darkness at all in Him, but we do have darkness in us.

Rather than the God of light making us all light, He reveals the element of darkness in us. He does not make our darkness deeper; the overflowing life does not make us worse sinners. But our darkness—our sin—does show up in stark relief, because the light of God now shines in our hearts.

According to Scripture, that is what light does. It reveals things as they are. It shows us reality. As Paul writes, "Everything exposed by the light becomes visible, for it is light that makes everything visible" (Ephesians 5:13, 14).

God in us shines light on our souls and shows exactly what is there, including our sin. This may be unpleasant, but it is also necessary, because sin can block the flow of God's blessing in and through us.

A doctor uses light both to diagnose and treat disease. Light shows up what is wrong, and it illuminates the operating field for surgical procedures.

I don't know much about surgery, but I do know that the ability to see clearly is often critical to fixing things. I have worked under many automobiles and have sometimes struggled, literally for hours, to install a single bolt. That was before my father-in-law went out and bought me a trouble light. Understand, I wasn't absolutely in the dark before. Some light filtered in, and I thought that was good enough. But what a difference it makes when one gets ample light. Suddenly you can see that your angle is off and there is no way that bolt is ever going to enter the threaded hole until you move the part up, up, up—no, that's a bit too far. Down, yes—almost—just a hair more ... got it! Remarkable how easily it goes when you get it right.

Believe me, if you have a problem of any kind and you are having trouble resolving it, the first thing to do is get more light on it.

Getting Enlightened About Sin

Those who are indwelt by God have a source of great light on man's most intractable problem, sin. There are two basic facts about sin that we all need to understand. The first is the one the Apostle John insists upon so strongly: *We have got it.* This contagious sickness that is epidemic in the human race has not bypassed either you or me. We are infected.

Do you think I am stating the obvious? Are you already quite aware of your sinfulness?

Well, maybe you are. I also thought I had my bolt lined up with the threaded hole. A little more light made it clear I hadn't seen things as well as I thought.

Question: When you are accused of anything, what is your reaction? Most of us tend to deny any wrongdoing, to be insulted and upset, to be defensive and perhaps to counterattack our accusers.

Why?

I have often heard Steve, my lawyer son, remark that "It looks as if there is plenty of fault to go around."

Legally, of course, one party might be in the wrong and the other in the right. Morally, too, so far as this particular proceeding is concerned. And I am not suggesting one ought not to defend himself or seek his rights.

What I am saying is that most accused people, even if they are totally innocent in the matter before the court, are far from innocent in fact.

It's just like a child who indignantly insists he did not do the thing his parents suspect him of doing, when in fact he didn't, but has done many things far worse that they don't know about.

My point is this: Why should we get up on our high horse over being accused of doing wrong, when in fact we have probably done more wrong than our worst accusers will ever suspect? If we do successfully refute any charges against us, it will be like getting off on a technicality. We are, in fact, as guilty as sin.

One reason we have so much difficulty in acknowledging this first fact about sin (our heavy involvement) is that we haven't sufficiently understood the second fact. John goes on to write about the second fact as follows:

> My dear children, I write this to you so that you will not sin. But if anybody does sin, we have one who speaks to the Father in our defense—Jesus Christ, the Righteous One. He is the atoning sacrifice for our sins, and not only for ours but also for the sins of the whole world.
>
> 1 John 2:1, 2

Observe, first, that the case described here is one in which the defendant is guilty. It says "if anybody does sin." It doesn't say if you are unjustly accused, poor thing, Jesus will defend you. So there's no need to play that innocent game with Jesus. He knows. And, remember, He is light in whom dwells no darkness at all, so He's not going to falsify the facts.

Observe, second, that Jesus Christ, our defense attorney, is also the judge's own Son, and His righteousness is unquestioned. What an advocate to have plead our case!

Third, an atoning sacrifice has been made for our sins. God can and does exonerate us on that basis; He pardons us.

When I am accused, then, my best course is to agree with my adversary that I indeed have demonstrated myself to be a wretched sinner. However, Jesus has taken my case, prevailed for me with the Father, and atoned for all my wrongdoing.

Even though the person accusing me may be (and probably is) as guilty as I am, I need not attack him in response. That will not help him, anymore than his attacks have helped me. But for God's grace, his attacks would have been a stumbling block to me, not a help. What he needs now is for Jesus to take his case, plead for him with the Father, and spare him judgment because Jesus atoned for his lovelessness. In other words, he needs the same grace I do.

Confession Is Good for More Than the Soul

Sometimes people are out to hang us, and there is no need for us to give them the rope. If we are accused of a specific act of which we are specifically not guilty, we would of course tell the truth. For that matter, even if we are guilty, we need not testify against ourselves in some self-flagellating manner. Jesus is the one who atoned for our sins. We cannot do so and need not punish ourselves in an attempt to do so.

Usually, however, people do not want our hides. They simply want us to acknowledge our humanity. They want us to admit we are sinners like everybody else.

That seems to be one thing Richard Nixon never understood. He said he would not grovel. But admitting one has done wrong, not simply made errors in judgment, is not groveling. It is walking in the light.

Dale Galloway, my pastor, once did something that offended me. I went to see him about it. I told him I felt he was using me to accomplish his purposes. I said I wanted to help him, but I didn't want to be used or be seen as a means toward his ends.

I don't know what I expected. A denial, perhaps. Maybe an "I'm sorry if it looks that way to you, but that's not true at all." From a less-principled and more manipulative pastor, I might even have expected the approach: "You must be out of fellowship with God, or you wouldn't feel this way. How much time have you spent in prayer and Bible reading this week?"

Dale simply said, "I'm sorry. Please forgive me."

In that moment, he gained lasting respect from me. Was he guilty of using me, as I charged? I don't know. Somehow it doesn't seem to matter. I didn't want blood from him. I simply wanted an acknowledgment of my feelings and my worth as a human being and brother in Christ.

In asking my forgiveness, in acknowledging his imperfection, Dale did not grovel. He walked in the light, which made it possible for us to continue having fellowship with each other, just as the Apostle John long ago said it would (*see* 1 John 1:7).

God's Wisdom and Our Need of Insight

God is omniscient, which is to say He knows everything. When the all-knowing God dwells in us, we wise up, too. The Apostle John says that the all-wise God is our personal inner teacher.

> But you have an anointing from the Holy One, and all of you know the truth.
> As for you, the anointing you received from him remains in you, and you do not need anyone to teach you. But as his anointing teaches you about all things and as that anointing is real, not counterfeit—just as it has taught you, remain in him.
>
> 1 John 2:20, 27

The idea of omniscience comes through strongly in the King James translation of verse 20: "But ye have an unction from the Holy One, and ye know all things."

Now, I must tell you in all honesty that I do *not* know all things. I don't even know the verses of Scripture just quoted; I had to look them up and copy them from the Bible to get them exactly right.

I don't know of anyone who claims to know all things, with the possible exception of some far-out fortune-teller. Christians don't make such claims. Even those who demonstrate the "gift of knowledge" only claim to know supernaturally about a few isolated situations or conditions, not everything.

William Alexander comments on the above-quoted Scripture as follows:

> A kind of spiritual omniscience appears to be attributed to believers. Catechisms, confessions, creeds, teachers, preachers seem to be superseded by a stroke of the

apostle's pen, by what we are half tempted to consider a magnificent exaggeration.[1]

If one presses the passage to its literal limits, ignoring the teaching of all other Scripture to the contrary, one would do away with the teaching agencies Alexander cites plus all study, inquiry, and learning, as well. What need of learning has one who already knows all things?

The Bible itself makes clear that this extreme view is false, for it says we are to "grow in . . . knowledge" (2 Peter 3:18). It lists teaching as one of the spiritual gifts (see 1 Corinthians 12:28). It says that "five intelligible words to instruct others" are preferable to ten thousand words in tongues, which do not instruct (1 Corinthians 14:19).

Since teaching and instruction are to proceed in the church, it is clear that one doesn't know all things simply by virtue of having the divine teacher within.

The Spirit Teaches Us Who Jesus Is

On the other hand, a divine teacher does dwell within those who partake of the overflowing life. The same Holy Spirit described as a river of living water also, according to Jesus, " 'will teach you all things and will remind you of everything I have said to you' " (John 14:26).

It seems likely that the Apostle John had these very words of Jesus in mind when he wrote his epistle. Jesus had said the Spirit "will teach you all things," and John says, in effect, that is what had happened.

This anointing that John says remains in you is surely the inner teaching ministry of the Holy Spirit, of which Jesus spoke. We have an authoritative teacher, and that teacher is God Himself, who dwells within us in the Person of the Holy Spirit.

Primarily, this inner teaching has to do with our knowing who Jesus is, as the context in both John 14 and 1 John 2 shows. I wrote in chapter twelve about this inner teaching, this insight and conviction that Jesus Christ is the Son of God, the Savior of the world. As Jesus said, " 'I know my sheep and my sheep know me' "

(John 10:14). Now, if we know Him, we don't need a teacher to tell us who He is.

In us is fulfilled the prophecy of Jeremiah 31:34. " 'No longer will a man teach his neighbor, or a man his brother, saying, "Know the Lord," because they will all know me, from the least of them to the greatest.' "

In 1 John 2, the Apostle is concerned about the spirit of antichrist, which "denies that Jesus is the Christ" or "denies the Father and the Son" (v. 22). He writes about "those who are trying to lead you astray" (v. 26). Some philosophical thinkers and persuasive talkers might "teach" us contrary to the Gospel truth about Jesus Christ, God's Son, our Savior. John says not to listen to such people. They may be more than a match for us in argument, but we have an inner teacher who will teach us the truth; He is the one to whom we must give heed.

The Spirit Teaches Us Gradually

While our inner teacher primarily reveals the truth about Christ to us, He also teaches us spiritual truth in other areas as we are able to receive it. Jesus said to His disciples, " 'I have much more to say to you, more than you can now bear. But when he, the Spirit of truth, comes, he will guide you into all truth' " (John 16:12, 13).

Notice the progressive nature of this teaching. We don't suddenly know all through a blazing revelation but are guided into truth. As we study God's word, pray, meditate, and consider the insights of other people with our inner teacher guiding us, we become more and more insightful in all areas of living.

Nobody except God has authority over our faith. We don't believe what some persuasive human teacher says; not even if he claims to base every syllable on the Bible. We are constantly asking our inner teacher to guide us into truth.

When we read the Bible, we often find things we cannot understand. A case in point is this phrase we have been talking about in 1 John: "ye know all things." We trust the Holy Spirit to interpret such difficulties for us, not magically, but through prayerful study and thought. As we have said before, God *in* us does not mean God *is* us. So we don't just know, as God knows; we learn from him by dialog with Him. Keeping in mind our inclination to color things, we try to set our preconceptions aside. We respect what other believers have understood the passage to mean. We consider what other passages of Scripture say, realizing that since all the Bible is the word of God, we must not do violence to any.

The Spirit Teaches Us How to Live

Through all of this process, we keep in mind that we are learning to live God's way. We are not primarily learning what position we should take on controversial questions. We are not learning what pronouncements we should make as to how everybody else ought to live.

Of course, it is possible that God wants us to become a prophetic voice to our generation. He may make known His will *through* us, but our first order of business is to learn what is His will *for* us. That is quite task enough for most of us.

The good news is that the Teacher stands ready to guide you, and you need not climb some mountain in far-off Tibet to inquire of Him. Not if He dwells within your heart. Seek His wisdom, rather than depending on your own.

> Trust in the Lord with all your heart and lean not on your own understanding; in all your ways acknowledge him, and he will make your paths straight. Do not be wise in your own eyes; fear the Lord and shun evil. This will bring health to your body and nourishment to your bones.
>
> Proverbs 3:5–8

Warning: Danger Ahead

Some people who talk about being indwelt by God and about partaking of the light and wisdom of God, mean something far different from what I mean. I've said that God's light reveals our sin as well as clearing us from guilt. I've said that God's wisdom teaches us in our ignorance.

There is an incredibly wide gulf between these biblical concepts and the "God-in-you, God-is-you" notions of new-age and spiritist religions.

They do not know Jesus as the unique Son of God, but think all of us are (or can become) sons of God, as He was. They are not realistic and serious about man's sin problem, as the Bible always is. And they glorify their leaders, almost as if they were God.

The sad thing is that these unbiblical and, in many cases, demonic religions gain adherents by offering people a false answer to a real need. People need the living water, the overflowing life, the fulfillment of the indwelling Spirit of God. Not having it, they are easily led to drink from the broken cisterns cleverly marketed by phony gurus, mediums, channels, and cults.

If you can't see the profound difference between what I have been setting forth in this book and the teachings of those who do not know our blessed Lord and Savior Jesus Christ, you must not be under the tutelage of that inner teacher of whom John writes.

I would not serve you well to let you think that everybody who talks of God knows God. As the Scripture says, "Satan himself masquerades as an angel of light. It is not surprising, then, if his servants masquerade as servants of righteousness. Their end will be what their actions deserve" (2 Corinthians 11:14, 15).

God will take care of religious phonies and servants of Satan. Their end will be what they deserve. I've lived long enough to see it happen more than once. Unfortunately, a few years later, new false prophets arise to lead astray new victims. I don't want you to be among the victims, if I can possibly help it. That's why I sound this warning.

But even more important than warning people about poisoned cisterns is leading them to living water, so they no longer thirst. That will continue to be our focus.

FIFTEEN

God's Holiness in You

A sad fact of life is that one can catch diseases from others, but one cannot catch health.

Holiness is one of those words that carries so much baggage one hesitates to use it. The word means different things to different people. To some, the word *holiness* is extremely intimidating; they are uncomfortable with it. To others, the word carries connotations of strictness, of regimented living and thinking, or of perfection.

Holiness is also a religious word, certainly not one most people would use in the course of normal everyday conversation. When was the last time you talked with anyone about holiness? People freely discuss being well, normal, healthy, clean, and whole, but they don't easily talk about being holy.

The Hebrew and Greek words translated as *holy* in the Bible basically mean to be "set apart." Many Bible scholars have said that *holy* therefore means to be set apart for, or unto, God. That idea certainly has some validity, but it also has some problems.

The first and foremost biblical use of the word *holy* is to describe God Himself. The single most frequent use is in the name Holy Spirit. Obviously, *holy* in these cases does not mean "set apart for God." The Holy Spirit is not a spirit set apart for God; the Holy Spirit *is* God. Similarly, when God is called holy, He is not being described as set apart unto Himself.

Another problem that arises indirectly out of the set apart to God concept of holiness is that it lends itself to a faulty concept of reality. One easily imagines a mass of people on the one hand and the set-apart people on the other. It is a short step from there to viewing the mass as the normative and those set apart as the oddballs, diverging from the normal.

I'm not saying the phrase "set apart to God" demands that view, but it's commonly taken that way. Even if we consider holiness to be a superior condition, we still tend to see it as abnormal.

Rather than defining holiness as "set apart unto God," we should define it primarily as "set apart from sin." That way—and only that way—does the term make sense when applied to God, as it so often is. God is apart from sin.

This definition of holiness as being set apart from sin also lends itself to a correct view of reality. To be holy is normal, not some strange variation from normal. Sin is a sickness in the human race; it is an abnormality. In times of epidemic, healthy people may be the exceptions to the rule, but they are still normal. Your temperature is normal when it is approximately 98.6 degrees, and that would remain true even if every other person in the world was running a fever of 104 degrees.

Do you want to be holy?

I ask that question because your answer to it probably reveals something about how you view holiness.

I believe there are hosts of Christians who, if they were honest, would have to answer that question negatively, or with a very hesitant and qualified yes, at best. They have distorted views of holiness; they equate it with being strange.

Do you want to be holy?

Before you answer, please understand that to be holy means to be set apart from sin so that you become well, normal, healthy, clean and whole.

If that is what you want, nothing will help you attain it as much as the presence and influence of the *Holy* Spirit in your life. Let's consider how holiness works.

Holiness Cannot Be Caught

I'm fighting a bad cold right now. It has been a long time since I had a full-blown, miserable, persistent, scratchy, stuffed-up, bleary-eyed, head cold like this one. I used to get them frequently, so this one reminds me to be thankful that bad colds are now a rare experience for me.

I'm not sure where or how I picked up this cold, but I do have a plan for getting rid of it. I know several people who are very healthy. I am going to hang around them and see if I can catch a case of good health.

I'm joking, of course, because whether I like it or not, a sad fact of life is that one can catch diseases from others, but one cannot catch health.

This phenomenon, where the bad is communicable but the good isn't, was first brought to my attention by the prophet Haggai. He asked the priests of his day what the effect would be if a person carrying consecrated or holy meat were to touch some other food. Would the other food become holy by virtue of contact with that which was holy?

The priests said no.

Haggai then reversed the situation. If a person were unclean because of contact with a dead body and he touched some food, would it become unclean?

The priests said yes (*see* Haggai 2:12, 13).

In other words, *defiled* was communicable, but *holy* was not.

What the priests said about ceremonial defilement and holiness is also true as regards:

- *sickness and health*
- *contamination and purity*
- *dirty and clean*

A person can get sick, contaminated, or dirty from contact with someone who is sick, contaminated, or dirty. A person cannot get healthy, pure, or clean simply by contact with someone who is healthy, pure, or clean.

The Source of Holiness

Cleanliness, health, and purity are what we might call first-stage conditions. They are always original, fresh, and new; they cannot be passed along from someone else. If we have them at all, they originate with us.

That is not to say that holiness originates *from* us, because it doesn't. We are not its source; God is.

That is where the overflowing life comes into the picture. The life (or "seed") of God-in-us is the source of any holiness we have. The Apostle John writes of holiness, or being set apart from sin, as another effect of having God indwell us.

"No one who is born of God will continue to sin, because God's seed remains in him; he cannot go on sinning, because he has been born of God" (1 John 3:9).

This verse may sound as if we are no longer subject to sin's contamination, but that cannot be the case. John had already written, "If we claim to be without sin, we deceive ourselves and the truth is not in us" (1 John 1:8). As we said in the previous chapter, God-in-us does not mean God *is* us. God is perfectly holy, but we are not.

Nevertheless, the presence of the holy God within us has definite implications for our own holiness. John writes that, "No one who lives in him keeps on sinning" (1 John 3:6).

These words are not so much an appeal as they are a description. John doesn't say one *should not* keep on sinning, but that one *does not* keep on sinning. A little further on, he says one *cannot* go on sinning who has been born of God (1 John 3:9).

We come out with two strong and seemingly contradictory statements from John about our sin.

- First, we all sin, and to deny it is not consistent with the in-dwelling of God, who is light.
- Second, we have a holy presence within us, and we cannot sin.

Here is my suggested solution to this seeming contradiction. If we change the second statement slightly, the contradiction will disappear: We have a holy presence within us that cannot sin.

Doesn't that remove the difficulty? It is God within us, the holy seed, that cannot sin; we can and do.

The only problem now is that John did not say that God-in-us (or the "seed" in us) cannot sin. He said that *we* can't.

In saying that *we* cannot sin, John is recognizing and honoring the vital union that exists between us and Christ. I have said repeatedly that we are not God. But neither do we simply have God present somehow within us. No, it is much more than that. We are joined to Him in one spirit. God is a separate entity dwelling within us, but we are united with Him as one.

Sin Is Alien

Sin—not God—is what we are to see as the separate and alien entity within us.

As I have written elsewhere:

> You should view sin as something alien to your true nature. Despite what we've said about God's holiness being far above ours even at our best, it's also true that sin is not native to the human species. Adam and Eve were not created as sinners. Sin entered from without. Jesus Christ came upon the scene as one fully human (as well as divine); yet he lived and died without sin.
>
> Even as a human being, then, you are not intrinsically sinful. Sin is an intruder, a cancer of the soul, an outside influence that has taken control.
>
> As a Christian, you are even less an intrinsic host to sin than you were as a child of Adam. You have been born again into the family of God. God's seed in you is holy and cannot sin. You are on your way to an eternal kingdom where "nothing impure will ever enter" (Revelation 21:27). You are going to feel at home there. Totally

169

at home, as you have never been before. You will not long for the old ways or the old days. You will not secretly miss your sins, for you will fully know that they were never really a part of you. They do not belong.[1]

When John writes that you cannot sin because you are born of God, he is viewing God-in-you as your true identity and sin as alien.

Paul writes from a similar perspective when, speaking of his own sinful behavior, he says, "Now if I do what I do not want to do, it is no longer I who do it, but it is sin living in me that does it" (Romans 7:20).

Under ordinary circumstances, if I heard anyone talk like that I would suspect him or her of making excuses. I might respond sarcastically, "Oh, no, of course it's not *your* fault when you sin!"

Considering this was the Apostle Paul, however, and considering his obvious anguish over his sin, as revealed by the context, I realize that the distinction he makes between the essential person and sin that dwells in that person is a legitimate one.

Both John and Paul insist that, although we are infected with sin, we are still holy in Christ. The holiness of the indwelling God is normative for us. Sin, though it is a troublesome and persistent inner adversary, is not normative for us.

In summary, then, this is the teaching. You cannot sin because you are born of God, but your problem now is to keep the alien force of sin that still works in you from exercising control. This will be your lifelong struggle, but one you will win when you rely on God's Spirit, who dwells within you. "So I say, live by the Spirit, and you will not gratify the desires of the sinful nature" (Galatians 5:16).

SIXTEEN

God's Love in You

Everyone who loves has been born of God and knows God. Whoever does not love does not know God, because God is love.

1 John 4:7, 8

Many years ago, when I was a boy, I got into a serious predicament one day. In disobedience to my parents' standing orders, my older brother, Ron, and I went to play on the logs in the river by the mill. It was a Saturday, and the mill was closed. Therefore, Ron assured me, the logs would not be moving and we would be safe. He knew because he had been down there before.

It was fun walking along the huge logs and stepping from one to another. They formed almost a solid raft, and I felt no danger. But then we came to a place where there were open stretches of water between the logs. I soon found myself on the wrong end of a log that extended into an open span of river. The log began to turn under my feet, and I fell in. I couldn't swim.

I came up, frantically grabbed for the log, and pulled myself over to it. Reaching both arms as far as I could over the log, I tried to pull myself up onto it. The rough bark bit into the tender flesh of my hands and arms. My wet clothes felt as if they were made of lead. I almost thought I was going to make it up onto the log, but it turned with my weight and dunked me again.

I called for help, but Ron said he couldn't do anything. If he tried, he would fall in, too.

"Work your way to the end of the log," Ron ordered. "That way it won't turn when you try to pull yourself out."

I pulled myself the few feet to the log's end. Ron was right. Not only did the log not turn, but there was a ledge protruding from its end, practically like a step, where the tree had been cut down. I clambered out, straddled the log as I scooted toward safety, and was soon back where the logs formed a deck.

Soaking wet and thoroughly shaken, I began sloshing toward home, only to come upon my folks. Coincidentally, they had driven out to the mill that day to get a trailer load of firewood. They drove a coupé, so Ron and I always rode in the trunk. This was to be no exception.

Maybe they thought I needed to bear the consequences of my actions. Maybe they didn't know I needed some comfort and attention. Maybe they just weren't about to squeeze a wet and naughty kid into the seat with them. Anyhow, I rode home in the trunk, wet and cold and miserable.

Some thirty years later, I pulled another foolish stunt. I was in Beirut, Lebanon, and our tour group was scheduled to visit the ruins at Baalbek that day. I was sick, but I went anyhow. (I used to always keep going when I was sick. I figured I would feel rotten, anyhow, so I might as well have something to distract me, rather than just lying around concentrating on my illness.)

I bravely boarded our tour bus and set out with the others for Baalbek. When we arrived, I summoned all my strength and trekked through the ancient ruins. However, by noon I was about as sick as I have ever been in my life. I could do nothing but lie on the backseat of the bus and suffer.

At midafternoon the bus stopped at a roadside inn and the others went in for refreshments. I was racked with chills and too sick to move. When the others returned, one of the women came to me with some hot herbal tea. "Here," she said, "drink this. It will make you feel better. And, please, move up here to the middle of the bus. This bumpy backseat is probably the least comfortable spot in the bus for you. Come on, now, I've got a spot all picked out for you."

I moved to the place she indicated. She covered me with a warm blanket. I sipped the hot tea. And I quietly wept with gratitude.

What did the one incident have to do with the other? I can't really explain it. I can only tell you that someone I barely knew showed me love when I had no one to blame but myself for my predicament. And that love was healing. It got me out of an old, cold car trunk and wrapped me in a warm blanket of love.

What I am saying is this: People who are hurting particularly need love. Often they are least lovable at the very time they need love most. Those who are sick, defeated, fallen, wounded, or confused are not very attractive. To the contrary, they are often decidedly unpleasant to be around.

Our choice in such situations is:
- to let hurting people suffer alone in car trunks and backseats of buses, or
- to show them kindness.

Marked as God's

According to the Apostle John, the overflowing life—the life of God-in-us—causes us to love. He writes: "Dear friends, let us love one another, for love comes from God. Everyone who loves has been born of God and knows God. Whoever does not love does not know God, because God is love" (1 John 4:7, 8).

What a beautiful list of attributes John has provided us as evidences of God's presence within us. It is quite different from those elements often made a priority by religious people. Where John emphasizes:

- *Light*
- *Wisdom*
- *Holiness*
- *Love*

people today often emphasize:

- *Sacraments*
- *Social concern*
- *Doctrine*
- *Emotion*

Each of the latter is good—even essential—in its place and in balance with the others, but religious people tend to major on one of the four, as if it were the sum and substance of godliness.

My own tradition is heavily weighted toward item three on the second list. The all-important thing for a Christian, I have always felt, is to hold correct doctrine. It is therefore difficult for me to accept what John writes: *Love* is the crucial thing. I can understand one needs love in addition to correct doctrine, for Christianity is a matter of the heart, not just the head. But I do not yield easily to the view that love, by its presence or absence, shows whether or not a person is born of God.

Yet that is just what John seems to say. "Everyone who loves has been born of God and knows God. Whoever does not love does not know God" (1 John 4:7, 8).

I want to respond, "What? Isn't the crucial thing to hold correct doctrine?"

I suspect others might respond, "What? Isn't receiving the sacraments of the church of paramount importance?"

"What? Isn't involving oneself in the struggle for social justice the test of true faith?"

"What? Aren't tongues and ecstasies and revelations and other manifestations of the Spirit the evidence that one truly knows God?"

The Case of the "Sinless" Woman

John seems to give love a primacy over everything else, and one wonders about that. Does he mean it?

An account such as the following by Corrie ten Boom, about her ministry with the mentally retarded, suggests how love may overshadow correct doctrine in importance.

> We were together in our church room and I spoke about the meaning of "sin."
>
> "Do you all know what the word 'sin' means?"
>
> They told me they surely knew. It was disobedience, bad words, and ugly thoughts. It was lying, killing, beating, swearing, unbelief in Jesus Christ.
>
> "Have you ever sinned?" I asked.
>
> "Never," was the unexpected answer from Marie, a poor, imbecile woman.
>
> Her whole face was radiant with pride. I tried to argue, but could not convince her. Then I spoke of the love of Christ and she told me:
>
> "I know that Jesus loves me so, that he died on the cross for me. I love Jesus and tell him everything." Her whole face was beaming with joy.
>
> I knew that Marie had only some months to live. She had cancer. I was not afraid that she was not ready to appear before God's throne. Why Jesus died on the cross she did not understand, but she was thankful for his love—perhaps more thankful and glad than many good, normal Christians, who have a sound theology but whose eyes do not sparkle as do Marie's eyes, when one speaks of Jesus' love.[1]

I still think doctrine is hugely important. An imbecile woman is hardly the standard for all of us. Elsewhere in this same epistle, even John insists on correct doctrine—at least concerning the identity of Jesus Christ as the Son of God. "No one who denies the Son has the Father; whoever acknowledges the Son has the Father also" (1 John 2:23).

Nevertheless, I think I am ready to yield the point that love is the most reliable indicator of God-in-us. As John says, "God is love." Love is God's very nature and essence. Those who truly know God, then, must also love.

Why Love Is Supreme

John is not alone among the biblical writers to give supremacy to love. Paul praises love as "the most excellent way." He declares that tongues, knowledge, faith, helping the poor—all religious exercises—are nothing without love (*see* 1 Corinthians 12:31–13:3). Even faith and hope are secondary to love (*see* v. 13).

And why is love superior? Because, again, God is love. It is in loving that we are like God. Faith and hope are not attributes to be found in God. They are immensely important to our human experience, but are not a part of the character of God, as love is.

Love is also superior because it is outgoing. Faith and hope are inward; they are elements of the abundant life. Love reaches out to others; it is the essence of the overflowing life.

Love is superior in a third way: It is eternal. Faith will someday give way to sight. Hope will end in the full realization of everything for which we have hoped. In heaven we will no longer need either faith or hope. But love will continue, only enlarged—a great ocean in which we will live and move and have our being.

Overflowing Death

Our theme throughout this book has been that we can have life in such measure and of such quality that it overflows in life-giving ways to others. The basis of the overflowing life is God-in-us. We are to be like God, not just by imitation, but because He indwells us.

When it comes to loving, therefore, John points to God's nature as its basis. We are to be like God, who is love. John also tells us we are to be unlike someone else.

John writes, "This is the message you heard from the beginning: We should love one another. Do not be like Cain, who belonged to the evil one and murdered his brother. And why did he murder him? Because his own actions were evil and his brother's were righteous" (1 John 3:11, 12).

As far as we know, at that time Cain and Abel were the only sons of Adam and Eve. Think of it! The whole world lay before them, uninhabited and unspoiled. Yet Cain would not allow Abel to go on living.

We hear all sorts of theories today about the causes of crime, conflict, war, and other forms of man's inhumanity to man. Poverty, crowded conditions, economic disadvantage are cited as root problems. Elimination of these problems supposedly would bring a cure.

However, Cain didn't kill Abel because of crowded conditions or economic disadvantage or poverty. Cain killed Abel "because his own actions were evil and his brother's were righteous."

The evil in Cain's heart overflowed into his world, killing his brother, Abel, and breaking his parents' hearts. Cain himself then became a fugitive and a marked man.

All this woe, all this suffering, was unnecessary. None of it would have happened if the love of God had filled Cain's heart, instead of envy and hatred. And it is lack of the love of God that to this very moment continues to blight the lives of both wrongdoers and their victims.

As J. C. Ryle wrote many years ago:

> Think, for another thing, what a happy world this would be if there was more charity. It is the want of love which causes half the misery there is upon earth. Sickness, and death, and poverty, will not account for more than half the sorrows. The rest come from ill-temper, ill-nature, strifes, quarrels, lawsuits, malice, envy, revenge, frauds, violence, wars, and the like. It would be one great step towards doubling the happiness of mankind and halving their sorrows, if all men and women were full of Scriptural charity.[2]

Do not be like Cain, the Bible says. Your alternative? To be like God, who is love. You can be like God because, and only because, God stands ready to give you the great gift of Himself. "God has poured out his love into our hearts by the Holy Spirit, whom he has given us" (Romans 5:5).

But here again we must "use the car," so to speak. We must put into action the love of God that is potentially ours. As John writes, "Dear children, let us not love with words or tongue but with actions and in truth" (1 John 3:18).

Love in Action

My great concern is that we will have words only—great, beautiful words about love—but little of it in practice.

That's how it has been down through the centuries. The law of love has been known much better than it has been practiced. Even in Moses' day, hundreds of years before Christ came, the law of love was known. " 'Do not hate your brother in your heart. . . . Do not seek revenge or bear a grudge against one of your people, but love your neighbor as yourself. I am the Lord' " (Leviticus 19:17, 18).

The people of Jesus' day knew about the law of love, even before He articulated it to them.

> On one occasion an expert in the law stood up to test Jesus. "Teacher," he asked, "what must I do to inherit eternal life?"
>
> "What is written in the Law?" he replied. "How do you read it?"
>
> He answered: " 'Love the Lord your God with all your heart and with all your soul and with all your strength and with all your mind,' and, 'Love your neighbor as yourself.' "
>
> "You have answered correctly," Jesus replied. "Do this and you will live."
>
> Luke 10:25–28

But though men knew the concept, they did not live in the love of God. They were too wrapped up in themselves and, often, in their religious views and practices. So Jesus told them a parable.

> "A man was going down from Jerusalem to Jericho, when he fell into the hands of robbers. They stripped

him of his clothes, beat him and went away, leaving him half dead. A priest happened to be going down the same road, and when he saw the man, he passed by on the other side. So too, a Levite, when he came to the place and saw him, passed by on the other side. But a Samaritan, as he traveled, came where the man was; and when he saw him, he took pity on him. He went to him and bandaged his wounds, pouring on oil and wine. Then he put the man on his own donkey, took him to an inn and took care of him. The next day he took out two silver coins and gave them to the innkeeper. 'Look after him,' he said, 'and when I return, I will reimburse you for any extra expense you may have.' "

Luke 10:30–35

After telling the parable, Jesus asked, " 'Which of these three [the priest, the Levite, or the Samaritan] do you think was a neighbor to the man who fell into the hands of robbers?' "

The answer of course, was the Samaritan.

We feel the full thrust of this parable only when we realize that priests and Levites were the religious good guys of the day and Samaritans were despised as heretics. Jesus seems to be teaching, as John did later, that he who loves is the one who knows God.

Words and Music Courtesy of God

Today, as in the days of Moses and Jesus, people know the words to God's song. The words are "You shall love the Lord your God with all your heart, and your neighbor as yourself."

Somehow, like others before us, we have not set the words to music. God's love does not sing in our hearts. Indifference and cruelty show themselves, even in the very citadels of faith. Ah, but then the love of God shows itself in some despised Samaritan, and light breaks through the clouds like sun after rain.

I read of such an incident recently. The account was written by a pastor whose wife had bravely refused an abortion.

Shirley had gotten pregnant after we assumed we would have no more children. She was older and after

179

several examinations the doctor told her that the pregnancy was in deep trouble. He gently explained the consequences of carrying the child and said, "I must frankly tell you the chances are very slim your child will be normal. I strongly recommend an abortion."

. . . We went for a long ride and she related what the doctor had recommended. I knew how my wife had suffered during her previous pregnancies. I also knew abortion is morally wrong. We were caught in a dilemma. The doctor assured us it would be totally secret and my church would never need to know. It was a simple procedure and could be handled at this early stage without concern. He felt we should do it.

Torn is the only word I can use to explain how I felt at that moment. I couldn't lose Shirley, I knew her welfare was the overriding concern of our caring doctor. What should we do? It was in that moment I said to her, "Darling, I love you more than any other human being. I don't feel I can tell you what to do. Let me pray with you for three days and at the end of that time you make your decision. Whatever decision you make I will stand behind you, even if it means losing my church or the ministry. I am committed to you."

Three days passed and we prayed. We again went for a ride and Shirley announced her decision. I'll never forget the tears she cried and how difficult it was for me to drive because I could hardly see through my own tears. "Ron," she said, "we will have the baby. I could not help but think, What if this child inside me is another Paul the Apostle? How could I stand the thought that I would have aborted him?" The decision was made and we told the doctor. He shook his head sadly and said, "All right, then we will do the best we can."

He did do the best he could, but still our baby died. Our little boy died in his mother's womb after seven months. Major surgery had to be performed to save her. I remember pacing the hospital halls, praying for my wife, knowing the great sadness we both felt. . . . Finally, after what seemed an eternity, the doctor came out to tell me my wife would make it. Then this kindly Jewish doctor said something that deeply moved me. I've seldom been as emotionally shaken as I was in that moment.

"Reverend," he said, "I baptized him for you. I thought that would be what you wanted."

I wept.

In my church we do not believe in infant baptism, but I was deeply touched by this good doctor's concern. He did not know that what he did was opposed to my theology. He simply wanted to reach out to my grief and somehow lessen my load. I will always love him for that act.

We told this to the Toronto reporter and he wrote the story. Then the fire storm hit. It was a reaction we were not prepared for. Livid Christians screamed at us and wrote horrible threatening letters. What had offended them the most is that we had even *considered* abortion. They couldn't understand how I would let my wife make the decision and then stand with her regardless. They felt I was morally weak and had no right to minister. They picketed my church. They wrote letters to the newspapers, saying my wife should be committed. Some pastors blasted us from their pulpits and said the best thing we could do for the ministry was to leave it.[3]

Why was it the Jewish doctor was loving but the Christian activists were vicious? Why is it always a Samaritan that shows love, while the orthodox are uncaring and cruel?

Ah, but it is not *always* that way. We who are orthodox in doctrine can be orthodox in love, too, but the awful danger is that we will not be. We need the warning implicit in Jesus' parable of the good Samaritan.

Maybe, too, Jesus selected a Samaritan as His example of a life touched by God's love in order to give hope to those yet outside the established fold. Maybe He wants to tell them—to tell you—that love marks the people of God. Maybe He wants you to know that in loving, you belong. You belong to Him and with His people.

Will God's people accept you? Yes, they will, and if some don't, maybe it's because they are not of God, for God is love.

So if you've been disappointed by "religious" people, if you have looked to them for love and found rejection instead, look again. You'll find love.

Showing Love

"Dear friends, let us love one another, for love comes from God," John wrote (1 John 4:7). John didn't say, "Well, either you have love or you don't, and if you have it, I'm sure it will show in your actions." No, he urged us to express the love of God that dwells in us if we know Him.

Our deeds of love may be "inappropriate" to the occasion, as was the Jewish doctor's baptism of the Hembree baby. Our deeds of love could be misunderstood or rejected. Or they may work a deep and lasting healing in someone's life that we will never even know about. To this day, the woman on the bus to Baalbek has no idea what her kindness meant to me. Maybe God will let her come across these lines and find out. I hope so.

But I wonder, how many people in the world remember receiving a loving touch from me? Or from you? Whether they remember or not, how many have received such a touch? That's the important question. For God remembers every act of love we have ever performed. "He will not forget your work and the love you have shown him as you have helped his people and continue to help them" (Hebrews 6:10).

He will not forget.

You see, love is important to Him.

—SEVENTEEN—

A
Sense
of Him

We must not view Bible reading, prayer, our faith, church attendance, or anything else we do as another deposit in the coin slot of a heavenly vending machine. If we do, we will likely end up pounding the machine with our fists and demanding to know why it isn't delivering the goods.

We have come a long way together since we began to speak of the little princess, Romeo and Juliet, the woman who lived with six men, and of the reality of a truly fulfilling life.

The claims of Jesus stand clear and uncompromising before us. There is no question that He offers an overflowing life. He said that if we come to Him and drink, a river of life will flow from within us.

"Does it really work?" someone might ask. "You have written sixteen chapters about the overflowing life, but do you have it? Does it work for you?"

Someone else might ask, "But can it really be mine? Is there any more you can tell me about how to make such a life my own? Is there a simple, step-by-step plan I can follow?"

If those questions are on your mind, you deserve some straight answers.

It Works

My answer to the first question—does it work for me?—is yes.

God came to dwell in my heart and life when I was a young man, and He has been making a radical difference ever since. What griefs He has spared me! What healing He has worked in me emotionally! What grace He has shown in my wandering! What liberation He has brought me! What truths He has taught me! What guidance He has provided through the labyrinths of life and religion!

So many times, the indwelling Spirit of God has made a critical difference in my life.

I would be less than honest, however, if I left you with the impression that my life is a continual feast. My heart is not always full of God. Streams of living water do not always flow from within me.

Sometimes it is because I am neglecting the gift of God that is in me. I keep thinking back to my earlier illustration about the car (*see* chapter twelve). To have *anything* in a practical sense requires that I use it. More than once in the writing of this book, I have been reminded that I have the overflowing life and what I need to do is claim it and use it.

I must keep in mind that to claim it and use it does not depend on better performance or more heroic effort on my part. We have said repeatedly that the overflowing life is God-in-you, but we still tend to forget that. To claim and use God-in-you is not a matter of heroics or effort, but of fellowship, spiritual sensitivity, and awareness.

Jerry Cook captured the concept I'm talking about and applied it to his ministry as a pastor. He wrote:

> The first year I was in the ministry, I became very frustrated. The church was growing and I was getting the credit, but I knew there was not the slightest relationship between what was happening and what I was doing. I

184

felt utterly useless and completely irrelevant. And I was. I could have dropped in a hole and God's work would have gone right on. Probably a little better.

The latter part of that year I landed in the hospital. I was 27 years old, had prepared for the ministry for nine years and, after less than a year of pastoring, I was in the hospital on a heart machine and there was some question whether I could even continue pastoring.

My ministry, so-called, had lasted less than twelve months and been totally ineffective.... I saw what had been happening. What I had built ... was gone. What God had built was standing. I understood that Jesus builds his church, that I not only don't have to build it but cannot build it. That was what had given me trouble. I'd been under the tremendous pressure of having to build a church.

The Lord said, "It's my church, Jerry; I'll build it."

"Well, Lord, then what am I for?"

"Just hang around and do what I tell you," he said. "Just be available ... and try to stay out of the way."[1]

This is what we need to do, also: relax, get off the performance trip, and simply be available to God.

Is There a Step-by-Step Plan?

Earlier I wrote about the necessity of prayer and faith. We need to pray that God will fill us with His Spirit. We need to pray in faith, not "trying to believe" but believing. We also read in Scripture that "faith comes from hearing the message, and the message is heard through the word of Christ" (Romans 10:17). It can be tremendously helpful to read the Scriptures and study them. I recommend memorization of key passages (as suggested in chapter seven), and frequent meditation upon God's message.

But we must not view Bible reading, prayer, our faith, church attendance, or anything else we do as another deposit in the coin slot of a heavenly vending machine. If we do, we will likely end up pounding the machine with our fists and demanding to know why it isn't delivering the goods.

God is not dispensed through a vending machine.

So we face a difficulty here. How-to information can be helpful, but it becomes a snare when (perhaps unwittingly) we begin to rely on the formula instead of on the Lord.

Or when we rely on a teacher or a book.

This book cannot confer the overflowing life upon you. It can only talk about such a life.

God Himself must quicken your heart.

And that is what I pray—and believe—will happen. The Spirit of God can come upon you, making real and vital what otherwise may be just print on paper or fuzzy ideas, at best. When the Spirit quickens your heart to God's truth, something happens, such as described by an unknown poet:

> 'Twas not the words you spoke,
> To you so clear, to me so dim,
> But when you came,
> You brought a sense of him.

A sense of Him—an inner awareness of the presence of God—that's what is essential.

Pray? Yes.

Read Scripture? By all means.

Claim God's promises? Good!

Trust God to hear and answer when you pray? Certainly.

Step out and take action to put your faith into practice? Wonderful.

Read this book again? Fine.

Do all of these things. They are as close to a step-by-step plan as I can give you. Do them in your search for the overflowing life. Or better yet, do them because you have already received overflowing life.

But don't imagine that these things *are* the overflowing life, or that the faithful performance of all of them will produce overflowing life, though they certainly may give God something to work with in your life.

What does it come down to, then?

A Sense of Him

What is the key?

Just what it has been all along: There must be a merger between you and the living God. A spiritual union must be established.

"You will seek me and find me when you seek me with all your heart," the Lord told the nation of Israel (*see* Jeremiah 29:13).

"Blessed are those who hunger and thirst for righteousness, for they will be filled," Jesus said (*see* Matthew 5:6).

I can tell you without a shred of a doubt where the overflowing life is to be found: It is in the Lord Himself. So seek Him. Seek, and you will find.

We have now come to the end of our time together. I still believe, more than ever, in the gift of God, and I very much hope that you do, too. We ordinary humans really can experience overflowing life, God-in-us, the God who is love. My prayer is that, for you, this "vision of a distant possibility" will be no longer distant, and no longer just a vision of a possibility either.

Instead, may you have the sense, the conviction, the knowledge that in your innermost being flows a river of living water and that, though it may not yet have flowed out from you very far, it will. It will.

Notes

Chapter 2

1. Alexander Maclaren, *Christ in the Heart* (New York: Funk & Wagnalls, 1902), 16, 17.
2. Ibid., 57, 58.
3. Ibid.
4. Jeanne Marie Guyon, *Madame Guyon: An Autobiography* (Chicago: Moody Press, n.d.), 72, 73.

Chapter 4

1. Malcolm MacGregor, *Your Money Matters* (Minneapolis, MN: Bethany House, 1977), 42.
2. Stanley C. Baldwin, *Bruised But Not Broken* (Portland, OR: Multnomah Press, 1985), 20, 21.
3. Ibid.

Chapter 8

1. Viktor Frankl, "The Will to Meaning," *Are You Nobody?* Paul Tournier, ed. (New York: John Knox Press, 1968), 26.
2. James D. Mallory, Jr., *The Kink and I* (Wheaton, IL: Victor Books, 1973), 114.
3. Ibid., 112.
4. Frankl, "Will to Meaning," 26.
5. Viktor Frankl, *Man's Search for Meaning* (Boston: Beacon Press, 1962), 108.
6. J. I. Packer, *Knowing God* (Downers Grove, IL: Intervarsity Press, 1973), 29.
7. Norman Cousins, *Anatomy of an Illness* (New York: W. W. Norton, 1979), 71, 72.
8. Ibid., 74.
9. Ibid., 79.
10. Stanley C. Baldwin, *When Death Means Life: Choosing the Way of the Cross* (Portland, OR: Multnomah Press, 1986), 32–34.

Chapter 10

1. Nathaniel Branden and E. Devers Branden, *The Romantic Love Question and Answer Book* (New York: Bantam Books, 1983), 151.
2. As quoted in Rodney Clapp, "What Hollywood Doesn't Know About Romantic Love," *Christianity Today* (February 3, 1984): 33.

Chapter 11

1. L. Jean Bogert, George McSpadden Briggs, and Doris Howes Calloway, *Nutrition and Physical Fitness*, ninth ed. (Philadelphia: W. B. Saunders Company, 1973), 225.

Notes

2. Guyon, *Madame Guyon: An Autobiography*, 81.

3. Ibid., 101.

4. Ibid., 126.

5. Ibid., 281.

6. Stanley C. Baldwin, *How to Build Your Christian Character* (Wheaton, IL: Victor Books, 1982), 86, 87.

Chapter 12

1. Stanley C. Baldwin, *What Did Jesus Say About That?* (Wheaton, IL: Victor Books, 1975), 21.

Chapter 14

1. William Alexander, *Exposition of the Bible* (Philadelphia: S. S. Scranton Co., 1903), 797.

Chapter 15

1. Stanley C. Baldwin, *When Death Means Life*, 128.

Chapter 16

1. Corrie ten Boom, *Common Sense Not Needed* (Fort Washington, PA: Christian Literature Crusade, 1975), 19.

2. John Charles Ryle, *Practical Religion* (New York: Thomas Y. Crowell Co., 1959), 123, 124.

3. Ron Hembree, *The Speck in Your Brother's Eye* (Old Tappan, NJ: Fleming H. Revell Co., 1985), 63–65.

Chapter 17

1. Jerry Cook with Stanley C. Baldwin, *Love, Acceptance and Forgiveness* (Ventura, CA: Regal Books, 1979), 74, 75.